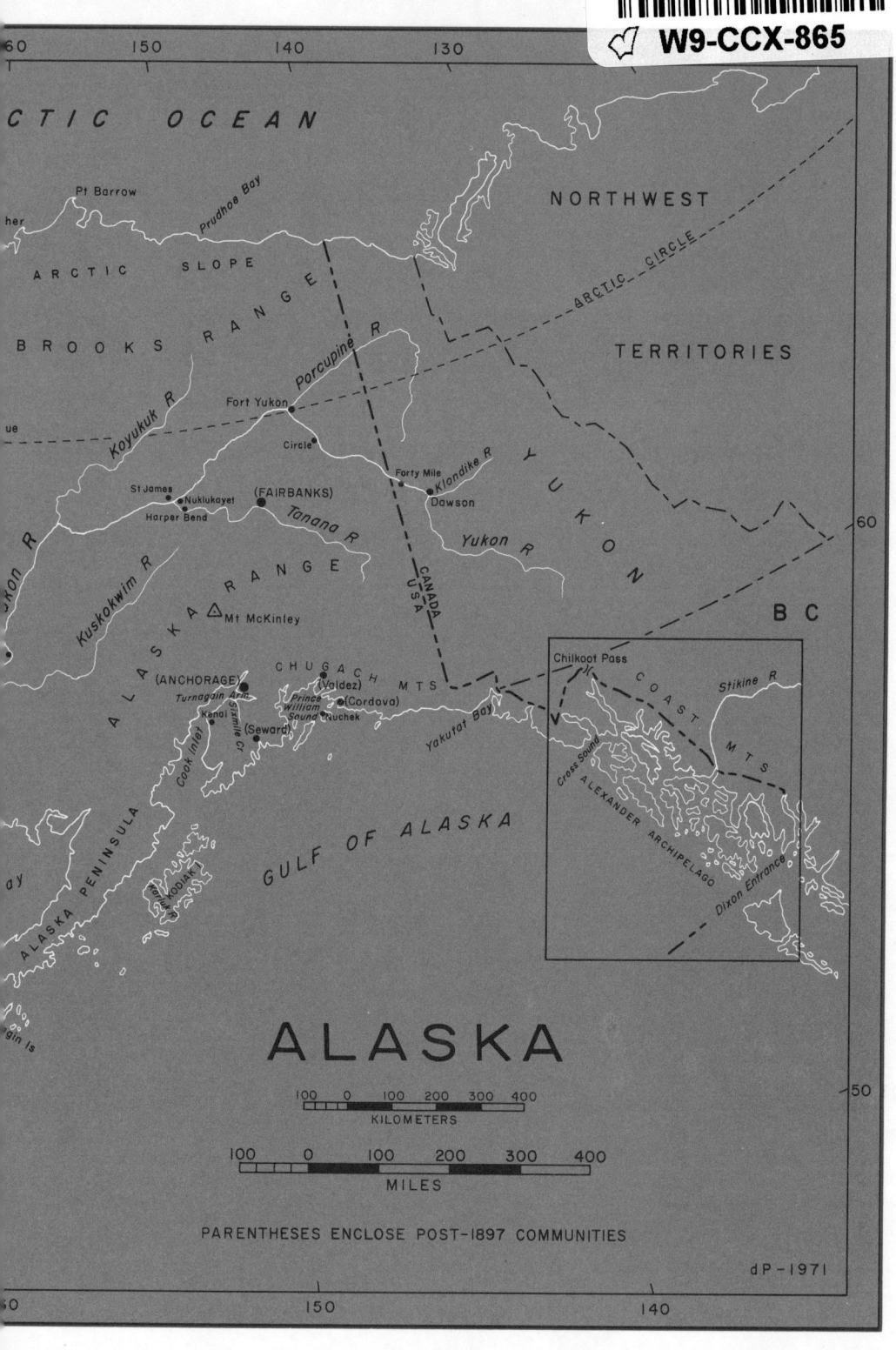

W9-CCX-865

ARCTIC OCEAN

Pt Barrow

NORTHWEST

Prudhoe Bay

ARCTIC SLOPE

ARCTIC CIRCLE

BROOKS RANGE

TERRITORIES

Koyukuk R

Porcupine R

Fort Yukan

Circle

St James Nuklukayet

Forty Mile

Klondike R

YUKON

60

Harper Bend

(FAIRBANKS)

Tanana R

Dawson

Kuskokwim R

Yukon R

CANADA
USA

Mt McKinley

BC

ALASKA RANGE

CHUGACH MTS

Chilkoot Pass

Stikine R

(ANCHORAGE)

(Valdez)

COAST

Turnagain Arm

Prince
William
Sound

(Cordova)

Cross Sound

MTS

Kenai

Kuchek

(Seward)

Yakutat Bay

ALEXANDER ARCHIPELAGO

Cook Inlet

ALASKA PENINSULA

GULF OF ALASKA

Dixon Entrance

Kodiak

ALASKA

50

100   0   100 200 300 400
KILOMETERS

100   0   100   200   300   400
MILES

PARENTHESES ENCLOSE POST-1897 COMMUNITIES

dP-1971

150   140

ucap,ustx F 908.H64

Americanization of Alaska, 1867–18

3 9153 01287355 2

DISCARD

The Americanization
of Alaska, 1867-1897

☆ ☆ ☆ ☆ ☆ ☆ ☆ ☆ ☆ ☆ ☆ ☆ ☆

The Americanization

of Alaska, 1867-1897

☆ ☆ ☆ ☆ ☆ ☆ ☆ ☆ ☆ ☆ ☆ ☆ ☆

Ted C. Hinckley

Pacific Books, Publishers
Palo Alto, California

The painting reproduced on the jacket is the artist's conception of the flag-changing ceremony in Sitka, October 18, 1867, when Alaska was transferred to the United States by the Czar's commissioner. The painting is copyright © 1967 by the Humble Oil and Refining Company and used with permission.

Endpaper map by Duilio Peruzzi.

Copyright © 1972 by Ted C. Hinckley.
All rights reserved. No part of this book may be used or reproduced in any manner whatsoever without written permission from the publisher, except in the case of brief quotations embodied in critical articles and reviews.

International Standard Book Number 0–87015–197–5.
Library of Congress Catalog Card Number 71–180900.
Printed and bound in the United States of America.

PACIFIC BOOKS, PUBLISHERS
P. O. Box 558, Palo Alto, California 94302

To Oscar O. Winther
Teacher and Friend

☆ ☆ ☆ ☆ ☆ ☆ ☆ ☆ ☆ ☆ ☆ ☆ ☆ ☆ ☆

Acknowledgments

THOSE WHO ENGAGE IN historical research owe an infinite debt to libraries, funding agencies, and an astonishingly wide range of people. For the author to credit here all those who have assisted him is impossible. From the Presbyterian Historical Society in Philadelphia to the University of Alaska, with numerous stops between, is quite a search. Hopefully, the sheer geographical extent of such a research effort can convey something of this historian's immense gratitude to scholars, antiquarians, and even polite gasoline station attendants. Without their aid, this book could never have taken form.

My bibliography cites those institutions that have been of particular value to me. The patient and capable staffs of these depositories have dug out their jewels for me, and while I assembled the mosaic, let it never be forgotten that *they* supplied the pieces. Particularly steadfast researchers have been San Jose State College librarian Christine Simpson, and Phyllis Nottingham of the Alaska State Historical Library, and their respective co-workers.

Other specific acknowledgments are mandatory. Graduate students Steve Larson, Vernon Mitchell, and Wynn Wachorst exhibited a surprising capacity for "academic dirty work." Over the years editors Robert E. Burke, John W. Caughey, Robert De Armond, Charles E. Cuningham, Emily E. Johnson, Lorrin Morrison, and Henry and Romayne Ponleithner have painstakingly retrieved me from investigative pitfalls and the slough of literary despond.

7

Surely, for a writer an ounce of encouragement is worth a pound of criticism.

A grateful salute to skippers Richard Sears and George C. S. Benson for helping chart those windward tacks. Likewise to Charles S. Gubser for timely aid in anchoring down valuable United States government publications.

Illustrations by photographers Franklin R. Dalkey and Richard F. Szumski, and cartographer Duilio Peruzzi, have dispelled much of the Great Land mystery that my words never could.

Gentle threats and affectionate bedevilment by a number of colleagues and old friends sustained my narrative's glacier-like momentum. Among the most persistent were Clifford Merrill Drury, H. Brett Melendy, H. Wayne Morgan, Morgan B. Sherwood, and Gerald E. Wheeler. Four who gave parts of this manuscript their precious time were historians Theodore Grivas, John Hawgood, Jack Miller, and anthropologist Dorothy Jean Ray. To Hugh P. Brady and his brothers and sisters, a very special thank you for permitting me to use them as a conduit to the past.

Generous assistance from the following organizations has helped support my research: the Alaska Centennial Historical Publications Committee, Alaska Methodist University, the American Association for State and Local History, the American Philosophical Society, Indiana University, the Presbyterian Historical Society, the San Jose State College Foundation, and the University of Washington.

Finally, a sweet-smelling rose for my dear wife. May God bless her and keep her mind and fingers nimble for years to come.

TED C. HINCKLEY
San Jose State College
San Jose, California

☆ ☆ ☆ ☆ ☆ ☆ ☆ ☆ ☆ ☆ ☆ ☆ ☆ ☆ ☆ ☆ ☆ ☆

Key to Abbreviations
Used in Notes

ACC – Alaska Commercial Company Collection, University of Alaska, College, Alaska.

AGP – Alaska Governors Papers, Federal Records Center, Seattle, Washington.

AHD – "Documents Relative to the History of Alaska," 15 vols., unpublished MS, University of Alaska History Research Project, University of Alaska Library and Library of Congress.

CCO – "City Charter and Ordinances," Alaska State Historical Library, Juneau.

CCP – "City Council Proceedings and Resolutions, Sitka, Alaska Territory," Alaska State Historical Library, Juneau.

CHR – Custom House Records, Alaska State Historical Library, Juneau.

JCorr – Sheldon Jackson Correspondence Collection, Presbyterian Historical Society, Philadelphia.

JGB – John Green Brady Collection, Beinecke Library, Yale University, New Haven, Connecticut.

JScrap – Sheldon Jackson Scrapbooks Collection, Presbyterian Historical Society, Philadelphia.

NA, RG 98 – National Archives, Microfilm Record Group 98, Records of United States Army Commands – Department of Alaska.

PUTS – "Sheldon Jackson Letters," Speer Library, Princeton Theological Seminary, Princeton, New Jersey.

TAP – National Archives, Microfilm Record Group 430, U.S. Interior Department Territorial Papers Alaska, 1869–1911.

Contents

CONTENTS

Illustrations

ILLUSTRATIONS

The Americanization
of Alaska, 1867-1897

☆ ☆ ☆ ☆ ☆ ☆ ☆ ☆ ☆ ☆ ☆ ☆ ☆ ☆ ☆ ☆ ☆

CHAPTER ONE

Introduction

I think we would do well in buying these possessions, for I never saw a place that was so much in need of buying as this; and as a place to emigrate from it has advantages possessed by none. — Harper's Weekly, *April 27, 1867.*

ALASKA WAS TOO OVERWHELMING for man. Possibly it was intended as a playground for the gods. Nature had given it a climate ranging from the frigid, isolated Arctic wastes to a southern littoral graced by the mildest of climates. As if such a diverse setting were not sufficiently awesome, Alaska was placed atop the earth's most prodigious and powerful feature, the Pacific Ocean, and commanded to unite Asia and America.

Physiography had dictated that Alaska should form a union for the earth's great continents, but it was restless man who consecrated the oath by marriage of blood — blood born of love and mixed with greed. Dreading the enormous unknown, yet irresistibly drawn eastward by a land so challenging, so virginal, Mongoloid people first crossed the Bering Strait some thousands of years ago. Subsequent centuries of occupation by Indian, Aleut, and Eskimo left the Great Land little changed.

By the 1700's, the expansiveness of Europe's nations had forced aside the Pacific Basin's few remaining geographic barriers. Mariners Vitus Bering, James Cook, and Jean Francois Galoup de la Pérouse revealed Alaska's relationship to Asia, America, and the greatest of oceans.[1] Each paid the supreme price for his curiosity.

Vitus Bering's groping coastal exploration of Alaska in 1741 had raised about as many questions concerning the vast projection of land thrusting westward from atop North America as it had resolved. The Dane's discoveries, his incredible perseverance, and his tragic death were little appreciated by his employer, the Russian government. However, among the Siberian fur hunters, Russia's reckless *promyshlenniki*, there was jubilation. Like their counterparts in New France, the *coureurs de bois*, and later America's mountain men, the *promyshlenniki* were avid fur hunters. News that the region was rich in fur-bearing creatures inflamed their cupidity, and, violent and voracious, they swept eastward over the Aleutian Islands. In their wake the *promyshlenniki* left havoc among the aboriginal peoples. By 1784 Kodiak Island had become a toehold base for Russian fur hunters. Alarmed at the frenzy with which his countrymen had exploited both human and animal life, and sensing that tax rubles were being lost, the Tsar belatedly moved to consolidate this extension of empire.[2]

Like Great Britain's Hudson's Bay Company in Canada, Russia's tool for controlling her huge North American dominion was a profit-motivated corporation. Chartered in 1799, the Russian-American Company never became more than a pale shadow of her English competitor. The Russian organization's redoubtable leader, Alexander Baranov, despite penurious home support, in every way equaled the most indefatigable of governors fielded by the neighboring Hudson's Bay Company. In 1802 a surprise amphibious attack by Indians totally destroyed his Fort Archangel base (not far from present day Sitka). Fort inhabitants not massacred were scattered. Costly ship losses compounded his grief. Undaunted, Baranov hung on and rebuilt. Hostile Tlingit Indians, magnificent if deadly marine warriors, and his own hard-drinking, half-starved, frequently mutinous employees should have been challenge enough. Baranov also had to face down British, Spanish, and American interlopers searching for the sea otter. By the time of Baranov's death in 1819, Russia's slender forces had launched commercial feelers as far as the Hawaiian Islands and Baja California.[3]

Baranov's successors never matched his zeal. By the mid-nineteenth century, Russia's interest in her New World enterprise had waned; her expansive energies had now become focused on Asia. Company profits were only fair, and actual Russian settlers in the distant possession were few. Baranov's effort to create a California base, Fort Ross, north of San Francisco Bay, had failed to meet expectations and was finally sold. Worst of all, accusations against the monopoly by both the Russian press and various governmental commissions weakened the organization's credit at home. The Crimean War, 1854–1856, revealed the colony's vulnerability to seaborne conquest. Had they wished, English fleet units could easily have seized Russian America's capital of New Archangel, or as it was by then occasionally called, Sitka.[4] Actually England had for some years benefited from the Stikine Territory Lease, a financial arrangement that enabled the Hudson's Bay Company to operate in Southeastern Alaska. By the sixties these factors, among others, had convinced St. Petersburg that the gigantic, isolated appendage had become a liability. Encouraged by harmonious diplomatic relations with the United States, seemingly the only nation willing to meet the purchase price for her colonial stepchild, Russia turned to Washington, D.C.[5]

When the United States bought Russian America in 1867, it further confirmed its historic desire to become a Pacific power. America's territorial lunge to the Pacific had been assured twenty years earlier after England withdrew from the Oregon Country and Mexico was driven from her northern holdings. By 1850 California had become a state. A few years later the jingoistic Young Americans were talking about United States dominance of Central America, Hawaii, Canada, and Russian America. Granted, any exuberance regarding the latter was relatively pallid, but during the administration of President James Buchanan it at least surfaced. From 1861 to 1865 dreams of Pacific empire were shelved as the Union, under Lincoln's leadership, endured its cruelest war — a civil conflict that finally resolved the question of federal supremacy.

William Henry Seward, ex-New York Governor and U.S. Senator, had served as wartime Secretary of State. The assassination plot that murdered Lincoln and catapulted Vice-President Andrew Johnson into the White House had also crippled Secretary Seward. Luckily, the Secretary survived the assault. Seward was a tough politician and one of America's most successful Secretaries of State. A man of distinguished bearing and surpassing intellect, a felicitous speaker in an age of skillful orators, Seward elucidated a breathtaking manifest destiny rhetoric. To the South, to the North, and to the West, he insisted the United States had imperial obligations. But Seward was fifty years in advance of his countrymen. His aspirations to see Old Glory snapping proudly over Caribbean islands, Hawaii, and Canada had to wait. On Russian America, however, Seward scored.[6]

The traditional notion that the acquisition of Russian America won little public support, drawing almost universal condemnation from the nation's press, has now been qualified.[7] To be sure, there were critics and carpers who snickered at the $7,200,000 purchase price. Certainly Thomas Nast's lampooning cartoons, which characterized the region as nothing but icebergs and polar bears, injured the Secretary's case. And who has not heard the invidious appellation "Seward's Folly"? Happily, Seward had allies — on Capitol Hill, throughout the press, within the Pacific Slope's commercial centers, and, most important, in the Russian minister. Far West Senators, such as California's Cornelius Cole, and influential Easterners like Republican Congressman Thaddeus Stevens sensed the economic advantages that must inevitably accrue from control of Russian America. Considerable senatorial opposition and apathy were overcome by the powerful voice of veteran Massachusetts solon Charles Sumner. It is noteworthy that it was not only Pacific Slope newspapers that comprehended the Far North's potentialities. The *Boston Herald* reminded its readers, ". . . those who know most about it, estimate it most highly. The climate on the Pacific side [at that latitude] is not to be compared to that on the Atlantic side of the continent. . . . The country is reported to abound in furs, forests and minerals, while its rivers and bays on its coast swarm with as fine fish as ever were caught." A century ahead of itself, the *Philadelphia Inquirer* conjectured, "A time may come, when the possession of this territory will give us the command over the Pacific, which our extensive possessions there require"[8]

Too frequently, those who analyze the circumstances surrounding the purchase of Russian America concentrate exclusively on the diplomatic and congressional aspects. Indeed, they are fascinating: Baron Edouard de Stoeckl, Russia's Minister to the United States, long-time Washington resident, impatient to sell, and Secretary Seward, just as impatient to buy, after weeks of negotiations, signing the treaty at four o'clock in the morning. The obvious has been slighted. As was true in Texas and Oregon, the proximity of land-hungry American adventurers to Alaska portended an ultimate Yankee occupation, diplomacy notwithstanding. This was the opinion of Russia's Minister to the United States. Writing to the Russian Chancellor, Prince Gorchakov, in mid-1867, Stoeckl declared,

[Americans] look upon that continent as their patrimony. Their destiny ("our manifest destiny" as they call it) is forever to expand. . . . They are the ones who gradually invaded Texas which later became a state of the Union. New Mexico and some other parts of the South were acquired in the same manner. It had been hoped that our colonies' lack of resources would keep them safe from the greed of the freebooters, but it was not so. Although the fish, the furs, some other comparatively insignificant products of our possessions certainly did not measure up to the rich valleys of the Mississippi and Rio Grande, nor to the gold-bearing plains of California, they did not escape the covetousness of the Americans.[9]

Here, below "Baranov's Castle," the American flag was raised on October 18, 1867. This photograph, taken in the 1880's, shows (left to right below the Castle) the Post Office, Custom House, and Army barracks.

Stoeckl was not alone in his anxieties about a northern push by resource-hungry Yankees. Just a few years earlier during the Fraser River gold rush, these "freebooters" had poured into neighboring British Columbia. It should not be overlooked that when in 1867 Great Britain created the Dominion of Canada, one of its major aims was prevention of American acquisition of Canada (four years later British Columbia joined the Dominion). For Russia, however, the year 1867 marked a time to sound retreat. Who changed the name from Russian America to Alaska, an Aleut word meaning "mainland" but popularly understood as "the Great Land"? Possibly Sumner or Seward deserves the credit; certainly the transfer of sovereignty made a new name mandatory.[10]

What is often misunderstood is that America's frontier experience in Alaska began promptly with the territory's annexation, long before Canada's Klondike magnet was electrified at the century's end. The three decades from 1867 to 1897 failed to produce any neat unfolding of America's traditional frontier pageant. There were parallels with the pioneer occupation of the huge trans-Mississippi West, to be sure, but in numerous and critical ways, Alaska's settlement was different.

The Americanization of Alaska in 1867 was borne northward neither by wagon train nor by railroad locomotive, but via the sea. Her pioneers yearned for no parcel of unbroken sod on a crop-producing prairie. They spun gossamer dreams of appreciating urban real estate and rich ore-bearing ledges. Only an uninformed handful of her immigrants, most of whom were drawn from Pacific Slope communities, visualized a future behind a plow. These fledgling Alaskans aspired to stand behind a store counter or, best of all, to seat themselves at a land speculator's desk. If simple survival demanded dirt under their nails, it would result from mining, not farming.

Hyperbole was a synonym for America's West. No matter how much truth there might or might not be to the anguished. protests at "Seward's Folly," the sheer immensity of the nation's Far North frontier seemed to promise wealth to those hardy enough to seek it. Had not San Francisco, the Pacific Coast's largest emporium, enjoyed trade relations with Sitka since before the Gold Rush? And who would fall heir to the Russian-American Company's far-flung fur-trading network? Rumors had it that the San Francisco firm of Louis Sloss and Company was preparing to do so. In 1868, whispers became audible when the ex-Forty-niner turned hide dealer, Louis Sloss, linked forces with the successful wartime business promoter, Hayward M. Hutchinson, and steamboat captain William Kohl, to create the Alaska Commercial Company. After 1870, when the Company obtained a federally granted monopoly of the Fur Seal (Pribilof) Islands, it did indeed make money. However, its economic impact on the newest American frontier was oblique at best. As in the case of Nevada mining, most of the Alaska Commercial Company profits ended in San Francisco.[11]

In 1867, to the minds of Alaska's enthusiastic boosters, prodigal size was a touchstone of American success. The victorious conclusion of the Civil War only two years prior to Alaska's purchase had confirmed the political indivisibility of the Union. Soon the completion of the transcontinental railroad would affirm the Republic's economic unity. Bigness and push had done it all. Who would be so bold as to question the prospects of a land that was larger than Texas and California combined? Many had already done exactly that. Reluctant to vote money to confirm the Senate-ratified treaty, House opponents of annexation loosed more than mere Parthian shots. Not until July, 1868, was the appropriation bill finally passed, and only then with ugly gossip of "bought" votes. How much bribe money was expended by Minister Stoeckl to oil the transfer machinery may never be known.[12]

Time would validate Seward's optimism. Still, those who originally opposed him were not purblind. Alaska was then an exotic, an undeveloped mass. Economically, Alaska was almost irrelevant. Gilded Age America was preoccupied with a mushrooming urbanization and a contiguous West rich in mines, farming, and cattle, everywhere being tied together by a burgeoning railroad network. Alaska's pioneers had in fact assumed a sideshow status. But they were Americans! To accept such "second-class citizenship" was unthinkable. The years would turn to decades and still Alaskans would never tire of asking themselves why they could not enjoy a prosperity relative to that which blessed Oregon and California.

The truth is frequently harsh. No matter how aggrieved their feelings, and notwithstanding all their formal and informal protests, Alaska was a noncontiguous acquisition. A four-day water passage from Washington Territory to points along Alaska's southeastern Panhandle cost both time and money. Although its landscape was no mere composite of glaciers and igloos, it was certainly no montage of apple orchards and citrus groves. Actually, it should have been labeled "Alaskas," not Alaska. Briefly, and all too simplistically, this prodigious expanse may be divided into five geographic regions. The southeastern coastal strip, commonly called the Panhandle, is favored by the same average temperature as that of Philadelphia. It is composed largely of islands, the Alexander Archipelago, and the mainland shore separated from Canada by coastal mountain walls. This Pacific mountain system, extending northward and then westward around the Gulf of Alaska, divides two of the other geographic sections. One of these, the Alaska Peninsula and its insular extension, the Aleutian Island chain, mark the culmination of the Pacific mountain system; the other, the third geographic region, is Alaska's south-central area, whose indented coastline is rimmed to the north by the gigantic Alaska Range.

The land's fourth geographic region is mid-continent Alaska, or the Central Plateau. Situated between the Brooks Range to the north and the Alaska Range to the south, it is drained by several large rivers. The Yukon, by far the most important of Alaska's rivers, crosses it and empties into the Bering Sea. This vast interior has a typical mid-continent climate with exaggerated winter low temperatures and summer highs. North of the Brooks Range, sloping gradually to the Arctic Ocean, is the fifth region, the Arctic Slope. This area, and the Bering Coast, are the home of that most remarkable of humans, the Eskimo. At Point Barrow, the United States' northernmost tip of land, the sun disappears from late November until late January. Only a fool can think of such a dominion in the geographic singular.

Many of the territory's most ardent admirers were slow to grasp its immensity and diverse physical conditions. Enlightened development was thus unnecessarily delayed. Her pioneer citizens' claim that "District ills can find their cause and cure in the nation's capital" was to a degree true. Yet, if Congressmen and public officials were frequently ignorant of Alaska's needs, so were her settlers. When some of these Americans tried to apply the standard rules of frontier development to what had been Russian America, the frustrations produced by geographic uniqueness were only intensified. No less misguided were those who viewed the 586,400 square miles as a colony. Until both the federal government and her pioneers appreciated Alaska's novelty and finally recognized how to coordinate its growth with the nation's social and economic maturation, regional maturity was impeded.

This study examines the men and women who carried United States institutions, habits, and attitudes to Alaska after 1867. Her aboriginal peoples and the Russian Americans who elected to remain are discussed but only as they relate to the Americanization. From the purchase to the Klondike rush, that is the era from 1867 to 1897, four general historical periods are discernible. First is "the occupation," the six-year span dating from the formal transfer ceremony at Sitka on October 18, 1867, to the collapse of Sitka's town council in 1873. By this latter date the most discouraging realities of the Far North frontier had become painfully apparent. Painful because until then the territory's friends had too often either stubbornly refused to face reality or had not bothered to inform themselves about its actual economic prospects.

The years from 1873 to 1877 marked a period of "retreat and consolidation." Despite the Army's withdrawal in 1877 and Sitka's economic doldrums, America's Alaska frontier development did not end. From the late seventies through the eighties, what is here identified as the period of "utilization and recognition," a more sensible exploitation of Alaska's resources was undertaken. In particular, mining, fish-canning, and tourism grew apace. By the century's closing decade, the Far North's Panhandle frontier displayed not only a modicum of internal vigor but a society that boasted a reassuring amount of law, order, and public civility. Quite as important and concurrent with this change was the nation's growing awareness of Alaska's peculiar limitations and very real prospects.

The Great Land's immensity and adjective-defying heterogeneity mock easy classification. Its annexation had produced no rupture of national feelings like those inflicted by the admission of California to the Union. Nor, after the passage of thirty years, did the utilization of Alaska's resources attract a residual population equaling even Nevada's. Yet what a colossal, unbelievably magnificent, physical stage Alaska boasted. And how variant its actors, and how unorthodox their script. The Alaska frontier from 1867 to 1897 presented a drama easily as spellbinding as any act in the Far West pageant.

NOTES

1. Two splendid studies that will introduce layman and scholar alike to Western penetration of the Pacific Basin are: Herman R. Friis (Ed.), *The Pacific Basin: A History of Its Geographical Exploration* (New York, 1967), and A. Grenfell Price, *The Western Invasions of the Pacific and Its Continents: A Study of Moving Frontiers and Changing Landscapes, 1513–1958* (Oxford, 1963).

2. The Russian story has most recently been told by the late Hector

Chevigny, *Russian America: The Great Alaskan Venture, 1741–1867* (New York, 1965).

3. Hector Chevigny, *Lord of Alaska: Baranov and the Russian Adventure* (New York, 1944); Adele Ogden, *The California Sea Otter Trade, 1784–1848* (Berkeley, 1941).

4. On all questions of geographic nomenclature the reader should consult the distinguished compendium by Donald J. Orth, *Dictionary of Alaska Place Names* (Washington, D.C., 1967).

5. An essential source for detailing annexation is: U.S., Congress, House, *President Johnson's Message . . . Russian America*, 40th Cong., 2d Sess., Exec. Doc. No. 177, Pt. 1. Of the numerous secondary studies tracing various aspects of the Alaska purchase, a few of the most helpful are: Thomas A. Bailey, "Why the United States Purchased Alaska," *Pacific Historical Review*, III (March, 1934), 39–49; Victor J. Farrar, *The Annexation of Russian America to the United States* (Washington, 1937); Frank A. Golder, "The Purchase of Alaska," *American Historical Review*, XXV (April, 1920), 411–425; C. Ian Jackson, "The Stikine Territory Lease and Its Relevance to the Alaska Purchase," *Pacific Historical Review*, XXXVI (August, 1967), 289–306; Anatole G. Mazour, "The Prelude to Russia's Departure from America," *Pacific Historical Review*, X (September, 1941), 311–319; S. B. Okun, *The Russian-American Company*, trans. by Carl Ginsburg (Cambridge, Mass., 1951); and Benjamin Platt Thomas, *Russo-American Relations 1815–1867* (Baltimore, 1930).

6. His most recent biographer is Glyndon G. Van Deusen, *William Henry Seward* (New York, 1967).

7. Donald Marquand Dozer, "Anti-Expansionism During the Johnson Administration," *Pacific Historical Review*, XII (September, 1943), 253–275; Virginia H. Reid, *The Purchase of Alaska: Contemporary Opinion* (Long Beach, 1940); and Richard E. Welch, Jr., "American Public Opinion and the Purchase of Russian America," *The American Slavic and East European Review*, XVII (December, 1958), 481–494. This latter article is reprinted in: Morgan B. Sherwood (Ed.), *Alaska and Its History* (Seattle, 1967).

8. Welch, "American Public Opinion . . . ," pp. 277, 283.

9. Quote in: Ernest Gruening, *An Alaskan Reader: 1867–1967* (New York, 1966), 46.

10. On the basis for the name "Alaska," two works by George R. Stewart are most helpful: *Names on the Land: An Historical Account of Place Naming in the United States* (Boston, 1967), and "The Name Alaska," *Names, Journal of the American Name Society*, IV (December, 1956), 193–201.

11. Information on the emergence of the Alaska Commercial Company may be found in: Gerstle Mack, *Lewis and Hannah Gerstle* (New York, 1953); and Richard A. Pierce, "Prince D. P. Maksutov: Last Governor of Russian America," *Journal of the West*, VI (July, 1967), 403–411.

12. One man's educated opinion on how the Russian minister may have lubricated passage of the appropriation bill is: William A. Dunning, "Paying for Alaska: Some Unfamiliar Incidents in the Process," *Political Science Quarterly*, XXVII (September, 1912), 385–398.

☆ ☆ ☆ ☆ ☆ ☆ ☆ ☆ ☆ ☆ ☆ ☆ ☆ ☆ ☆ ☆ ☆ ☆

CHAPTER TWO

Occupation
1867-1873

*LET US HAVE PEACE! This is the watchword of our Alaska merchants
and traders for 1871. For the past three years they have quarrelled like cats
and dogs over the juicy bones in that territory. Now the lambs and the lions
junket in harmony. Blessed are the peacemakers, for great shall be their
rewards in codfish and in salmonfish, in sea otters and in land otters, in fur
seals and in hair seals, in minks and in martens, in whales and in whisky—
when they get to San Francisco.* —The Alaska Herald, *July 1, 1871.*

BY LATE 1867, United States soldiers and civilians had begun
to sort themselves out across Southeastern Alaska. The
greatest concentration of these pioneers, in company with
some 200 troops, disembarked at Sitka in mid-October. On
October 18, standing at attention in parade review and fac-
ing their Russian counterparts, the men in blue witnessed the
transfer ceremony. The verbal formalities were laconic.
United States Commissioner, General Lovell H. Rousseau,
reported: "The Salutes being completed, Captain Pes-
churov stepped up to me and said: 'General Rousseau, by
authority from his Majesty the Emperor of Russia, I transfer
to the United States the territory of Alaska,' and in as few
words I acknowledged the acceptance of the transfer and the
ceremony was at an end."[1]

The treaty had stipulated that those Russians who wished
to remain in Alaska would gain "all the rights, advantages
and immunities of citizens of the United States." For many

Alaska's southeastern Panhandle enjoyed a mild climate, quite different from that of the winter-locked Yukon. This view of the Haida village of Howkan on Prince of Wales Island shows (center) the natives' shift from their massive hewn log structures to the balloon frame bungalow of the white man. Probably taken about 1880. (Smithsonian Office of Anthropology, Bureau of American Ethnology Collection)

the prospect of Americanization was not appealing. Over the next two years "some went to British Columbia, some to California, most went to Russia." The bulk of these people were probably "Creoles," that is, inhabitants of mixed native and Russian ancestry. The identification "Creole" was a contemporary classification and like "half-breed" occasionally had racist overtones.[2] Accustomed to what had been a slow-paced, paternalistic living pattern, these Russian Americans would suffer almost as serious an acculturation shock from the new owners' commercial vivacity and ethnocentricity as would the aboriginals.

Alaska's total population in 1867 can only be estimated. Lumped together, all of the military and recently arrived civilian personnel could hardly have totaled more than 900. At Sitka the number of people once employed by the now defunct Russian-American Company oscillated, for added to the several hundred "old Sitkans" were Russians from posts scattered across the Great Land. They descended on the capital and then, in many cases, left the District forever. The territory's entire native population, from the Arctic Slope to Dixon Entrance at the Panhandle's southern tip, in all likelihood did not exceed 30,000.[3]

The Indians (Tsimshians, Haida, but primarily Tlingit) who lived in Southeastern Alaska were concentrated in coastal villages throughout the Alexander Archipelago. In 1867, probably the largest of these aboriginal centers was Sitka's Ranche, as the capital's Indian quarter was called. Panhandle indigenes, unlike the wandering, unencumbered Great Plains horse Indians, had accumulated numerous physical possessions. Long before the Europeans arrived, the temperate climate and lush flora and fauna of Southeastern Alaska had stimulated among the natives both a high degree of social stability and esthetic creativity. Almost invariably eighteenth-century explorers had been impressed by the aboriginals' skill in crafting the cedar and spruce that surrounded them. Once the Haida and Tlingits' materialistic propensities were whetted by such popular trade items as Russian iron goods, Hudson's Bay Company blankets, and American ("Boston Men") knick-knacks, their already acquisitive nature was abnormally magnified. By the 1860's, the virile Northwest Coast Indian had in considerable measure been supplanted by a town-dweller, captivated by industrial-age comforts. In native villages like Howkan and Kassan, and at Sitka, they were more inclined to emulate the white man's frame houses than to construct the stately war vessels of their elders.[4]

Curiously, the Panhandle Indians' affinity for village life approximated the life style increasingly evident across nineteenth-century America. Even as the nation's center of population continued to move west, greater numbers of Americans were shifting from the independence of the farm to an interdependent existence within a city. Mining towns, cattle towns, rail towns, towns of every description — the vast majority of which would never win the cherished "city" status — for the nation as a whole it presaged a higher standard of living. For too many of Alaska's Indians, urbanization meant not a higher standard of living but social erosion.

During 1867–1868 few of the bumptious passengers who strode ashore at Sitka gave much thought to the perplexities of acculturation. Some came north merely to scout out a business prospect and then return. Hayward M. Hutchinson, wasting no time and obviously well financed, went directly to the Russian-American Company managers. "I bought everything they had," he later recalled, steamers, fishing boats, wharves, salt, furs, and facilities located at Sitka, the Pribilof Islands, Kodiak, Unalaska, and distant northwest trading posts as well.[5] All this was transacted months before Uncle Sam rendered actual payment for the Great Land. Indicative of the ignorance of Alaska's new sovereign at what had in fact been bought was the postponement in clarifying who owned what in the vast mid-continent Yukon River Valley. Not until the fall of 1869 did Captain Charles W. Raymond, U.S. Corps of Engineers, journey far up the Yukon River. On August ninth, after taking careful sightings through theodolite and quadrant, Raymond informed the Hudson's Bay Company agent at solitary Fort Yukon that his station was in the territory of the United States. The Hudson's Bay Company men acquiesced, and the Stars and Stripes replaced the Union Jack.[6] It would be a long time before anyone felt like quarreling over so remote a region.

Even across the Panhandle it was anything but clear what the nation had acquired. One visitor to the capital found neither "white nor Indian who had crossed from one side of Sitka Island [Baranof Island] to the other, a distance of not over twenty miles. . . ."[7] Geologist Alfred H. Brooks later reflected that the enormous bulk of "interior Alaska was known only through the reports of a few traders."[8] Some months before the actual October transfer, the federal government had initiated action to chip away this wall of ignorance. Directed to carry out a scientific reconnaissance along Alaska's coast was George Davidson of the United States Coast Survey. United States Revenue Marine Captain W. A. Howard, who would transport Davidson's staff northward, was ordered to ascertain "the most available channels of commerce. . . ."[9] Certainly if ever a sustained coastal trade was to materialize, accurate information on the new land's poorly charted coastal maze was imperative. Alaska had not been in American possession for a year before the lack of such knowledge extracted its cost. The U.S.S. *Suwanee*, a side-wheel double-ender, struck a sunken rock in Queen Charlotte Sound, and despite her $5/8''$ iron hull, had to be abandoned.[10] Although lost in British Columbia waters, the *Suwanee* would have too many successors along the Panhandle's Inside Passage. While those who directed the Davidson-Howard cruise sought to prevent such maritime accidents, they also wished to convince the American public, and congressmen in particular, that Alaska was worth the purchase price. Accomplishing this would take quite a few scientific reports. Alaska-damning cartoons, the "Seward's Folly" label, a massive noncontiguous question mark, the possibility of still more Indian wards — whatever the criticism

—too many Americans believed the nation had hung an albatross around its neck.

Upon his return to San Francisco, George Davidson spoke favorably of Alaska's fur, fish, and mining prospects. On the subject of her agricultural potentialities he was restrained. It was just as well; Alaska's 1867 frontiersmen had steamed north with carats, not carrots, dancing before their eyes. Then, and in the months to follow, appeared prospectors whose picks had torn into Nevada's Comstock Lode and ore veins from Arizona to Idaho. Some of these same Yankee goldseekers had joined the Fraser River rush in neighboring British Columbia. For most, that 1859 quest had failed to pan out. Yet western miners were Micawber's sons—frontier Alaska would lack homesteaders but never sanguine, hard-drinking, itchy-footed bonanza-seekers.[11]

Indispensable to the western prospecter was the boom town and its residents who supplied his wants. For all their scabrous appearance and wanton sensuality, these mining camp spores occasionally sprouted into permanent and prosperous centers of human habitation. In 1867 it seemed reasonable to assume that on the Alaskan frontier Sitka would become the hub of territorial affluence. Here, as in other protean Far West communities, land speculation and merchandising went hand in hand. An *Alta California* correspondent reported, "Among the civilians on the way to Sitka is a California forty-niner . . . with an outfit of whiskey and tobacco, the proceeds of which he will invest in lands about the promising town. . . . He has an undoubted faith that in a dozen years Sitka will contain fifty thousand inhabitants."[12]

During the fall of 1867, eager promoters "squatted over the whole vicinity of Sitka—preempted the Governor's house, and one godless individual" even recorded a claim for the church and church lands! Competing stores, ten-pin alleys, and, of course, saloons rattled the sleepy village. Sitka, the company town of Russian days, was overwhelmed by the free market economy "of the inevitable Jew and irrepressible Yankee," to quote one observer.[13] Could Sitka really aspire to become a trading hub matching Helena, Denver, or Sacramento? Her ardent boosters envisioned nothing less. Didn't their quaint community have historic roots leading into the eighteenth century? Was it not graced by a truly beautiful harbor with an arc of snow-capped mountains towering nearby? Why shouldn't they reach for an opulent future? Wasn't it just eighteen years since the Golden Gate metropolis itself had been little more than a rag-tag cluster of shanties and rude frame structures?

Sitka's profile in 1867 was undeniably more solid than frenzied San Francisco's had been in 1848. The surviving Russian-American Company buildings impressed an *Overland Monthly* correspondent as "very large and constructed of ponderous hewn logs." Among these were "the Governor's residence, Saw-house, hospital, barracks and warehouses." A touch of spiritual solidarity was added by the presence of the faded, blue-grey Russian Orthodox Cathedral of St. Michael.[14] To be sure, the stockade dividing the town from the Indian quarter, the Ranche as it was labeled, was rather dilapidated. Decades before, after Baranov's reconquest of Sitka (then appropriately renamed *New* Archangel), the barrier had represented the difference between life and death. Now the palisade's rickety antiquity conveyed a sense of historic security; not since 1855 had Sitka's natives forcibly tried to drive out the white invaders. Taking no chances, American soldiers paced sentry duty along the stockade. Sounds from their challenges and changing of the guard quickly became as regular a part of nocturnal Sitka as the nightly hubbub emanating from the Ranche.[15]

Although contemporaries commonly identified the new possession as a "Territory," Alaska was not one. To speak of the territory (note the small "t") as a geographic component of the national domain was correct. Notwithstanding all the official and unofficial reports and statements then referring to the Territory of Alaska, the Great Land did not

The Russian Orthodox Cathedral of St. Michael, Sitka, Alaska. The Cathedral was destroyed by fire during the 1960's. (Bancroft Library, University of California, Berkeley)

become a Territory until the next century.[16] Since Thomas Jefferson's day, settlers in the new additions to the national domain had confidently assumed that they would one day win statehood and thus gain constitutional equality with their sister commonwealths. But Alaska had no Organic Act, no Governor, not even the promise of one. A Military District and United States Customs District were the legal perimeters granted by Congress.[17] Nor was President Andrew Johnson any help. In his final State of the Union address, Johnson devoted a single sentence to the Far North territory: "The acquisition of Alaska was made with the view of extending national jurisdiction and republican principles in the American hemisphere."[18] Exactly what all this might really portend, no one knew.

Charged with keeping the peace over this constitutional enigma was 39-year-old General Jefferson Columbus Davis. Davis, despite a checkered Civil War record and the misfortune of coincidentally bearing the first and last name of the late Confederacy's president, was a capable career officer.[19] He had no illusions about the get-rich-quick adventurers that had accompanied him north. Most likely, Davis presumed that just as types such as these eventually had been restrained by the "better-half" on dozens of other historic frontiers, so would the devil-may-care element ultimately be integrated into Sitka society. Certainly he would attempt to promote civilian rule, but for the moment and until such authority asserted itself, he and his men had the job of maintaining law and order.[20]

Accounts left by the military personnel reveal that for them, be their Alaska duty station Fort Tongass, Fort Wrangell, Sitka, Fort Kodiak, or remote Fort Kenai one hundred miles up Cook Inlet, they generally reconciled themselves to their Far North sojourn as a normal part of soldiering. The mixed reactions of Emily McCorkle Fitz-Gerald, wife of the post surgeon, were typical of most of Sitka's army wives. "There is a dirty little town scattered around the post full of Russians. Then, off to one side, is the Indian village. The Indians are not allowed in the garrison until after nine in the morning and are obliged to go out again at three." The Tlingits were "the most horrible, disgusting, dirty hideous set I ever saw. Their faces are all painted and they have rings through their noses and chins. Some of them paint their faces bright yellow, some red, some blue, and some jet black." Yet Emily extolled her serene surroundings: "Everything is beautiful. The Bay is so full of lovely islands, the beach so pretty . . . green fir so fresh looking, and such lovely moss and fern, and all so new and strange, that though I know that life here after awhile will be dull and doleful and awfully tiresome, I did enjoy it this morning. . . ."[21]

Army folk might ease the rigors of their present assignment by speculating about future duty in Maryland or California, but among members of Sitka's new civilian populace such a psychological flight was to be rejected. For all its striking natural charm and stolid if unpretentious qualities, Sitka's future could be assured only by permanent residents. The Americans intuitively sensed that if the capital of old and new Alaska was to prosper, community loyalty was mandatory. This demanded a steadily rising number of citizens, consumers and producers who, unlike the town's peripatetic miners and military personnel, would make the Far North capital their home. Alaska's transformation from a vague frontier to a thriving settlement depended on men like John H. Kinkead.

John Kinkead was no Davey Crockett; neither was he a latter-day Alexander Baranov. Except for his above-average height and calm wide-set, downward-slanting eyes, Kinkead's appearance was totally undistinguished. Fundamentally he was a small-town merchant with a veneer of legal training. Like Leland Stanford, he had arrived in California among the tardy forty-niners. While his hands sported few callouses, Kinkead was unafraid to gamble. Win or lose, he would keep thinking big. In 1867, Alaska's glimmering potentialities proved irresistible.

When Kinkead was born in 1826 in Pennsylvania, America's West ended at the Rockies' crest. Because his parents subsequently took up various residences in Ohio, the lad grew accustomed to family mobility. In 1845 the youth found himself in St. Louis, Missouri, clerking in a dry goods store. Four years later the California gold rush swept him as far as Salt Lake City. He arrived in California during the mid-fifties, but Nevada's Washoe craze drew him eastward. Like other westward-migrating Americans, Kinkead mixed business and politics.[22] Indeed, such tyro politicians seem to have been almost as commonplace "in the territories" as Eli Terry clocks. If the faster minute hand represented money, it but marked the time when the slower hour hand would register public preferment. During the Civil War Kinkead had tasted territorial politics and worked as a member of Nevada's Constitutional Convention. Neither Nevada Territory's government nor commercial opportunities sated his wanderlust. During the summer of 1867, as he later recalled, "I found myself . . . out of a job and ready for almost any adventure."[23] Alaska promised plenty of the latter. Kinkead also smelled mercantile money and political power wafting from the north. Telegraph connections with John Conness, an old California friend and one of the merchant-miner breed then serving as a United States Senator, produced a postmastership. For $12.00 per annum, Alaska acquired its first postmaster.[24] Thus enforced, Kinkead boarded the *John L. Stephens* and sailed for Sitka with the original band of American settlers. Undismayed by the primitive community that greeted him, Postmaster Kinkead purchased a store of goods, finagled an appointment as post sutler, and "at once opened with a tempting display of woolen pants, and shirts, calicoes, knives and trinkets." By handing out "some trifling bauble after each purchase," he monopolized for a time "the Indian trade."[25]

At Sitka, Kinkead encountered enterprising nomads like himself, men inured to frontier crudity and quite willing to gamble sweat and money on the capital's prospects. Next to General Davis, the minuscule settlement's most important personality, a booster who loved nothing so much as giving a patriotic address, was Alaska's first Special Agent of the Treasury Department, William Sumner Dodge. Easily matching Dodge's effervescence was tailor-journalist Thomas G. Murphy. So smitten was Murphy with printer's ink that when type and press were unobtainable, he laboriously scribbled out copies of Alaska's first newspaper, *The*

Sitka Times, in longhand.[26] Murphy's *nom de plume* was "Barney O'Reagan." Whether he had needle or pen in hand, "Barney" appears to have been the embodiment of every nineteenth-century town-builder. A contemporary described him as

> . . . a politician, lawyer, priest, editor, printer, author and poet . . . Genial, jovial, full of story, bubbling with an excess of the product of the Blarney-stone, he was everywhere, knew everything, and was first and foremost to execute all things. He was the exuberant, irrepressible spirit of the country. Strongly imaginative, full of faith and hope, possessed of an organ of self-esteem that knew no abasement, he leaped at once to the front of events and astonished all with ideas he advanced, the schemes he proposed and the strategy he displayed in their execution.[27]

There were others who, if less colorful, were equally eager to see Sitka flower, citizens such as grocer C. B. Montague, who bragged about his "scarce eggs at $1.50 a dozen," and lawyer William Wood, who saw dollar signs in future land title squabbles, and Army surgeon Alexander Hoff, who kept talking about the necessity for wide streets and civic planning.[28] These men wore no coonskin caps nor did they talk tough, but they were frontiersmen and they had carried north a great tradition: the firm conviction that business could not advance without a democratically constituted system of law and government. An auxiliary belief, one no less enthusiastically subscribed to, was their opinion that Sitka's electorate must be educated. Being "educated" bespoke their faith in the infinite worth of the public school and the Protestant verities it then communicated.

Although he lacked a high school diploma, John Kinkead had "read law." His most practical education had been participating in frontier Nevada's transition to Nevada Territory. Now, in 1867, while his wife, Lizzie Fall Kinkead, assisted with the organization of those pioneer indispensables, a Sunday School and a public school, he joined with William Dodge, Thomas Murphy, and others in meeting "the need of this country . . . the organization of Civil

Government with a general code of legislation." Such a structure, affirmed his co-workers, would "in a few years repay tenfold the cost of the purchase besides extending well towards the coast of Asia the Genious [*sic*] of Republican institutions."[29] In 1864, Kinkead had helped clothe Nevada in statehood without the requisite 60,000 citizens. Then President Lincoln had "played politics": the Commander in Chief had gravely sought all the wartime support he could muster. Was it now too much to hope that this enormous Far North frontier, or at least the Panhandle, might not also be covered with the cloak of territorial government? To Kinkead and his fellow boosters, anything but an affirmative reply to such a query would have been heresy. Before the purchase year had ended, the Sitkans requested "Territorial government for the Territory [*sic*] of Alaska."[30] Historically, the first step toward statehood required a federally constituted Organic Act, judges, and a Governor. To secure a delegate, that is a nonvoting voice in Congress, 5,000 eligible male voters were required.

The District did not have even one-tenth that number. But this was the Great Land, and people thought expansively. The Alaskans' claim that their remoteness from the rest of the country made a representative at the nation's capital mandatory was interpreted by congressional lawgivers as typical Western bombast. But in fact an informed Alaska lobbyist, resident at Washington, D.C., was urgently needed. Not until the 1880's would this critical need be filled. And then he would be merely an aroused volunteer.

On October 21, just three days after the cession, Sitkans were invited to attend a meeting "to consider the propriety of organizing a civil government for the Territory." The announcement was signed by Thomas Murphy. The gathering "was attended by a few persons; a preamble and resolutions were drawn, expressive of civil liberty and declaratory of civil rule, and Murphy was declared the head of the government." Even for boomers this was too abrupt. Within three days a second public gathering occurred. Murphy was shorn of office, and a committee was formed to draft government resolutions for a proposed city charter. One pioneer recalled that "upon inquiry it was found that not a single copy of the Constitution of the United States, nor a single state, not a copy of any municipal charter or ordinance, not a law book, nor a statute of any kind, save one, which Murphy had — Wharton's Criminal Practice — was obtainable."[31]

The accumulated political experiences of the town-builders surmounted this hurdle with little difficulty. On November 11, Sitkans gathered in convention at Thomas Murphy's tailor shop to discuss the proposed charter. Officers from the Army, Navy, and Revenue Marine were present as spectators. No doubt they came out of curiosity; some styled the assemblage "a usurpation of authority unwarranted in law." Not in the slightest cowed, the settlers continued with the cutting and pasting of the proposed municipal charter. Properly amended, the resolutions were "adopted section by section." It was then moved that a committee of two give literary grace and unity to their work and submit the charter for final convention approval. Thomas Murphy's name was joined for this task to those of N. J. T. Dana and William Dodge. Three days later the convention reconvened, this time in the Club House. After listening to the stylistic creation of Dana, Dodge, and Murphy, it was "ratified by the convention and ordered submitted to the people for adoption by ballot. . . ." Before disbanding, "the people in convention" nominated candidates for the offices created under the charter. William Dodge was their choice for capital mayor.[32]

On November 25, Sitka had its first municipal election. The charter was enthusiastically adopted — how could it be otherwise when "All American citizens before voting will be required to have signed the Charter."? To no one's surprise the town's first mayor was William S. Dodge. With one exception the convention's candidates for councilmen (five), recorder, and surveyor were unanimously approved.

Apparently Murphy was not entirely happy with the results. He and some of his supporters politicked to jettison one councilman. This may explain why Murphy took the trouble to have eighteen Russian Americans certified as United States citizens. Whether they were so entitled under the annexation treaty was not yet clear. However it was clear that the new government could not afford to overlook the talented Tom Murphy. He was soon appointed city attorney. Luckily, the town's first marshal, Paul B. Ryan, proved to be "a good and noble man . . . [who] discharged every duty faithfully and well."[33]

Only in part would Sitka's new government reflect the historic tripartite divisions: executive, legislative, and judicial. The Council "passed all laws necessary to the public weal, revised all official accounts, directed all public improvements, levied all taxes . . . authorized all contracts and all disbursements of moneys." The executive arm, initially Mayor Dodge, "presided over the Council . . . approved or vetoed all laws passed by that body, superintended all improvements [public]" and exercised all those duties "generally conferred on Mayors in other municipal corporations. The executive and judiciary branches were vested in one. In addition to his Council duties, Sitka's mayor was given jurisdiction to sit as judge presiding over a mayor's court. His authority extended only over "criminal cases and cases of action arising from a breach of the peace."[34]

General Jefferson Davis promptly endorsed the town fathers' local government.[35] Quite as positive was the General's response to Mrs. Kinkead's pleas regarding the desirability of establishing a temperance society. Indisputably the rising rate of street brawls, thefts, and unseemly incidents with Indian squaws and Russian American "ladies of love" was all too frequently linked with excessive drinking. One of the first of a number of surprises that Davis had encountered upon assuming his Alaska command was that Congress had dried up Alaska. Davis knew the rationale for such a legal prohibition: liquor plus Indians produced explo-

The United States Custom House at Sitka during the Army period. (Bancroft Library, University of California, Berkeley)

sions. But to insist that *no* spirituous drink enter so vast a Customs District—rigorous enforcement of such an order was folly.[36] An old Army man, the General resolved impossibility by the art of bureaucratic procrastination, that is, memorandums to headquarters asking for clarification, random jailhouse scapegoats, and paper threats. If he never attended Lizzie Kinkead's temperance meetings, the officer did what little he could to keep the local Tlingits from firewater.

Army wives and assorted townswomen composed the distaff side of Mrs. Kinkead's life. They viewed their isolation as not markedly different from earlier western experiences, except for the ubiquitous Sitka mist. Life in mining camps and frontier forts, midst climates ranging from a burning Arizona sun to a howling Dakota blizzard, had left these women not only adept at adjustment but learned in the art of keeping constructively occupied. The ofttimes riotous brawling of drunken miners, soldiers, and Indians was commonplace enough. Equally traditional were the church and classroom which the ladies instituted to shield their children from such barbarities.

These ancient agencies for melding mind and morality had existed under the Russians. After the transfer, Russian Orthodox religious services continued as usual at Sitka's Cathedral of St. Michael, as well as at lesser Russian Orthodox enclaves scattered along Alaska's western periphery. In conjunction with their worship, priests struggled to sustain educational programs. Sitka's Dean and Archpriest Paul Kedrolivansky dejectedly informed his Bishop on the 1869 school attendance decline. "At the beginning of the year we had 16 boys and 14 girls, but after the middle of the year almost half of the children, particularly the boys dropped. Some of the more mature," the priest observed, "enrolled in the American school . . . or went to work as house servants in the American homes . . . others dropped because they were kept at home by their parents under various pretexts. . . ."[37] In sharp contrast to this parental

45

somnolence was the literacy-conscious society represented by the Kinkeads and their fellow pioneers. A Lutheran church had existed under the Russians, and it was in this building that the Army Post Chaplain, Reverend J. O. Rainer, a Methodist, initiated Protestant Sunday services.[38] Later a Baptist Chaplain, William H. Van Horne, succeeded him. His son, Ira Van Horne, assisted with the public school.[39]

On such pedagogical and religious imperatives, civilian and military leaders were in general agreement. Young Van Horne's role is noteworthy not only because of the District's later union of public schools with Christian missions, but also because it highlighted how America's nineteenth-century pioneers fused training in the traditional three R's with the fourth R of the Christian (which usually meant Protestant) religion. Lizzie Kinkead attempted to have the Russian priest re-establish a similar "practical" program for his flock. Her exertions to revive the almost forsaken Indian chapel that lay alongside the palisade proved some-what more successful.[40]

Quite as aroused at the need for elevating the quality of life was Mayor Dodge. So was tailor Thomas Murphy, the ink-stained "Barney O'Reagan." Murphy imported a printing press, eager to commence the District's first type-set newspaper. Unfortunately the ebullient printer ran out of capital. Mayor Dodge salvaged the endeavor financially, made Murphy editor, and on April 23, 1869, *The Alaska Times* at last afforded the capital a real news organ.[41] Dodge was no less energetic on the public school question. Nine days after the transfer he joined his fellows in purchasing a "suitable building for the use of the city as a public school. . . ." General Davis agreed to heat the structure and help pay the teacher's salary. Assured that the facility might also be used for their meetings, Sitka's Masonic Lodge pledged its support. By mid-1868, and no doubt badgered by the town's mothers, Dodge had argued his sister-in-law Addie Messer, then resident in Illinois, into coming north to re-lieve the teacher shortage.[42] The fate of Addie Messer and her public school teacher successors delineates the advance and ebb of America's first frontier community in Alaska.

During the 1867–1868 school year the salary paid various substitute teachers hovered around $50.00 a month. When Miss Messer began teaching in the fall of 1868, she was granted $75.00 a month by the City Council. Miss Addie departed in June 1870. What had happened to her salary may explain why she left. By February of 1870, Sitka's economy was sagging badly and with tax revenues falling, John Kinkead, now a councilman, recommended that the Clerk "inform the school trustees of the reduction in the Teachers pay" to $25.00.[43] Possibly it was because Irish-born, 31-year-old Catharine Murphy had four children to support that she obtained $50.00 a month for the 1870–1871 term. Two years later, however, Sitka's economy wallowed in fiscal doldrums; it appears that male teachers Ira Van Horne and A. C. Allen had to be satisfied with $35.00 a month, portions of which were virtually donations. As the dispirited civilians drained off after 1869, the number of students likewise declined, along with the drop in teachers' pay. The military, however, was not free to pick up and leave Sitka. After July 1873, Major J. Stewart's daughter assumed the task of shepherding the few remaining youngsters.[44] That same month, Dodge, long since a Californian, commented with some asperity, "It is evident . . . that with a decrease of the population from about 700 at the date of the cession to less than 300 now, the school should have dwindled down to almost nothing. If so it has only shared the fate which has befallen every other enterprise attempted at Sitka, and every individual with generous impulses who ever settled there."[45]

What had happened? The steady evacuation from late 1867 to early 1869 of many old Russian-American Company personnel had distressed Kinkead, Dodge, Murphy, Montague; in fact, it had worried all of Sitka's fledgling frontiersmen.[46] Most acutely they sensed that this loss of consumers must be not only matched but exceeded by a steady infusion of Yankees. Without a ballooning population, their individual aspirations would fail. Throughout 1868 and 1869, notwithstanding discouraging economic portents, they labored to supply traders, troops, and Tlingits. And, as the conscientiously penned "City Council Proceedings and Resolutions" testify, their commendable civic-mindedness did not falter. Yet, despite all his community labors, Kinkead's mercantile efforts with Frank K. Louthan refused to quicken. In October 1869, their partnership was dissolved.[47]

By spring of 1869, Sitka's municipal fitness, financial as well as physical, was in a serious condition.[48] Dangerous swine in the streets, accident-inviting boardwalks, disturbing reports from Health Officer Alex Hoff on filthy backyards, desperately needed welfare for an "old blind-lady" and a "little Boy and Girl," requests for a "partition for the school water closet," one and all, large and small, all these costs had to be met.[49] Simple humanity demanded it. Scissors-like, these rising expenses were complemented by a dwindling tax base. It was with some humiliation that Sitka's mayor felt compelled to go to General Davis "to obtain his views." Although the General went so far as to declare that the taxes were excessive, he platitudinously advised the Council of the need for a "just and proper tax to protect the resident merchants and of raising the revenue for city purposes."[50]

The truth of the matter was that even with the military payroll there simply was no longer enough commercial activity funneling through the District capital to match the exalted dreams of the Yankee Alaskans. What perplexed and doubly frustrated these urban pioneers was that overall the Great Land's economy had not suffered such financial embarrassment. Yet nowhere else had Alaska witnessed such high hopes as it had in the illusory economic foam that first bubbled over Sitka.

Psychologically incapable of pricking their own booster bubbles, Sitka's organizers chose to cast their splenetic darts at a variety of readily available targets. Sometimes it was the

"damned damp climate" or "degenerate Indians." After
1870, when the Alaska Commercial Company secured its
lucrative 20-year monopoly of the Pribilof Islands' fur crop,
it became a popular goat. Sitkans joined Anglophobia to
financial frustration by blaming any vicissitudes in the
Indian trade on Hudson's Bay Company competition.[51] But
the primary target of the settlers' fulminations and complaints was, first and always, the United States government.
Like the Montana settlers who later damned James Hill
after his Great Northern Railroad had transported them
west and financed certain of their basics, Alaskans never
tired of condemning the lawmakers in Washington, D.C.
Their imprecations have ranged from charges of "total dis-
interest" to "dictatorial rule." In the pioneer period it was
usually the former.[52]

Among the settlers' half-pleading, half-recriminatory
protests at their government's callousness, three denunciations stand out. First was the indictment that Congress had
failed to provide them an Organic Act, thereby blocking the
territory's civil growth. Washington had indeed been cava-
lier. Yet Alaska's pioneers chose not to recall those enormous
geo-political blocks of the Louisiana Purchase, inhabited by
many more real citizens, that had waited decades before
receiving official territorial status. Understandably, the
formation of a territorial administration was never fast
enough for business speculators, especially those who also
harbored political ambitions. Ultimate statehood was the
politicians' payload; it glittered with sinecure nuggets.
Political prospectors Kinkead and Dodge were in excellent
historical company. Great Americans like Andrew Jackson
and Sam Houston had made superb use of frontier politics
in their climb to the Olympian heights. Yet with few excep-
tions, vast western regions like the Louisiana Purchase Territory and the Mexican Cession usually had not been sliced up
into various territories, that is, embryo states, until their
respective economies evidenced durable and widespread
viability.[53]

The varied dress of these Haida and Tlingit men shows what was happening to Northwest Coast culture by the late 1860's, approximately when this picture was taken at Fort Tongass. Two of the three men wearing the handsome Chilkat blankets appear to have dressed their sons in white man's clothes. (Bancroft Library, University of California, Berkeley)

A corollary to this proposition formed frontier Alaska's second major grievance. Permanency was impossible, insisted her settlers, because the most fundamental of all pioneer institutions was lacking: America's historic quarter-section. Much has been made of Congress's failure to provide homestead rights promptly for Alaska's settlers. Surely nothing was more sacred to nineteenth-century American society than the yeoman farmer and his quarter-section of land. But the mortise of public ideals and the tenon of legal reality rarely, if ever, coincide. Congressional leaders were painfully aware that ever since the Old Northwest had been constituted in 1788, and in fact earlier, troops had frequently been required to expell excessively eager sodbusters from unsurveyed land. Historically, policing this federal land, as well as the adjudication of aboriginal claims, had cost the public a great deal of money. In Alaska this was further complicated by the cession treaty, which specified "the inhabitants of the ceded territory . . . shall be maintained and protected in the free enjoyment of their liberty, property and religion." The Great Land lacked any detailed record of survey. Should Congress, therefore, welcome District land claimants, it would also invite prolonged and expensive legal contention.

If Sitka, Wrangell, and other regions of settlement had quickly obtained bona fide plats, Alaska's petty capitalists would definitely have been fortified. At first the absence of fee simple ownership failed to deflate civic optimism. Businessmen like grocer Montague and trader Kinkead easily located structures to carry on their merchandising. However, when Dodge engrossed land, commercial property, not farm land, and the "Record of Deeds" shows he more than any other assiduously sought to do so, who could he sell it to—other tradesmen?[54] Men so adaptive and imaginative flirted with yet another economic panacea: honor the hallowed farmer by giving him a Far North homestead; Alaska will have its vital consumer; business will prosper; and all will be well. But, not only was the Panhandle unsurveyed, its soil was agriculturally uninviting. Finally, what were hypothetical husbandmen to do with their cash crops if a green thumb should bless them? Ship their produce to Washington Territory? Handling and transportation costs denied them such an outlet, not to mention the superior agricultural conditions that already favored Washington-Oregon competition.

And so the last of frontier Sitka's constantly reiterated gripes: "Isn't there something that can be done to improve the transportation and mail services with Puget Sound, Portland, and San Francisco?" Postmaster Kinkead was disgusted no less than his neighbors at the territory's miserable mail service. Once a month he sorted a postal shipment, and though his clientele were delighted at receiving a wad of letters, they often evidenced it with testy grunts. "Cripple Creek got mail every week." "Even Fort Colville gets news from St. Louie in a week's time." Against such growls the logistics of economic reality proved impervious. Be the coastal carrier sail or steam, if it was to operate with frequency it must enjoy an income-producing trade along its line of commerce. In this matter, as well as their two other chronic remonstrances, Alaska's pioneers were partly justified. Congress's failure to subsidize a weekly postal delivery was inexcusable. Yet, consider for a moment the District's enormous size, its small and widely dispersed population, the scattered economic activities, and the fact that all significant transportation had to be by sea. Seen in this light, the quantity and quality of Alaska's early transportation links seem somewhat more reasonable.

Unquestionably, the vernal years of Sitka's first frontier were 1868 and 1869. Americanization meant promulgation of "school house, God's house and court house," and many a wit would have added, bawdy house. Americanization also meant the pleasure of recreational customs and national celebrations. It is not without significance that the "Masonic Fraternity held the first celebration ever witnessed in this city." Following a community picnic, the

Masons arranged an egg hunt for the children and adult entertainment for their parents, "started by Gen. Davis and his accomplished lady, the Music struck up some beautiful airs and dancing commenced." Sitka's Russian Orthodox citizens were at first no less zealous in maintaining their various semi-religious holidays.[55] Some of them appreciated that on certain matters related to Alaska's new masters their fellow-Slavs should be properly informed. Thus, when the capital rocked with its first Independence Day celebration on July 4, 1868, "Joseph Lugebil (a citizen of Russian birth) [agreed] to address his people in their own language, explaining the character of the occasion." And of course there had to be a parade.

Battery E, Fifth Artillery, and Company D, Ninth Infantry; the post fire engine manned with a soldier company; a Liberty Car with a Russian girl as the Goddess, and another as Columbia; another car, decorated and seated full of young ladies dressed in white, representing the States and Territories, while an infant child, supported among the others, portrayed Alaska as the youngest of the sisters, the weakest and most dependent upon the grand cordon of States constituting the American Union—these, with citizens on foot, made up the procession.

Mayor Dodge was selected as "Orator of the Day" and gave his audience the same kind of stirring address then being repeated in thousands of American hamlets, of past heroics and the thrilling prospects that inevitably awaited their present sacrifices.[56] The Mayor made certain his remarks were reprinted in booklet form and broadcast where they might do the most good.

In the spring of 1869, Dodge played his trump card. Even now, a century later, one cannot help but admire his imaginative gamble. William Henry Seward had masterminded the Alaska purchase. He had only recently stepped down as Secretary of State, and America at long last had just completed its transcontinental Union Pacific Railroad. Dodge was all for a Pacific union—specifically Alaska's unity with the Union. Accordingly, Dodge convinced Seward—the tired warrior needed little convincing—that he should rail west and then come north and visit "his purchase." How Dodge journeyed to Chicago, met the great statesman, and brought the Seward party to Alaska is a fascinating story. For the Republican veteran it was one exuberant welcome after another—a heartwarming thank-you from a grateful nation. For Dodge the results were heartbreaking.[57]

Vainly the Mayor had hoped that Seward would somehow be able to apply congressional leverage and resuscitate his drowning Sitka investments. Notwithstanding Dodge's Sitka hospitality and the Mayor's gift of nearly 7,000 feet of cedar for Seward's Auburn, New York, home, the retired Secretary could do nothing. A March 1, 1870, letter from Dodge to Seward summarizes what had befallen him: "Very soon after you departed General Davis took from me all the balance of the buildings which afforded me an income, leaving me prostrate financially. . . . I am now practicing law [at San Diego]. . . . I hated to leave Alaska. . . . All the citizens are discouraged and very many have left. They consider the action of the Government as unwarranted and despotic. . . ." And then the essence of Dodge's grievance: "What we all desire is stability to our titles so we can buy and sell with safety."[58] In light of Dodge's initial avidity for Sitka's commercial property and the generally confused state of affairs, he may have deserved the harsh handling he got from Davis. Whatever the case, Dodge's luck, for all his civic dynamism, had run out.

Pelt merchant Emil Teichmann visited the embryonic Alaskan capital during these early years and noted three categories of citizens. The "respectable class," that is the officers, married non-commissioned officers, and the Kinkeads' circle; a "second military class, of a much lower standing, that comprised the traders, keepers of billiard saloons and dealers in spirits . . . carried on a more or less illicit trade with the soldiers and Indians, evaded customs and excise duties and were liable to prosecution at any moment had the administration of the law not been so lax"; and a third group of "adventurers who were to be found in all new settlements . . . of various grades." It was this latter body that rose like a miasma before the aspirations of men like Dodge and Kinkead. Teichmann's description of Sitka's rabble would have found its likeness in backwater ports from the China Coast to Baja California.

Whilst to outward appearance there was no difference between them, with their torn and tattered clothing and general air of being down on their luck, some quite decent people were to be found amongst them—shipwrecked seamen, who were waiting for a chance of returning to the south, and gold-miners who had not been successful in their prospecting and were now without resources in this remote region. But most of them were the so-called "Rowdies," professional loafers, who only waited for an opportunity to take to their evil courses and looked searchingly at every respectable passer-by. I was always uncomfortable when any of these fellows were about, the more so as they made a practice of openly displaying their weapons. . . .[59]

It gave small comfort to couples like the Kinkeads that community toughs like Laubacoff, Rusoff, and Booth were thrown into the military jail by action of the Mayor's court. With each passing month he and Lizzie became ever more conscious that their neighbors, the town's stable element, were returning whence they had come. Sitka's rowdy strain grew bolder and more disgusting.

One of the economic props upon which the ex-Nevadan had built his mercantile hopes had been the American Russian Commercial Company (not to be confused with the Alaska Commercial Company), commonly called the Ice Company. Initiated at San Francisco in the 1850's, the firm had for a time offered an ice trade with Russian America.[60] After the transfer, the organization continued to function, although by then it was primarily importing fish and furs. No teetotaler, Kinkead had nevertheless been troubled by the District's liquor control quandary, and for his temperance-conscious wife, the sale of liquor to the natives was utterly reprehensible. At first he had tried to avoid involvement in this nefarious trade. Because his white customers demanded hard liquor, and in order to meet the local competition, Kinkead began to handle it. Kinkead was either too honest or too slow. Customs Collector William Kapus nailed him; he was fined and his liquid stock confiscated.[61] Early in 1870 Kinkead learned that the Ice Company with whom he had had considerable dealings, was supplying "rum, wines as well as malt liquors to the Indians [sic] of Bellisofski [Belkofski]." Sitka's Collector reported that "during some of their holidays, the whole tribe is reported to have been drunk. . . ."[62]

There is no way of knowing exactly when John and Lizzie Kinkead first asked themselves if things might not be more auspicious back in Nevada. Possibly a letter from his brother in San Francisco or from Kinkead's loyal Carson City friends urging him to come home and get into politics may have set such thoughts into motion. Whatever that first stimulus, it was a catalyst too long suppressed midst mounting frustration. He had to admit the truth. Later he would declare, "From a sanitary point of view we found Alaska in a very bad condition. The Indians were dirty and vile, the lower class of Russians and Creoles were not much better. . . ."[63] Among Sitka's Muskovite strain, the shock of national and cultural shift had itself been harsh, but when they realized that the pioneer American community was itself in decay, many sank into despair, which resulted in an excessive sickness among the Russian-American population, climaxed by an abnormally high death rate. There were other manifestations of social collapse. "We most earnestly invite," declared the *Alaska Times*, "the liberal consideration of our citizens to the impoverished condition of many Russian families residing among us. . . . They are willing to work, but there is no labor to offer remuneration or reward." A shocking number of their wives "gave themselves up openly to prostitution."[64] In September of 1870, the San Francisco-published *Alaska Herald* noted:

Our merchants have shown a commendable enterprise in their efforts to develope [sic] the resources of Alaska, and a large amount of capital has been invested in the trade with a reasonable hope of realizing handsome return. But, alas for human expectations! These hopes have not always been verified by experience. It appears that the employees of the expeditions have, in many cases, wasted the property of their employers in riotous living, gambling, drunkenness and in the demoralization of the natives. Some have, in fact, gone so far as to make their vessels places of prostitution. As a consequence, our merchants have become discouraged, and have been forced to close trading posts which would otherwise have yielded a large trade and good profit on the investment.[65]

Standard accounts of Sitka's degeneration throw most of the blame on the American soldiers. This is foolishly simplistic. Teichmann observed at that time:

If the Russians were to be believed, this sad state of affairs began with the arrival of the American troops. It is possible that this may have aggravated the evil, but it seems quite evident that a very low state of morality reigned in the colony previously. . . . the men not only disregarded the shameful trade plied by their womenfolk but in some cases even openly promoted it in order to gain a profit for themselves.[66]

To indict the United States, as some do, for the destruction of Russian "culture" in Alaska is no less questionable. At any one time Russia never had more than a thousand active citizens in all of Alaska. Judging by the relative paucity of Russian words and institutions that remained after 1867, Slavic blood and the Orthodox Church excepted, there was really not a great deal to destroy. Good evidence exists that the Company's apogee had been reached years before, and all the United States inherited was a cultural husk.[67]

In April of 1870, John Kinkead regretfully tendered his letter of resignation to the City Council. His civic efforts were on record, as he later jested, "the accumulation of honors was distressing." But duty as councilman, Mayor, and a reputation as a "fair judge" had turned not a dollar. In his forties, Kinkead realized that his future demanded a reasonable economic acceleration. Yet on every hand he and his wife witnessed community retrogression. The city treasury was so low that its marshal frequently had to be

Mist-shrouded, sleepy Sitka in the mid-1870's. Right of center are St. Michael's Cathedral and the Army parade ground. To the left, next to the water's edge, is a stretch of the old stockade. Farther back are two guard towers reminiscent of the Russian fear of another 1802 massacre.

laid off; Thomas Murphy was soon to move his *Alaska Times* to Seattle, leaving the territory without a newspaper; rumors that Alaska's touted San Francisco ice market would soon have to compete with artificial ice doomed prospects for even this District staple.[68]

The Kinkeads had given three good years to Alaska. That was enough. What were John's thoughts as their southbound steamer began the return trip to San Francisco and thence to Nevada? Judging by later events he probably mused over still another spin of the wheel mixing business and politics. His brother, who for a while had joined him at Sitka, now assured him of a San Francisco partnership. Beyond that lay mercantile, mining, and milling activities in Nevada's Humboldt and Lander counties. In 1878, Kinkead's financial success would be capped by no less a political plum than Nevada's governorship. What would have been the sojourner's reaction if someone had told him upon his departure that he would one day return as Alaska's first Governor? John Kinkead probably would have enjoyed a hearty laugh.

Poor Sitka could only groan. Unless the loss of men like Kinkead, Dodge, and Murphy, and their industrious women folk was reversed, the community was doomed. It would become nothing but an oasis of soldiery, a blighted settlement, about which swirled a social dust exhibiting faint decorum and the meagerest solicitude over building a great North Pacific emporium.

In 1870 and again in 1872, Sitka's Army officers carried out a census of the capital's populace. During this period the town lost more than 20 percent of its non-Indian inhabitants (394 down to 314). The number of prostitutes had fallen from a high of 34 to 18.[69] The more respected institutions of civilization, school, and church had declined even more alarmingly. The root cause of the port village's slump could be found in the Custom House receipts. Between late 1867 and July of 1869 the capital had sufficient maritime traffic to produce more than $21,000 in duties. In 1870 the duties registered a total of $449.28, and three years later sank to $155.25.[70]

On February 18, 1873, the Sitka City Council held its last meeting. Examination of the official "Proceedings" indicates that the hardy remnant of politicos did not then realize that their adjournment marked a constitutional *finis* to America's first Far North urban outpost.[71]

Writing in July, 1873, when he had become bemusedly reconciled to his Alaska losses, William Sumner Dodge (a cryptic *nom de plume* identifies the author, but it surely must have been penned by Sitka's first Mayor), scanned the Alaska adventure:

Our company was not wholly made up of expectant officeholders; there were some who were content to seek new avenues of trade and industry, without a thought of being made Governor or even Justice of the Peace; but it may as well be confessed that most of us thought that political greatness would be thrust upon us, and we were prepared to submit gracefully.

General Davis was no longer the central villain of the Sitka melodrama. "Military rule was established, and soon the idea of a civil government for that vast region ceased to be entertained with favor. Those who for a time cherished fond hopes of political honors were actuated by a worthy ambition; but were they not somewhat premature in their plans and short sighted in their vision?" And then in utter candor, "Some of them think so now, when it is too late. They staked their all and lost. Well, life is a game of chance, and as the wheel of Fortune turns out our prizes or blanks, we must cheerfully accept our 'luck.'"[72] Fortunately for Alaska, the United States had a plenitude of gamblers.

NOTES

1. U.S., Congress, House, *Message in Relation to the Transfer of Territory from Russia to the United States*, . . . 40th Cong., 2d Sess., House Exec. Doc. No. 125, p. 5.

2. Hector Chevigny, *Russian America: The Great Alaskan Venture, 1741–1867* (New York, 1965), 260. For a useful analysis of the Creole, see:

OCCUPATION 1867–1873

Henry Wood Elliott, *Our Arctic Province: Alaska and the Seal Islands* (New York, 1886), 104 ff. When official Russian Orthodox Church reports used the term, they evidently meant people part Russian, part native.

3. There are various estimates of Alaska's 1867 population: Ivan Petroff, *Report on the Population, Industries and Resources of Alaska*, 46th Cong., 3d Sess., House Exec. Doc. No. 40, and K. H. Stone, "Populating Alaska—The United States Phase," *Geographical Review*, XLII (July, 1952), 384–387.

4. Good introductions to the forever fascinating Northwest Coast culture are: Philip Drucker, *Cultures of the North Pacific Coast* (San Francisco, 1965), Aurel Krause, *The Tlingit Indians*, trans. by Erna Gunther (Seattle, 1956), and Albert P. Niblack, *The Coast Indians of Southern Alaska and Northern British Columbia* (Washington, D.C., 1890).

5. Gerstle Mack, *Lewis and Hannah Gerstle* (New York, 1953), 31.

6. Clifford Wilson, "The Surrender of Fort Yukon One Hundred Years Ago," *The Beaver*, Outfit 300 (Autumn, 1969), 49.

7. Theodore A. Blake, "Notes on Alaska," *Proceedings of the California Academy of Sciences*, IV (January, 1868), 13.

8. Alfred H. Brooks, *The Geography and Geology of Alaska* (Washington, D.C., 1906), 121.

9. Morgan B. Sherwood, "George Davidson and the Acquisition of Alaska," *Pacific Historical Review*, XXVIII (May, 1959), 144.

10. C. L. Andrews, "Marine Disasters in Alaska," *Washington Historical Quarterly*, VII (January, 1916), 23.

11. Pre-Klondike Alaska mining history begs for research and synthesis. For an introduction, see chapters in: Alfred H. Brooks, *Blazing Alaska's Trails* (Caldwell, Ida., 1953), and T. A. Rickard, *Through the Yukon and Alaska* (San Francisco, 1909). On the peripatetic nature of mid-nineteenth century miners, use the excellent study by Rodman Wilson Paul, *Mining Frontiers of the Far West 1848–1880* (New York, 1963).

12. *Alta California*, October 26, 1867.

13. *Ibid.*, November 23, 1867; *New York Daily Tribune*, July 17, 1868, and Frederick Whymper, *Travel and Adventure in the Territory of Alaska* (New York, 1869), 103.

14. C. Delavan Bloodgood, "Eight Months at Sitka," *The Overland Monthly*, II (February, 1869), 179.

15. Useful on the United States Army's early responsibilities are: U.S. Army, *Building Alaska with the United States Army: 1867–1962* (Anchorage, 1962), and Valerie K. Stubbs, "The United States Army in Alaska 1867–1877: An Experiment in Military Government" (unpublished master's thesis, The American University, May, 1956).

16. The distinction is further explained in: Max Farrand, "Territory and District," *American Historical Review*, V (July, 1900), 676–681, and George W. Spicer, *The Constitutional Status and Government of Alaska* (Baltimore, 1927), 24–25.

17. The classic account of how Alaska finally gained full territorial status is: Jeannette Paddock Nichols, *Alaska a History of Its Administration*

... *During Its First Half Century under the Rule of the United States* (Cleveland, 1924). For a recent historical overview of this whole question, see: Jack E. Eblen, *The First and Second United States Empires: Governors and Territorial Government, 1784–1912* (Pittsburgh, 1968). Although it does not examine Alaska, the award-winning study by Earl Pomeroy helps to place the Far North's demands in a more realistic frame of reference; Earl S. Pomeroy, *The Territories and the United States, 1861–1890* (Philadelphia, 1947).

18. James D. Richardson (Ed.), *A Compilation of the Messages and Papers of the Presidents* (22 vols.; New York, 1911), 3886.

19. Allen Johnson and Dumas Malone (Eds.), *Dictionary of American Biography* (New York, 1959), III, 131.

20. Students of early Alaska law enforcement, military and civilian, will benefit from the compilation of Tom Murton, "The Administration of Criminal Justice in Alaska 1867–1902" (unpublished MS, University of California, Berkeley, 1965).

21. Abe Laufe (Ed.), *An Army Doctor's Wife on the Frontier: Letters from Alaska and the Far West, 1874–1878* (Pittsburgh, 1962), 42–44.

22. John H. Kinkead, "In Nevada and Alaska," (unpublished MS, Bancroft Library, University of California, Berkeley); *The National Cyclopaedia of American Biography* (New York, 1899), XI, 201.

23. *The Alaskan*, May 30, 1891.

24. Melvin Ricks, *Directory of Alaska Post Offices and Postmasters* (Ketchikan, 1965), 58.

25. *Alta California*, September 26, 1867 and February 11, 1868.

26. Extant copies may be enjoyed at the Bancroft Library, Berkeley, California.

27. *Alaska Herald*, July 9, 1873.

28. Fragments drawn from *The Sitka Times*, 1868.

29. Letter from William S. Dodge to Hugh McCulloch, Secretary of Treasury, January 16, 1868, Custom House Records, Alaska State Historical Library, Juneau, Alaska. This collection hereafter cited as: CHR. Details of the first Organic Act's evolution may be found in: Ted C. Hinckley, "The United States Frontier at Sitka, 1867–1873," *Pacific Northwest Quarterly*, LX (April, 1969), 57–65. The best source is, of course, the actual "City Charter and Ordinances," which contains the entire 1867 Sitka Charter and Organic Act for the City of Sitka, Alaska State Historical Library, Juneau, Alaska. Hereafter this is cited as: CCO.

30. Resolution No. 31, December 13, 1867, "City Council Proceedings and Resolutions, Sitka, Alaska Territory." This volume is also located in the Alaska State Historical Library. Hereafter this is cited as: CCP.

31. *Alaska Herald*, July 9, 1873, contains a wonderful description of the pioneer politicians at work. In addition to the early town government holdings at the Alaska State Historical Library, there are also germane documents in the John Green Brady Collection, Beinecke Library, Yale University, New Haven, Connecticut. Hereafter this is cited as: JGB.

32. *Alaska Herald*, July 9, 1873.

33. *Ibid.*

34. CCO, 5 ff.

35. Communication from J. C. Davis to Citizens of . . . Sitka, November 16, 1867, National Archives Record Group 98, Records of United States Army Commands — Department of Alaska, Roll 2, A Volume Entitled Treaty Reports . . . 1867–1876. Hereafter this collection is cited as: NA, RG 98. This approval also is found in: CCO, 6.

36. Morgan B. Sherwood, "Ardent Spirits: Hooch and the Osprey Affair at Sitka," *Journal of the West*, IV (July, 1965), 301–344, explains the liquor dilemma after the purchase. For its inception, see: F. W. Howay, "The Introduction of Intoxicating Liquors Amongst the Indians of the Northwest Coast," *British Columbia Historical Quarterly*, VI (July, 1942), 159–169.

37. Report of Dean Paul Kedrolivansky to Bishop Paul, February 25, 1870, "Documents Relative to the History of Alaska" (10 vols.; unpublished MS, University of Alaska History Research Project, 1936–1938), II, 368. Hereafter this is cited as: AHD.

38. Toivo Harjunpa, "The Lutherans in Russian Alaska," *Pacific Historical Review*, XXXVII (May, 1968), 144; Bloodgood, "Eight Months at Sitka," 180; *Alta California*, November 19, 1867.

39. *The Alaskan*, May 30, 1891.

40. Bloodgood, "Eight Months at Sitka," 180; Kinkead, "In Nevada and Alaska," 10.

41. *Territorial Dispatch and Alaska Times*, May 22, 1871; *Alaska Herald*, July 9, 1873. Indispensable to any investigation of Alaska's journalistic history is: James Wickersham, *A Bibliography of Alaskan Literature, 1724–1924* (Cordova, Alaska, 1927).

42. *Alaska Times*, April 30, July 16, and October 9, 1869; *Alaska Herald*, July 24 and September 9, 1873. CCP, Council Resolution, October 5, 1969.

43. *Ibid.*, Council Resolution, February 23, 1870; *Alaska Herald*, July 9, 1873.

44. *Ibid.*, June 13, 1874; "Census of Sitka, Alaska [1870]" NA, RG 98, Roll 2, A Volume Entitled Treaty, Report . . . ; "Sitka Records" Memorandums: December, 1870, January 11, 1871, June, 1872, July 2, 1872, and February, 1873, JGB.

45. *Alaska Herald*, July 9, 1873.

46. *Ibid.*, January 1, 1869; "Sitka Population," AHD, II, 14.

47. *Alaska Times*, October 23, 1869.

48. *Alaska Times*, June 25, and July 16, 1869.

49. Unclassified Sitka Reports, 1868–1869, JGB; Council Resolution, July 5, 1870, CCP.

50. Letter from General Jefferson Davis to Sitka Mayor, April 20, 1870, NA, RG. 98, "Letters, 1867–1870"; CCP, May 18, 1869.

51. Suspicion of the Hudson's Bay Company encroachments began

early. See, for example, *New York Times*, May 3, 1867. The dispute continued for years. The Custom House Records, Alaska State Historical Library, Juneau, Alaska, contain numerous such Panhandle complaints.

52. For an excellent twentieth-century echo of this opinion, see: Ernest Gruening, *The State of Alaska* (New York, 1954), Chapters V–IX.

53. This is further developed by: Ted C. Hinckley, "Reflections and Refractions: Alaska and Gilded Age America," *Frontier Alaska: A Study in Historical Interpretation and Opportunity*, Ed. by Robert A. Frederick (Anchorage, Alaska, 1968); William H. Wilson, "Alaska's Past, Alaska's Future: The Uses of Historical Interpretation," *Alaska Review*, IV (Spring and Summer, 1970), 1–11.

54. Robert De Armond, "Summary of Sitka Record Book-Deeds," (unpublished manuscript, Alaska State Historical Library).

55. *Alta California*, August 5, 1868; CCP, July 2, 1868; *Alaska Times*, June 25, 1869; and *The Sitka Post*, January 20, 1877.

56. *Alaska Herald*, July 9, 1873; and W. S. Dodge Address, JGB, Sitka 1868 Box.

57. Frederick W. Seward, *Seward at Washington, as Senator and Secretary of State* (New York, 1891), 402–434.

58. Letter from William S. Dodge to William H. Seward, March 1, 1870, William Henry Seward Collection, Rush Rhees Library, The University of Rochester, Rochester, New York.

59. Emil Teichmann, *A Journey to Alaska in the Year 1868*, ed. by Oskar Teichmann (New York, 1963), 189–190.

60. Ivan Petroff, "Questions" (Unpublished MS, Bancroft Library); Hubert Howe Bancroft, *History of Alaska, 1730–1885* (San Francisco, 1886), 587; and E. L. Keithahn, "Alaska Ice, Inc.," *Pacific Northwest Quarterly*, XXXVI (April, 1945), 121–131.

61. *Alaska Herald*, December 20, 1869.

62. Letter from Jefferson C. Davis to William Kapus, July 22, 1870, CHR, Vol. 6.

63. Kinkead, "In Nevada and Alaska," 11.

64. *The Sitka Times*, September 19, 1868; Bloodgood, "Eight Months at Sitka," 184; *Alaska Times*, June 11, 1869.

65. *Alaska Herald*, September 17, 1870.

66. Teichmann, *Journey to Alaska*, 187.

67. Chevigny, *Russian America*, well summarizes the view that the United States destroyed a culture. For a differing interpretation of the sagging vitality of Russian America before the purchase, see: S. B. Okun, *The Russian-American Company*, trans. by Carl Ginsburg (Cambridge, Mass., 1951); see also Anatole B. Mazour's review of this work in the *Pacific Historical Review* XXI (May, 1952), 190. Suggestive of what awaits a social historian is Helen A. Shenitz, "Vestiges of Old Russia in Alaska," *Russian Review*, XIV (January, 1955), 55–59.

68. *Alaska Herald*, January 20, 1871, Wickersham, *A Bibliography* . . . , 33.

69. "Census of Sitka, Alaska [1871 & 1872]," NA, Micro. Gp. 98.

70. William Gouverneur Morris, *Report upon the Customs District, Public Service, and Resources of Alaska Territory,* U.S., Senate, 45th Cong., 3d Sess., Exec. Doc. No. 59, 11.

71. CCP, February 18, 1873.

72. *Alaska Herald,* July 24, 1873.

☆ ☆ ☆ ☆ ☆ ☆ ☆ ☆ ☆ ☆ ☆ ☆ ☆ ☆ ☆ ☆ ☆ ☆ ☆

CHAPTER THREE

Consolidation
1873-1877

It would probably have been easier to get a bill through Congress organizing an expensive Territorial Government . . . than to have obtained a recognition for the self-supporting municipality of Sitka, because one was the "regular thing" and the other an anomaly. — The Alaska Herald, October 24, 1873.

IN THE EYES of too many Pacific Slope investors, the first American frontier in Alaska had flopped. One San Francisco editor growled, "Our capitalists are disgusted with affairs in Alaska, and assert that business is gone to the dogs. They have been severely bitten by untrustworthy agents and injudicious investments of capital. . . . Money so invested will prove a dead loss."[1] In truth the collapse of Sitka's government in 1873 no more marked the demise of the Alaska frontier than would the "winking out" of hundreds of other Far West boom towns foreshadow the eclipse of Colorado, New Mexico, or Washington Territories. Alaska had failed only to live up to its advance billing. One section of General Davis's preliminary 1867 "Military Orders for Alaska" had reassured him that "Mail and telegraph communications will very soon be established between Sitka and San Francisco, and thence with all parts of America, Europe and Asia. With these facilities for trade and commerce . . . this new territory must soon become what nature intended it to be . . . 'The New England of the Pacific.'"[2]

Regrettably, such pretentious bombast had been matched by sapient generalizing. For the nation at large, Alaska would too long remain as one book title described it, *Our Arctic Province*. New York's Senator Roscoe Conkling revealed the depth of public ignorance by agitating for a railroad to run across Alaska to the remote Bering Sea Coast.[3] Other various southside legislative bodies recommended that the District be transformed into a national penal colony, a United States Botany Bay. Particularly vociferous in urging that the Far North become a dumping ground for felons were a number of 1874 California legislators — some, possibly, embittered over Sitka's recent fate.[4]

Town-building usually registered the success or failure of America's changing late nineteenth-century Far West frontiers. Yet a budding urban center could only germinate and flower when the soil in which it was planted proved economically viable. For the first two years after the transfer, Sitka's initial commercial bustle had provided this nourishment. By 1873 the military payroll loomed disproportionately large in sustaining the languid port village.[5] Uncle Sam's pay chest might hearten the disillusioned Sitkans, but tradition had dictated that private capital be the major factor in building the American West. Across the Great Land, as over the historic West, two aggressively independent, exploitive institutions preceded the actual American occupation. Fur-trading and mining form classic chapters of the frontier narrative. These inheritances from America's past, as well as the romantic whaling industry, were functioning in Alaska well before the Sitka boomers rushed north. Indeed, the economic consequences of this mighty triumvirate, when weighed against Sitka's significance, made the capital's destiny rather unimportant.

Whether through fear of being inundated by uncontrollable filibusterers or from lack of information, Alaska's Russian owners had done virtually nothing to develop the country's mineralogical potential.[6] Ultimately, the seduction of gold attracted more Americans to the Far North country

The whaling steamer Mary *lying at Port Clarence in 1886. (Bancroft Library, University of California, Berkeley)*

than any other single lure. That is, until World War II defense spending and installations outdrew even gold.

Because precious minerals had been found up and down America's Pacific Slope, it was normal that among Sitka's initial settlers were prospectors inspired by golden dreams. Despite a variety of tantalizing "gold discovery" reports emanating from the District capital, no major lode was uncovered. The newspapers and mining equipment merchants of West Coast cities were not reluctant to play upon every rumor of Alaska mineral wealth. At Sitka, Fort Wrangell, and Tongass, reported the *Portland Bulletin* of August 30, 1872, "Everybody in that region talks of nothing now but mines, and all are speculating in them." More restrained was the San Francisco-published *Alaska Herald*, "Should further prospecting turn out well, Sitka will soon find that she is not by any means 'out of the world.' Business and bustle will take the place of her present quietness, and the dreams of her early American settlers will be realized."[7] Not Sitka but her neighboring Panhandle community, Fort Wrangell, benefited from the first substantial wave of Alaskan goldseekers.

Pick and pan appear to have loosened British Columbia's Stikine River gold as early as 1861, and as at Canada's Fraser River rush two years earlier, Yankee miners were in the vanguard. The Stikine's channel thrusts into Alaska's coastal mountain range south of Sitka. Because it cuts deep into the interior, the Stikine is essentially a Canadian waterway. Approximately eight miles from its mouth lay the trading village of Fort Wrangell. Originally established as Fort Dionysius by the Russians to block Hudson's Bay Company encroachment, it became Fort Stikine when the English firm leased the area. In 1867 two companies of American troops arrived, and the name was changed to Fort Wrangell. Although the military abandoned the post in 1870 (the Army reoccupied it again from 1874 to 1877), the historic up-river trade with the Indians continued.

Among the trader-prospector types who influenced the

village's destiny was the New Yorker Ames T. Whitford. With others of the Civil War generation, Whitford had chosen to gamble on mining profits rather than martial glory.[8] While his countrymen tore themselves to pieces at Gettysburg, he prospected along British Columbia's Stikine River, exposed a paying bar, and returned to Victoria with close to $2,000 in gold dust. When Alaska's transfer occurred, only about thirteen whites still scratched for the illusive pay dirt in the vicinity of Whitford's lucky bar. By that date his own gleanings had been washed away in other futile mining ventures.[9] Whitford was one of those who had hustled to Sitka in 1867. Wiser than certain San Francisco dudes, he became "a dealer in trash and Indian curiosities."[10] He seems not to have made much, but when others quit, he stuck. Unlike Kinkead, he had fallen unmovably in love with the gigantic geographical Amazon called Alaska. Like Kinkead, Whitford had to learn that it was more remunerative to supply miners than to be one, and the liquor trade with the Indians, if risky, was quite rewarding.

During 1873, galvanic reports sped down the Stikine River, "Gold on the Cassiar [Dease Lake region would have been more correct] at the headwaters of the Stikine." To join what came to be known as the Cassiar Rush, Whitford headed south to Fort Wrangell, the logistical jumping-off point for the gold field. That the pay dirt was again located not on American soil but Canadian deterred him not the slightest. In January, Fort Wrangell had only three white residents, the U.S. Army having temporarily withdrawn, but by the time Whitford arrived, a throng of miners had activated their panoply of saloon, gambling hall, and bawdy house. Ex-Sitkan Whitford must have envied the profits being banked by his old British Columbia associate, veteran steamboat captain William Moore.[11]

Moore had been born in Germany in 1822. By 1851, he had become an American citizen and joined the California stampede. Thereafter his Germanic industriousness propelled him through a succession of business vicissitudes from Peru to British Columbia. During the summer of 1873, assisted by his sons, Captain Bill cleaned up five thousand dollars from mining in the vicinity of Dease Lake. The following spring, as the Moore party journeyed to their Dease Lake camp, they encountered the usual miner throng wending its way to the diggings. As one of Moore's sons later recalled, "With the passing of time, many of those on the trail, were becoming excited and over-anxious to get to the diggings, and locate, before all the ground had been staked. A great quantity of supplies were strewn along the trail, where men had thrown them away to lighten their loads, so that they might travel faster."[12] Having staked their claim the preceding year, the Moores traveled with greater deliberation. They were aware that those who jettisoned food and equipment on the trail were the same ones who would soon be begging their aid. The discarding of baggage en route "was very foolish," observed his son William Domingo Moore, "as it would require all their supplies to carry on work after reaching the diggings. But this is the history of all new mining camps. The great majority spend and waste more, getting to a new gold camp, than they ever recover from their efforts."

The Moore men decided they could parlay larger profits by transporting and supplying the gold-hungry crowd champing to travel upriver to Telegraph Creek, or to "the head of navigation." From that point the miners would have to pack overland to the Dease Lake diggings and thence throughout the Cassiar region. With his husky lads, Moore built the box-like steamer *Gertrude* and purchased the *Glenora* primarily for the Stikine River run. The *Grappler* was acquired to link up with Victoria.[13] Until the steamer traffic faded out in the early eighties, the Stikine run was rarely lacking in drama. The current in the river's upper canyons was turbulent; canoe travel required nine days to get as far as the fall line, while even the steamboat took three days. During passage, steamers tied up at the river bank each night, thus enabling travelers to go ashore and sleep. Insomnia from a vibrating hull was not the problem; these small vessels were so stuffed with men and cargo that there simply was not sufficient room for all the passengers to lie down at one time. The down-river return voyage was wild—"the steamers made the 150 miles in 8 to 12 hours, the machinery reversed much of the time, to restrain the boat from going entirely with the mad current."[14] To meet the need of a reliable pack trail from Telegraph Creek to Dease Lake, that is, the stretch nature denied his steamers, Captain Bill signed a special contract with the British Columbia authorities. The job was completed ahead of schedule. After the Canadians certified the trail as safe, Moore was allowed to collect two cents a pound for toll, fifty cents per head for horses and cattle, and twelve and a half cents per sheep. Packer competition had been charging a much higher sum. Little wonder that by the fall of 1874 there were thousands of miners, among them 300 Chinese and 50 Negroes, working throughout the Cassiar District. When the United States Customs tried to complicate Moore's shipments moving through Fort Wrangell, he merely operated his *Western Slope* directly from Victoria to the boundary on the Stikine.[15]

Whitford should have been more circumspect about the likely oscillations of this latest rush, but he again came down with gold fever. It was a familiar cycle and one to which he was fully inured. An early February departure from Fort Wrangell demanded snowshoes and hand sleds, for the ice held into March. One slip at some points along the trail meant a watery burial in river rapids far below. Active digging began in May. Freezing of the sluices in September closed the season. Winters were spent either at Fort Wrangell, "Wrangell" many a prospector labeled it, or at more decorous coastal cities to the south like Victoria and Portland. By 1877, U.S. Collector M. P. Berry reported that 900 white men, 250 Chinese, and 700 Indians were bound for the Cassiar fields through Fort Wrangell. Actually by that date the country was largely "panned out," that is, the less difficult placer mining was coming to an end.

Henceforth quartz mines and expensive machinery would produce the larger profits. According to the British Columbia Minister of Mines, approximately $1,000,000 in bullion was taken from the Cassiar Mining District in the peak year of 1874. At the decade's end, less than half that amount of gold was being mined, and this primarily by determined Chinese. Whitford returned to Sitka financially weakened, but inoculated against further argonautism.[16]

Before his departure from Wrangell, Amos Whitford may have witnessed the execution of miner John Boyd. It was the old story: consumption of too much "forty rod," an argument with a fellow prospector over a slut, and a murder, in this instance, Thomas O'Brien "shot through the heart" in the billiard saloon — "hurdy-gurdy" house. But for the intervention of some who preferred the niceties of a "trial," a mob would have hung Boyd forthwith. The District had no judicial system, so a miners' meeting was convened. In typical fashion a sheriff was elected who officially arrested the now sobered Boyd and charged him with murder. A judge (one journalist reported three judges) was likewise selected, and he appointed attorneys for the prosecution and defense. Next he ordered the sheriff to impanel a jury. Two days later the condemned man confirmed the craftsmanship of Wrangell's carpenters, several of whom probably had built gallows from Pecos to Salt Lake City. The *San Francisco Chronicle* detailed the venerable, if ugly, event.

The morning of the execution was a bright and beautiful day. Boyd was looked upon as being dangerous, having been engaged in several disgraceful broils at Wrangel and in the mines. Nothing is known of his birthplace or relatives: he spoke of neither. Very little is known of his past history, save that in Idaho he bore a bad name and was quarrelsome. . . .
A short while before the appointed hour Boyd asked for liquor and water, which were given him, and after smoking a cigar said, "I am ready." He followed the guard with a firm step, and at 9:30 ascended the rude scaffold. He was perfectly resigned and cool, and being asked if he had anything to say, merely said "he was sorry, and that he had not intended killing O'Brien." The noose

Nuklukayet, a dozen miles below the confluence of the Tanana and Yukon Rivers, was one of the first American trading posts in interior Alaska. A decade after the Alaska Commercial Company established this post in the late 1860's, its appearance had changed only slightly. Note the stern-wheel river steamer icebound for the winter. (Bancroft Library, University of California, Berkeley)

was then adjusted, the black cap drawn over his eyes, and at a signal from the Captain of the guard John Boyd was launched into the dread eternity, paying the just penalty of his merciless deed by "a life for a life."[17]

While such scenes as these evidenced Alaska's Americanization, another tiny trickle of goldseekers was penetrating mid-continent Alaska, that is, the enormous Yukon River Valley. Recall that Captain Charles Raymond had raised the American flag over remote Fort Yukon in August 1869. With the departure of the Hudson's Bay Company men, "Here before Christ" as they jocularly described themselves, the Alaska Commercial Company fur traders inherited the stockaded post. But for the nearby Yukon River, their station was an utterly desolate wilderness domicile. Luckily, their aboriginal clientele, the Tanana, Yukon, and Porcupine River Indians, although widely dispersed, usually were not hostile. Fort Yukon's 20-foot-high palisade offered only the frailest of shields against these Athabascan Indians. In times past, fierce Athabascans had ranged all over North America. They had devastated both Russian and British trading posts; America's fierce Apaches were of Athabascan stock. By 1869 many of Alaska's Athabascan peoples had been weakened by the shock of European encroachment. The mid-continent Indian, unlike his Northwest Coast brother, was not yet in virtual thrall to the white man's trade goods. With each trading season, however, the interior aboriginal's dependence upon gunpowder and manufactured goods increased. In 1869, Captain Raymond had journeyed upriver aboard the diminutive stern-wheeler *Yukon*, the first steamboat ever to appear on the great river.[18] That vessel, like all of the technological space-destroying marvels eventually introduced by Americans, cared not an iota for nature nor the creatures served by nature. Although the Indians who stood in wonderment gazing at the smoke-belching *Yukon* were not cognizant of it, that awkward 50-foot craft represented an onrushing end to the isolation of even this remote land.

75

Leroy Napoleon McQuesten arrived at Fort Yukon in August, 1873. McQuesten and his three partners, one of whom, Alfred Mayo, was an ex-circus acrobat, came not by steamboat but by canoe. The Raymond party had come up-river from the Bering Sea. These roamers had paddled downriver from Canada. "There were three men at Fort Yukon in the employ of the A.C. Co.," wrote McQuesten, "M. Mercier was in charge. We were treated like kings. We remained two days. Some of us had not had such good living in ten years. It was there we saw the first repeating rifle."[19] When McQuesten first arrived at Fort Yukon in 1873, he had already roamed over much of Alberta, British Columbia, and Canada's Northwest Territories. Roamer is about the only noun one can employ to describe the likes of McQuesten. Prospector, trapper, trader, steamboat captain, he and his partners were peripatetic adventurers, men split from the same stump as Ames Whitford and Captain Billie Moore. But where Whitford and Moore invariably fell back on town life, McQuesten's ilk often shunned it. Possibly the cruel natural environment in which these men labored ruined them for the company of urban living, gadget-crazy, modern man. Being handcuffed to desk and machine would have destroyed McQuesten. Brutal climatological conditions never could. Shrewd, tough, philosophic free spirits, men such as he really seem to have feared the strictures of success. Had they stopped rolling and unremittingly applied themselves to any one of a variety of different tasks on the Alaska frontier, many probably would have acquired capital and relative comfort. Any genuine serenity clasped by McQuesten's type would be ephemeral, won after surviving a stubborn environmental challenge — a biologic contest from which frontiersmen Dodge and Kinkead would have fled.

Another such fascinating roamer was the powerfully built Arthur Harper. Like Jason in search of the Golden Fleece, Harper had left Ireland to pursue the yellow stuff to California, along the Fraser River, and ever northward to Cassiar country and beyond. He arrived at Fort Yukon along with Mayo and McQuesten in 1873. During the early seventies, after extensive placer mining up and down the Yukon proved unremunerative, Harper, McQuesten, and Mayo went to work for the Alaska Commercial Company.[20] The vast valley might be parsimonious with her mineral wealth, but for the present at least she was quite generous to trappers and traders, and the thought of retreating to the "outside," to Portland or points south, left some of them colder than the 70 below zero temperatures which they occasionally endured. For such men, the need for recreation could be sufficiently gratified at lonely St. Michael, where the Yukon River's muddy waters mingled with the Bering Sea and the Alaska Commercial Company sustained a major distribution base. An 1870's visitor remembered how the "half-dozen whites here . . . appear to enjoy life, . . . they are not completely exiled, as they go down to San Francisco on a furlough once in every two or three years."[21] Personalities stamped from the McQuesten mold probably took the trip as much to satisfy their curiosity as for any other reason.

Gilded Age Americans were equally disinterested in visiting Alaska in the years immediately after its acquisition. Citizens who cared to examine their atlas might have deduced that Alaska's Bering and Arctic seas were more isolated than the Great Land's enormous interior. Yet years earlier, in the 1840's, while the Upper Yukon River remained insulated from the sounds of Russians at New Archangel, Russian America's Bering and Arctic coasts were echoing with the shouts of Yankee seamen. These New Englanders were, of course, American whalemen. They had first rounded Cape Horn and begun Pacific whale-hunting at the end of the eighteenth century. During the 1830's the Kodiak grounds, sometimes called the Northwest Coast Right Whaling Grounds, had been exposed by Barzillai Folger, a Nantucket captain. Throughout the next decade, Russian America's principal whaling grounds from the Aleutians across the Bering Sea and finally the Arctic Ocean were discovered and utilized primarily by Americans. The year 1846 marked the height of this maritime industry north of the 50th parallel: in that season almost three hundred vessels chased humpback, bowhead, sperm, killer, and their various whale cousins.[22]

Alaska's great age of whaling was already in decline when the United States acquired the territory. Throughout the sixties, Pennsylvania petroleum had steadily reduced the demand for whale oil. Civil War destruction had proved terribly costly: forty whaling ships were purchased, loaded with stone, and sunk to blockade Southern harbors; and the Confederate raider *Shenandoah* burned or captured dozens of whaleships off Russian America's northern coast. Yet despite changes in consumer fashion and the havoc of war, a reduced whale fleet remained in operation after the annexation.[23]

Like the prospectors who mined Vulcan's realm, the men who labored across Neptune's domain were a polyglot mix. Herbert L. Aldrich, who sailed with them, wondered:

Was there ever a better place to study character than in the forecastle? Portuguese, Scandinavians, Germans, Spaniards, Englishmen, Irishmen, Americans; almost every nationality can be found there. The Americans we had were bright fellows, mostly ranchmen. Of course, there was the man who did the tattooing, the accordion-jammer, the yarn-spinner, and the rest of the famous sailor kind. Many of these fellows found a home in the forecastle such as they had not known for a long time, if ever; not only good shelter, but plenty of wholesome food, and, if needs be, warm clothing.[24]

Waiting for favorable weather to beat through the Aleutian Islands might add a week to the long, hard voyage to the whaling grounds. To command a whaler, especially above the Bering Strait along Alaska's icy coast, demanded consummate skill. "To maneuver a ship from lead to lead, and among large cakes in an ice-floe," affirmed Aldrich, "is a lesson that sailors of much ability and experience have to study long and hard to learn." Whalemen enjoyed bragging how a veteran master, called up to testify on the loss of an Arctic whaler, handled the adjuster, also an experienced seaman. Offering tit for tat, the whaling captain finally asked the adjuster:

"Suppose you were on a lee shore in a gale where it was impossible to tack ship, where there was not room to wear ship, and you could not anchor, what would you do?"

"Expect the ship to go ashore," said the adjuster.

"I wouldn't," said the old whaleman, "I would take in the after sails, haul everything hard aback and boxhaul her," (that is, back the ship out). The insurance was paid without further question.[25]

Whether it was the over-confidence of such superb seamen or the whimsy of Neptune miffed at such pride, the year 1871 affirmed the awful vulnerability of wooden ships to Alaska's treacherous northwest shore. Eager to pursue their quarry and aided by a favorable wind, a large number of whalers entered a lane of water that had opened between the land near Point Belcher and the ice pack. Whales proved plentiful and the ships rapidly filled with bone and oil. After repeated warnings by both the local Eskimos and Nature herself, the ice pack relentlessly drew its trap. Thirty-four ships were crushed to pieces. Amazingly, not a man from the ill-fated fleet was lost. Despite their reduced ranks, the whaling craft continued their operations. Apparently not satisfied with the 1871 destruction, Nature again shut her icy maw in 1876, and twelve more whalers were consumed. This time lives were lost. Some crewmen chose a slow death aboard their doomed vessels to what they were certain would be a torturous death at the hands of the local Eskimo. As it transpired, those who turned to the natives for succor survived.[26]

When one considers what the whalemen had visited upon the Eskimo, it is not hard to understand why some of the seamen had so little confidence in the aboriginals' humanity. The whale hunters were ruthless predators, men little dif-

The adoption of modern ordnance eliminated many of the hazards formerly faced by walrus hunters, just as it had for whale-men. As the walrus along the Arctic Coast were slaughtered, the specter of starvation loomed larger for the Eskimo.

ferent from their contemporary, the Great Plains buffalo hunter. Both were sojourners who gave slight thought to the possible extinction of their mammal quarry. Neither worried about the beast's wasted, discarded carcass. As for the impact their ecological ravages might have on Eskimo life, few seem to have cared.

Alaska's annual whale hunters did indeed come from outside the District, and after they had filled their ships with a marine harvest, they sailed for a distant home. Until the mid-1870's, this was usually New Bedford, Massachusetts. Increasingly thereafter it was San Francisco, where ship and crew took winter rest. A typical San Francisco news note during November and December would read:

On the 13th instant the brig *Tropic Bird,* Jernegan master, 19 days from the Aleutian Islands, brought 450 barrels of oil, 4,000 lbs of whalebone, and 1,000 lbs of ivory—consigned to master. On the same day the schooner *Parallel,* Jacobson master, 13 days from the same Islands, brought 125 barrels of walrus oil, 75 lbs of whale bone, 1,000 lbs of ivory, and twelve fox skins, to A. Crawford.[27]

The whale bone cargo was baleen whose plasticity made it excellent for corset stays.

Armed with whaleguns and harpoon-bombs, these whalemen were eminently more efficient than the sea hunters of old, fishermen who were forced to approach the snorting aquatic giant in an open boat and then literally stab him to death. Now, should a whale season turn poor, whalemen turned their rapid-firing rifles that killed repeatedly, and from a distance, against walrus to fill their oil tanks. The walrus's ivory tusks weighed as much as five pounds a pair and, like all white gold, possessed universal value. During the 1870's the whalers' entire walrus kill was estimated at 100,000 animals.[28]

Possibly as wantonly destructive was the natives' improvidence, which the whalers had induced. The Eskimo had been introduced to the rifle early in the seventies. Like the portable whalegun and whale bomb, a few of which would fall into native hands, it caused the Eskimo to slight the ancient habits of thrift for the baubles obtained from easy killing. What matter the unused, rotting walrus carcass when the white man would supply them with tempting trade items: steel drills, metal cooking utensils, and always additional bullets — factory-made weaponry so that they could more quickly dispense with their crude weapons like the harmoniously balanced bone and slate-tipped harpoons.[29]

To judge from contemporary outcries, the most explosive of imports were not munitions but alcoholic beverages. Ivan Petroff, because of his extended governmental information-gathering activities in Alaska, expertly summed up the appalling social tragedy encouraged by the whaler-trader.

. . . the trading vessels coming to this region . . . have carried such quantities of alcoholic liquor that the natives have acquired a craving for the same that can no longer be subdued, and this causes them to look for no other equivalent for their furs, oil, and ivory than the means of intoxication. At the same time they become utterly reckless in their pursuit of fur-bearing and other animals, thinking only of satisfying their desire for the present without the slightest thought of the future; and if this state of affairs be continued the extermination of the people, consequent upon the exhaustion of their means of subsistence, can only be a question of time.[30]

Ironically, a considerable number of the ships exchanging contraband along Alaska's Arctic Coast had their origin in the Kingdom of Hawaii, mid-Pacific islands whose inhabitants had for over half a century suffered similar culture shock.[31] George Wardman, an agent of the United States Treasury who visited Alaska during the seventies, snapped that the smuggling "about Cape Prince of Wales and Clarence Sound between 'pirates' and the Eskimos" supplied the natives with rum and breech-loading rifles. "The result," wrote Wardman, "was not conducive to the welfare of the natives, profitable to the revenues of the country, nor just to legitimate traders who have scruples against infraction of the laws of the land and morals."[32]

Although the Gilley Massacre occurred two years after the

1876 whaling fleet's devastation, it may explain why a number of the entrapped whalers were not sanguine about Eskimo hospitality. Unquestionably the sorry affair underlay the Petroff-Wardman apprehension. According to George Gilley, Captain of the brig *William H. Allen*, he had come north

. . . on a whaling and trading voyage . . . a canoe load of Prince of Wales natives came along-side, and the chief waved a skin on a pole indicating a desire to trade. When he got on board he wanted ammunition. I got some, and, after he had shot at cakes of ice for awhile, he asked me to give him five cartridges for his repeating rifle. This I refused to do . . . although I offered to trade. It was quite noticeable that he and some of his followers were under the influence of liquor. . . . All began to ask for rum, but I told them that I had none. They said that they knew I had, for all ships with two masts had it.

Recrimination burst into flaming anger and fighting began. Ammunition exhausted and their canoes adrift, the Eskimos "all crawled under the t'gallant forecastle. . . . Seeing no other alternative," testified Captain Gilley, "I posted men above them, and when a native showed his head, he was clubbed and thrown overboard. Toward the last we hauled them out with gaff hooks. The three canoes had contained about twenty warriors but not one of them had escaped."[33]

Utterly detestable episodes like the Gilley outrage seem to have been inevitable on the outreaches of civilization, particularly if people deficient in the techniques and trinkets of the invader had become desperate to obtain them. Thankfully, such sensational massacres were the exception, not the rule, for where violence was habitual, commerce would not follow. This was a rubric as quickly comprehended by buyer as by seller.

By 1867 the lucrative and celebrated trans-Pacific fur-trading epoch between the Northwest Coast Indians and "Boston Men" and "King George's Men" had vanished into the pages of maritime history.[34] Consumer demand for Alaska's pelts, however, had not disappeared. After the

United States occupation, some of the Russian-American Company's trappers and traders elected to depart. Others, frequently with more aboriginal than Russian blood, chose to remain in Alaska and become "independent traders." They would trap or trade as whim and weather dictated. Hardly distinguishable from the natives among whom they lived, these men appear to have been scattered from St. Michael south, along the Great Yukon and Kuskokwim rivers, spotted throughout the Aleutians and ranging between Kodiak Island and the country about Cook Inlet. Russian Americans living east of the Kenai Peninsula, and throughout the Panhandle, seem to have been more prone to try new careers or sink into the torpor of town life.[35]

Just as it is dangerous to generalize about the men who sought the Far West's elusive beaver (try, for example, to compare "Cannibal Phil" and the Bible-reading Jedediah Smith), so must one be wary in categorizing Alaska's traders and trappers after 1867. Certainly when it came to the art of survival and dealing in pelts, these men were easily the equal of Jim Bridger or Thomas Fitzpatrick. Alaska had no Cheyenne horse warriors, but a solitary fur collector was fair game for silent, snowshoe- or canoe-borne predators. Furthermore, a trader who had survived many a winter imprisonment in Colorado could be driven quite mad by the terrorizing white silence laid down by 50 below zero temperatures over Alaska's huge, monotonous Yukon Valley.

After 1867 the vast bulk of actual trapping was still done by Alaska's native peoples. Across the mid-continent, after the spring thaw permitted the interior rivers to become navigable, the indigenes transported their season's catch to a trading station. A United States Treasury officer, an expert in checking cargoes, described an Indian's arrival at St. Michael:

The bidarra sailed up to the beach, the mast was sent down, and the contents of the boat began to find their way ashore. Twenty-three women and children and two dogs were first landed. Then tents, camp equipage, and salmon, fresh and dried for the party. After that the men commenced carrying off shoulder loads of dressed sealskins, neatly put up, five in a bundle, till forty-eight large and forty-one of the smaller size were landed. Five bundles of sealskin thongs, lashings for boat building nails being used— were carried off next, followed by two sealskins of oil, and bundles containing five hundred marmot skins for fur robes. All this came out of an open skin boat twenty-five feet long by eight feet beam,— flat bottom of course.[36]

In Alaska experienced mountain men such as McQuesten, Harper, and Mayo often mingled fur and gold hunting. As a result they eventually acquired a knowledge of the upper river and its tributaries without which the later Yukon River goldseekers and town-builders would surely have had to endure even rougher hardships than those extorted by climate and physiography. How strange a paradox: the wilderness trader who so abhorred the crush of civilization by his very activities accelerated its arrival. Unlike the rapacious miner and whale hunter, or for that fact, the slogan-mouthing town-builder, such frontier precursors as Mc-Questen preferred Alaska much as it was before steamboat and coastal traffic sped up socio-economic change. This essentially conservative attitude affected their relationships with indigene customers. Live and let live meant exactly that. McQuesten never forgot how he fell out of a loft at his trading post. "I broke one of my short ribs. It was two weeks before I could move, and I was in great pain. . . . There were three bands of Indians within days travel . . they would send a messenger every day to hear how I was getting along." His neighbors were not being completely selfless. Their shaman made "medicine for me to get well . . . they thought if I should die that they might be blamed for killing me as there was no other whiteman in this part of the country."[37]

No trader could afford to take the aboriginal for granted. A veteran prospector and trader and a respected Alaska Commercial Company employee, George Holt thought he understood both Alaska's Panhandle natives and the Athabascan of the interior. Indeed, it may have been Holt who in the mid-seventies succeeded in crossing over the Dyea Pass through the dangerous Chilkat Indian country and thereby inaugurated a circuitous route opening Panhandle traffic to the Upper Yukon River Valley. For all his wilderness acumen, Holt was unable later to escape death at the hands of a murderous Copper River Indian.[38] McQuesten's intuitive grasp of what he could and could not expect from his native clientele was an instinct that some of his peers never mastered. Trader James M. Bean arrived at St. Michael only two years after the purchase. In the late seventies, accompanied by his family, Bean journeyed up the Yukon and Tanana rivers to a place where Arthur Harper had once built a cabin, Harper Bend as it was latter dubbed. Here he began a new trading post. Bean refused to tie himself to any company and drove a tougher barter than any of his interior competition. McQuesten had warned the headstrong Bean against bringing his wife and children into Tanana country — the Indians were definitely not reliable. Only a few months after he had set out his stock of goods, Bean rejected a request for food from two young Indians. It was a mortal blunder. They returned, and while his wife sat eating breakfast, shot her down. Actually they had presumed their bullet would pass through Mrs. Bean and fell her husband as well. Luckily, Bean escaped with his children.[39] Arthur Harper, with three of his Indian employees, had the grim job of fetching the body. The Indian assassins "did not take but very little of the goods and those they afterward returned," recalled McQuesten. "The murderers were never punished for the crime and they used to come down to the Station every spring, but there would only be two or three traders and they didn't think it was safe to attempt to arrest them as the Indians had always threatened to rob the Station most every spring."[40]

Far to the south, along Alaska's Panhandle, aboriginal hostility toward Sitka and Wrangell traders was becoming less blatant. There were, of course, occasional acts of passion "in the bush" and out, and village "Indian scares" had not fully abated. Usually the presence of the soldiers calmed all but the most nervous of the whites. It was an open secret that some Alexander Archipelago merchants had even encouraged these alarms. Pleas for help meant United States Revenue Marine or naval vessels with spendthrift crews.

Possibly the most exasperating Indian challenge confronting Sitka and Wrangell pelt dealers was getting an Indian to make up his mind. For the Tlingit and Haida the annual exchange of his furs bore carnival-like overtones. He had labored long and hard to garner his catch, and to barter it away in minutes was foolish. After pitching camp some distance from the white man's town, a few days were always spent in ceremonial visits with resident Indians. Finally the Indian would select a store, stalk up to the counter, and silently deposit one pelt. The trader would then pick it up, shake it, smell it, rub it, twist it first one way and then another, then smooth it down again on the counter "with an air of cunning and shrewdness beautiful to behold." It was essentially a ritual. Once a price was quoted, the Indian silently picked up his fur, tucked it under his blanket and walked out. George Wardman was confident "that each of the ten store-keepers of Wrangell handles and appraises every skin brought for sale in this way." Frequently, to complete the sale required not only a tempting array of dry goods, guns, and ammunition and molasses (a splendid liquor base) but finery for the females and candy and nuts for the children.[41] When a fur shipment at last reached San Francisco, ultimately to be transshipped to points east and abroad to Europe, it received but curt attention in the press: "132 Silver Fox; 21 Red Fox; 7 Cross Fox; 4 Sea Otter; 38 Land Otter; 8 Beaver; 104 Sable; 1 Mink."[42] A routine newspaper inventory, to be sure, yet what book could recount the half-comic, half-tragic story that might lie behind each pelt — skins garnered from a region whose geographic extent equaled the distance from Los Angeles to Savannah, Georgia.

It was understandable that with Russian America's annexation the merchants of San Francisco had moved to
dominate her fur trade. After all, commerce between Sitka
and California was over half a century old.[43] In 1870, Captain Leonard Hartwell, a whaling captain of New Bedford,
reported that San Francisco not only was importing codfish
and salmon from Alaska but "that the very last season there
were some 28 vessels engaged in trading between San Francisco and Alaska in furs such as sable, fox, mink, otter. . . ."[44]
With Alaska's purchase, San Francisco businessmen envisioned Sitka as a potential Far North emporium, an *entre-
pot* to receive the District-wide fur harvest and an equally
thriving market for the distribution of their California
exports. As already noted, 1873 climaxed this dream. At
year's end the *Alaska Herald*'s editor counseled, ". . . the
principal trade of Alaska is, and will probably continue to be,
in the hands of San Francisco merchants. . . . The fur trade
is necessarily hazardous, requiring courage, judgment and
capital; and the few firms and individuals who continue it
have undergone an apprenticeship which has not cost them
lightly. . . ."[45]

"Not cost them lightly" was something of a euphemism.
However, by that date the entire nation's financial community was reeling from the doleful aftershocks of the Panic
of 1873. There had been nothing fundamentally wrong with
the San Franciscans' confidence in Alaska; they simply had
invested too much of their time and money in the wrong
community. The first editor and publisher of the *Alaska
Herald* was an erratic Slav named Agapius Honcharenko.
From his four-page sheet Honcharenko spread lies about
Alaska Commercial Company mismanagement and corruption. Maybe the Company had become a hate substitute for
his Old World enemies.[46] Whatever the psychological explanation for his monomania, he was right on some matters
when a majority held otherwise. In his January 1, 1869,
issue of the *Alaska Herald*, Honcharenko had urged that "The
future capital of Alaska should be centrally located and the

Island Kadiak [Kodiak] appears to be most eligible from its position. Sitka is a miserable, barren, rainy, foggy place, while Kadiak has a healthy and pleasant climate." How curious that his corporate *bête noire*, the Alaska Commercial Company, was the principal firm to concur with Honcharenko's insight.

Well before the retreat of the Dodge-Kinkead crowd, the Alaska Commercial Company saw that Sitka, while not necessarily a useless economic appendage, was definitely not central to Great Land development. If these San Franciscans were to succeed in their ambition, and they envisioned nothing less than filling the vacuum left by the Russian-American Company, they must do more than merely think big. The Alaska Commercial Company management comprised more than petty capitalists irresponsibly inflating each other's ego with booster gas. It united hard-headed businessmen glad to discard old-fashioned and wasteful proprietary ideas for the cost savings and steady yields of a modern corporation. When the firm secured its 20-year monopoly over the Pribilofs (Fur Seal Islands), located north of the Aleutians, there was another rudimentary reason for not being tied to Alaska's traditional port-capital. Sitka was neatly located for San Francisco freight, but it was way out of line with the fur empire the Company wished to dominate. The Russian-American Company had pushed its early administrative base from Kodiak to Sitka to better block foreign encroachment into what was then a pelt-laden Panhandle; now the San Franciscans would shove their commercial centers west and to the north, thus reversing Russia's historic course of empire. It was a gamble, but an intelligent one.

Capital, trained personnel, equipment, an efficient organization, political connections, a secure source of raw materials and a suitable market — had Andrew Carnegie studied the mercantile edifice erected by Hayward M. Hutchinson, William Kohl, Louis Sloss, and others, he must surely have grunted, "Good." To begin with, these men pooled both their managerial and financial wealth. The subsequent dividends confirm the soundness of their initial "capital position." To the ranks of men like McQuesten, Holt, and dozens of skilled Russian American and aboriginal employees, they added trained personnel wherever and whenever needed. For example, they early brought Captain Gustave Niebaum into the Company for his long-time shipping

Alaska Commercial Company field agents like trader Walker of the Yukon region, and their native co-workers, were indispensable in opening the interior to settlement. Indian George (above) had witnessed the murder of Bishop Seghers. (Bancroft Library, University of California, Berkeley)

experience throughout Alaska and British Columbia waters.[47] To serve as General Agents in Charge at such places as their Kodiak District, they hired cool, capable, and generally humane men. When one lonely Nuchek trader lost his nerve before some surly natives grumbling for credit, his General Agent superior duly reported the clerk's "cowardice" and then switched him to a safer post for he was "an honest and industrious young man."[48] Note has already been made of the prompt and energetic means by which Hutchinson in 1867 scooped up the Russian-American Company's equipment, both ashore and afloat. As for its political connections, the firm finessed admirably. Accorded the presidency of the Alaska Commercial Company was none other than San Francisco's Collector of Customs. When John F. Miller resigned this collectorship to accept his new corporate responsibility, he possessed more than just a knowledge of West Coast shipping. A one-time Indiana lawyer who found the California rush irresistible, later a brevet major-general with a Civil War combat record — in truth, Miller had connections leading right into the White House.[49]

A detailed, comprehensive analysis of the Company's successful field organization and the way in which, during its 20-year monopoly, it wisely assured itself of future resources and a competitive market position is yet to be written. Enough is now known to respect what the San Francisco directors accomplished.[50] By the mid-seventies they could point with pride to such commercial communities as those sustained on Kodiak Island, Unalaska (Eastern Aleutians), and the Pribilof Islands, as well as the string of Yukon Valley trading posts ancillary to St. Michael. Their annual fur seal operations on the Pribilofs were efficiently geared to diverse seasonal company business across the Great Land. Its general merchandising and fur-trading stations rarely functioned like clockwork, but the Home Office and Special District Agents ceaselessly labored to reduce internal mismanagement. Each station agent (trader) was required to keep a Record Book to be:

used at the station like a "Logbook" on board a vessel, for the entry, from day to day, of all events, as for instance:
The arrival or departure of vessels.
Accidents.
The state of the weather.
Transactions.
Purchase of Furs, etc. with respective payments for same, — as far as possible.
The fitting out of hunting parties, number of people belonging to same, where they are directed to: their return and catch. . . .[51]

At its remote insular stations where the Company maintained a year-round work force, it provided an improved standard of living, both medically and educationally, for native as well as white.[52] From its San Francisco headquarters the Russian Orthodox Church sent out an annual payroll in excess of eleven thousand dollars to priests scattered from Kodiak to St. Michael. Company vessels delivered the cash to these widely dispersed clergy.[53] With such sound public relations and business astuteness, is there any question why San Francisco's banks were also annual recipients of palmy Company returns?

Angered at the profit-producing Pribilof lease awarded Sloss and his associates, and embittered at their own Sitka losses, the Company's San Francisco enemies finally succeeded, during the seventies, in getting a congressional investigation of the "frightful monopoly." Before the dust had settled, Honcharenko and those who had abetted his lies were publicly humiliated. After a thorough inquiry, the congressional committee stated, "there is no just ground of complaint against the Alaska Commercial Company. . . ."[54]

Except for itinerant coastal trading craft, in the main schooners and barques, and random calls from United States Revenue Marine and Navy vessels, it was the Company's fleet that supplied any communicative unity to sprawling, geographically divided Alaska. Fortunately, a mail contract provided for a regular link between the District capital and southside. In July, 1875, "the wharf still being a wreck," the *California* dropped anchor offshore. Before the flukes could break the harbor's calm waters, "up went a shout from the soldiers and storekeepers, 'Is the paymaster on board?' "[55] Little wonder, for as the District Customs officer declared, of the Alaska Commercial Company's "large fleet of steamers and other vessels," none were documented at Sitka. "They have virtually abandoned Southeastern Alaska, and have no direct or pecuniary interest in that portion of the Territory."[56]

The Company's downgrading of the Southeastern region was strictly commercial, for just as the Yankee whaleman's penchant for trade had accelerated cultural change among Alaska's Eskimo, so did their mercantile-minded counterparts to the south continue to alter native socio-economic mores. Be the trader corporate or independent, afloat or ashore, he presented the Indian an inventory whose delights were ineffable. And again it was too frequently guns and liquor, and especially the latter, that aroused the aboriginals' desire. Because of the sordid and sensational effects of the frontier peddler's firewater, his image, whether in the Far West or the Far North, is rarely good.[57] This easy stereotype does an injustice to the unheralded traders whose advice, medicine, and numberless humane acts broke down barriers of race and language. A reading of the correspondence of the Stikine River firm of Callbreath, Grant and Cook makes it clear that although these men trafficked in liquor, they preferred not to pander to the natives' appetite for alcoholic drink.[58] Liquor could transform some natives into drunken clowns, but others could as quickly become murderous. Sadly, and despite the social tragedy it abetted, business competition assured the ubiquity of "ardent spirits," federal law notwithstanding.

Even with the best intentions, it was difficult for a trader not to employ dangerous quantities of alcoholic drink as a trade item with the natives. Their thirst for Hoochinoo, or Hooch as the Panhandle brew was later called, was if anything more unquenchable than that of their relatives on the

Great Plains. Everyone drank more in Alaska.[59] In fact, were it not for the extensive Custom House records, one simply could not accept as fact the Niagara-like flow of liquor that washed into this ostensibly dry territory. Treasury Department Deputy Collectors were assigned to half a dozen port communities. Like figures in a Russian short story, these customs officers labored in despair to stanch the flood that seeped in along Alaska's coastline maze. Among Alaska's Indians, Hoochinoo probably exceeded the Hudson's Bay Company four-point blanket as a common barter medium; however, unlike the durable blankets, it failed to survive passage through many hands.

Maritime traders probably exploited the aboriginals' insatiable thirst in their mercantile exchanges to a larger extent than their rivals ashore. In fact, these intermittent vessels were often a storekeeper's competitor as well as his supplier.[60] Most of them were not registered in Alaska. They operated out of ports extending all the way from British Columbia to Latin America to Hawaii, and unlike the representatives of the Alaska Commercial Company and the independent traders ashore, their skippers rarely worried over the social explosions that would result from an irresponsible disposal of liquor. Because they flaunted federal law enjoining the importation of liquor, they were rightly categorized as smugglers.

After the purchase, such seaborne storekeepers moved quickly to expand their illicit activities along the shores of the vast Far North market. Here was a sales territory that invited law-breaking, not only because of its labyrinthine coastline, but because of grossly inadequate policing and vague District law. Writing from the Pribilofs in 1868, Revenue Marine Captain J. W. White fretted to General Davis, "There was also landed at this place the cargo of the Hawaiian schooner 'Prince' shipped . . . from the Sandwich Islands. Said schooner came directly here discharging her cargo and returned . . . without touching at any port of Entry in the United States."[61] Although Davis had problems ashore, he had no compunctions about seizing the barque *Peru* and the schooners *Thomas Woodward, Lewis Perry,* and *Caldera* for smuggling liquor into the Panhandle. He doubtless suffered some vexation when a letter from the District Collector censored one of his staff who had recently imported eight kegs of whiskey, containing ten gallons each and marked as "private stores." Seeing a good thing, firemen and deckhands on such steamers as the *California* and *Gussie Telfair* equipped their pants legs with long pockets.[62] As it transpired, the territory's ranking customs officer, the District Collector, became so swamped with liquor prohibition headaches that the position became little more than a revolving door for the men holding the farcical job.

By 1870 the Secretary of the Treasury felt compelled to take more action.

The Department is in possession of information that a Mr. Levi, Master of the Schooner "General Harney," purchased a "Still" and . . . landing the same at Cooks Inlet, and there commenced the manufacture of rum. . . . You are instructed to ascertain whether the "still" is, or has been in operation at the point named, or at any other place in Alaska, and take such steps as will prevent an infringement of the law. . . .[63]

But how to "prevent an infringement of the law"? The District never had more than a few hundred troops, and these were virtually powerless because of their immobility. Certainly the Collector and his handful of deputies could not be expected to check the omnipresent liquor smuggling, even when they were reinforced by an occasional Revenue vessel. Congress had made the District "Indian Country" to clarify its historic intent to keep the indigenes from the bottle, but there it stopped. No territory-wide administration enforced the law, and incredible though it was, no one was certain what laws applied in Alaska and precisely which Pacific Coast courts had jurisdiction over what.[64] Making the territory one grand penal colony would have solved the problem of law and order; fortunately that half-canard, half-legislative absurdity had not won popular support. Oregon's Senator

John H. Mitchell advocated that Alaska be annexed to Washington Territory. This proposal to make the Great Land a noncontiguous county of a United States Territory would have been an intriguing if dubious governmental experiment, to say the least. As 1876 began, the *Alta California* ridiculed the gigantic Far North territory of less than "fifty whitemen" and urged the evacuation of Alaska's inhabitants "so we might close out the concern."[65]

Such facetious geo-political game-playing may have enlivened Pacific Coast drawing room conversation, but these satirical schemes aided General Davis and his successors not an iota. Sitka's economy had slumped. Wrangell's streets evidenced all the noisy superficiality of a miners' boom town, nothing more. White sojourners might come and go, but Alaska's Russian American and aboriginal inhabitants were there to stay, and both bodies posed grievous social quandaries for their military administrators. Sitka's "municipality expired," noted *The West Shore*, "and the military governor became stepfather to Sitka. As is generally the case, the stern stepfather rules with an iron hand."[66] In truth, not even in the District capital did the commanding officer "rule with an iron hand."

To Army officers had fallen the Sisyphus-like labor of maintaining law and order—law and order for law-abiding frontiersmen like Captain Billie Moore's family, and, it was hoped, law and order for the lawbreakers like pitiable John Boyd, and even Russian Americans and Indians struggling in the throes of harsh culture shock. Writing in the late seventies, William Gouverneur Morris grieved that "the condition of the Russians and their descendants today in Sitka is truly lamentable. They exist in a most pitiable state of poverty; in fact, most of them are in absolute want. They are subjected to all kind of ill treatment and contumely by the Indians." Morris exaggerated, but not much when he bemoaned, "They have no means of livelihood save what the sea brings forth and small patches of cultivated ground . . . the majority are in a state of starvation."[67] Another informed observer, writing of Sitka's "Russian half-breeds, quarter-breeds, octoroons, etc.," in 1877, opined that "as a class they are not distinguished by industry or energy; they are fairly letting the buildings in which they live rot above their heads."[68] An article in *The West Shore* indicated that this latter statement was not merely a literary phrase.

Another notable edifice [in Sitka] is the "Doubledecker," a two-story log house, tottering on its base, windows all broken, grimy, slimy, and dilapidated, in which nearly a hundred of the most wretched half-breeds of both sexes congregate making night hideous by their brawls, and day disgusting by their appearance, and both disagreeable by divers unqualified smells emanating from the unclean mass of filth in and about the house. It is the "Five Points" of the northern metropolis.[69]

The culture shock endured by Alaska's non-Yankee populace was not simply a burden of Americanization. The European's diseases, like his fiery liquor, had long preceded the 1867 transfer. In the gantlet of acculturation, no blows were more horrendous for Alaska's aboriginals than the ravages left by smallpox, measles, and their deadly bacilli cousins. Disease registered the same dreadful mortality rate throughout Alaska that European-borne bacteria had effected elsewhere across the Pacific Basin and the Americas. In 1837, Priest Jacob Netzvetov told how "Over 700 Aleuts died at Kodiak during the last year from an epidemic of smallpox."[70] It was a depressingly familiar report, and as the white man moved out among Alaska's native peoples, the circle of devastation widened. By the 1870's there were few areas of the Great Land that had not been swept by cruel epidemics. At least by then the frequency of their visitations had decreased. Nevertheless, measles and smallpox could still create havoc within an isolated native community.

Anthropologists may yet decide that by far the worst obstacle in accommodating a "weaker" culture to a more powerful one is the harrowing psychological adjustment. The soldiers were neither anthropologists nor social psychologists. Indeed, few if any of their fellow Americans then understood the curse of cultural staleness. Aboriginals were viewed as "wards," or at least this was how nineteenth-century white Americans had increasingly come to visualize them. It was a policy shaped by racism, apathy, greed, and genuine benevolence. Civilians in the Interior Department enunciated the virtues of civilizing the red man by annuities (gifts of food, blankets, etc.), thereby ending his nomadic, raiding life and transforming the "savage" into a reservation-bound farmer. To the Army, however, fell the dirty job of making certain the process was initiated even when opposed by the Indian—as it often was.[71] When they came to Alaska, Army officers who previously had been part-policemen, part-welfare workers among western Indians did not quickly discard all that their Far West experience had taught them. Luckily for Great Land indigenes, the richly endowed marine environment of the Alexander Archipelago eased any serious food deficiency commensurate with that confronted by horse Indians existing on the fast-disappearing Great Plains buffalo. In Alaska, ironically, the Army's food handouts—nobody seems to have called them annuity goods—went to Sitka's Russian Americans. An unofficial action, the welfare was spurred by simple humanity. Some capital merchants objected, and the soldiers' largess was terminated.[72]

The Army's response to the liquor control dilemma met the same fate. During 1875, Major James B. Campbell, one of General Davis's successors, issued instructions reaffirming "Indian Country" restrictions in Alaska and required both license application and $5,000 bond to trade therein. "The strictist provision of the Indian Intercourse law will hereafter be rigidly enforced," Campbell stoutly insisted. "The object," editorialized the *Alaska Herald*, "is more effectually to prevent the sale of whisky and firearms to the Indians. If this cannot be accomplished under the laws which have been extended over Alaska . . . it probably will not be effected by making the military commandant at Sitka an Indian Agent. . . ."[73] Keenly conscious of this threat to their unbridled commerce, the traders protested to General Oliver O. Howard, Commandant of the Department of the Columbia. Howard was a famous one-armed Civil War hero, popularly called the "Christian General" because of his religious and educational endeavors. He was accustomed to storekeeper hypocrisy. No doubt the sanctimonious cant about "Campbell's arrogant treatment of civilians" and "we never supply the Indians with firewater," annoyed him. Yet Howard was also painfully aware of the hard realities of law enforcement. It was always easy for an area commander to issue an order, but could it be enforced — and by the Army? He promptly informed Major Campbell that his attempt to license traders "be suspended." Impatient with the Far North perplexity, Howard urged his superiors, "I recommend speedy legislation . . . that either it be *without question* under military authority, or, far better, that it may be organized under a civil government."[74]

Civilian or military administration, the grinding process of native assimilation would not have been much different. His Northwest Coast culture long since in disarray, his mind and body assaulted by unfamiliar institutions, customs, and attitudes, the Indian struggled to adjust. At times he could be "silly." When for instance, Major Campbell tried to please a Chilkat chief by "getting him a soldier's cap with all the fixings — crossed cannon, pompon, etc." the Indian became indignant upon its presentation. Only after he secured an officer's cap was he placated.[75] The Indian could also be "crazy." After six Tlingit crewmen were lost from the sealer *San Diego*, their friends demanded reprisal or they would "at once kill six merchants."[76] At times the native could be "funny," as, for example, the occasion when a male, arguing with a squaw, tore off her clothes and took her blanket, "leaving the luckless creature in a perfect state of nudity and an immoral picture of curiosity to every passerby."[77] But more often than not, the aboriginal was a "problem."

First of all they were a problem to themselves. Bewildered, humiliated, and cheated, they drank too much. If sufficient surcease from their misery was not secured from intoxication, or possibly because of it, they concluded an evening in a fraternal row. Such an altercation could be doubly dangerous should the inebriated natives encounter a white man as they staggered home. The indigene adhered to "an eye for an eye" code of justice. Because he was not particular whose eye, an innocent white man might pay for an insult that one of his race had recently heaped upon a native. This was the explanation for the untimely death visited upon two Sitka traders by Kake Indians. The Kakes, infuriated at the treatment some of their people had received from the Sitka soldiers, killed the two men and set off what some newspapers headlined the "Kake War."

Even before Alaska was paid for, the *New York Tribune* had speculated what it would cost to subdue Alaska's aboriginals. Noting that it had cost the government $115,000 to kill one Indian on the Nebraska plains, the *Tribune* estimated in Alaska it might run as high as "$300,000 a head to kill Seward's Indians."[78] Happily, General Davis and his successors were not cut from the same martial cloth as their contemporary, George Armstrong Custer. There were instances in which a few soldiers appear to have gained satisfaction in killing a Tlingit or Haida, yet it seems clear that among the ranking officers the policy was to intimidate belligerent Indians and seek to avoid bloodletting. Whether this was due to compassion, the fear of unfriendly Portland and San Francisco newspaper correspondents, never ones to pass up a story about "drunken soldiers in the northern wasteland," or merely common sense, it is impossible to tell.

Convinced that the Kakes must be punished, as much to warn other Indians as to quash any more Kake violence, General Davis called upon Captain Richard W. Meade, commander of the U.S.S. *Saginaw*, to assist him. Davis and Meade were well aware how a few years earlier shipboard cannon of the H.M.S. *Clio* had shelled refractory British Columbia natives, forthwith ending their proclivity for "trouble making."[79] Taking some two dozen soldiers aboard the *Saginaw*, the joint Davis-Meade force steamed for Kuiu Island and the Kake villages.[80] In his official report Davis stated:

I had determined upon my arrival there to demand the surrender of the murderers. If this was not complied with, I then intended to seize a few of their Chiefs as hostages till they were given up. Upon reaching the first village, we soon discovered that the Indians had all left, except a small party known as the Thickehanny family, who are quite well civilized, and have been known for some years past to be very friendly to the whites, and having almost lost their identity with the Kake Indians. From these friendly Indians I learned more of the particulars of the murder and the perpetrators. They reported the whole party who committed the murder as very bad Indians, but that two of them committed the deed; the others were only accessories. After committing the murder they all returned to their villages, and stated what they had done. This threw the whole tribe into a state of excitement, and they stampeded, in anticipation of our vengeance. Nothing was left to be done except to burn their villages, which I ordered to be done. Their villages, containing in all twenty-nine houses, were destroyed. One house was left to the Thickehanny family, and the property they claimed as belonging to them. Quite a number of canoes were also destroyed. Where the Indians fled to we were unable to ascertain.[81]

Meade later told a reporter that "three villages were destroyed by fire and shell. A stockaded fort was also destroyed. . . . There was no loss of life on either side—it was a bloodless war."[82]

From beginning to end, the Army's Alaska duty had been one gigantic conundrum, a riddle for which no one had an answer. The truth was these fighting men had embarrassingly little to fight or to do. General Davis had not hesitated to employ his men on Sitka's civil works, and some soldier convicts were forced to build roads on distant Kodiak Island.[83] Still the fact remained, the one "war" in which they participated had been essentially a navy operation. Major John Tidball might believe the Panhandle Indians to be "savage and possess the villanous traits of character of that class," but veteran non-coms knew better.[84] Jailing intoxicated Indians failed to offer any of the glory then being won

Critics of the purchase of Russian America in 1867 derided it as a Polar Bear Garden. Ten years later, when the United States Army withdrew from Alaska, Thomas Nast still lampooned the Great Land in his Harper's Weekly *cartoons.* (Harper's Weekly, *April 21, 1877, p. 309*)

by their comrades galloping after Sioux and Cheyenne. Commander Davis, as well as his successors, must have recognized that the most feared enemy their command would ever confront would be troop ennui. Had Sitka been ringed by hostile Apaches, the soldiers would have been honored as saviors. As it was, they were cursed for debauching the natives. Who can doubt that Davis was delighted when he received orders to report to Portland and assignment to the Modoc War? For those Cassandras who continued to bewail Sitka's defenselessness before a likely Indian massacre, Davis is purported to have snapped, "There is no danger whatever from the Indians."[85]

During the seventies one Army commander followed another. Each tried his best to maintain military morale. Sitka's annual Independence Day parade, daily saluting the colors, monthly dances, one was called the "Hoochinoo Club Hop," and numerous other traditional and innovative activities were resorted to to keep the men reasonably content. With time hanging on their hands, soldiers commenced two semi-monthly news sheets, the *Alaska Bulletin* and the *Sitka Post*. Villagers applauded their journalistic ambitions as they did the soldiers' minstrel show and community theater productions, "Grandmother's Parrots" and "No One Averts His Fate."[86]

By February of 1877, the troops grasped at anything to remind them they also were fighting men. When a fugitive wounded Indian threatened to lead an assault against them, "the military authorities prepared their Gatlings and other light Field Guns and placed them in favorable positions for defense . . . two companies, 25 men each, of the Russian inhabitants of the town were organized and armed with Springfield muskets." Attempts to organize a company among the Americans were greeted with bemused apathy. Little wonder, for as one observer had commented, the Indians' "prowess and importance has been overrated; . . . [they] possess but a few guns and those ill-conditioned and of obsolete pattern."[87] No Indians attacked—then or later. That same February, when Gatling gun gasconade had seemed necessary to sustain a semblance of martial strength, a destructive fire wiped out the officers quarters. A United States Special Centennial Commissioner who came north to evaluate what Sitka's founding fathers had accomplished returned disillusioned. "There was but little change in the appearance of the place since my visit in 1869, but what there was appeared to be for the worse and showed by the apparent neglect . . . that the officials were already contemplating a removal of the troops and an abandonment of the post."[88]

The fate of the military occupation force was sealed in the spring of 1877. Orders to withdraw did not produce unanimous rejoicing; the *Sitka Post* ridiculed the budgetary justification for their evacuation. The *Chicago Tribune* was probably correct when it reported that, "it is the testimony of those most familiar with the condition of affairs . . . that the soldiers are of no use whatsoever. The Indians of Alaska are not of a troublesome character, and even if they were the troops could do nothing to suppress disorder." In the eyes of the *Alta California,* the Army's departure was "one of great humanity."[89] Some of the men had become actual Alaskans. Their wives had enlarged the territory's sparse non-native population, and notwithstanding Sitka's dampness, they had developed a warm affection for the land's harsh magnificence. A few of the enlisted men, earlier discharged at the capital, would remain behind as the spouses of Russian American ladies, but for the men still in uniform, the 1877 orders were final.

General O. O. Howard was quite relieved that the military occupation had ended. From first to last it had been a source of embarrassment to the Army.[90] Professional integrity, not to mention the welfare of the civilians left behind, required of him a recommendation for future territorial policing. The *New York Times* correctly reported Howard's opinions on how to enforce the law on the Far North frontier. "He thinks a gunboat should be sent there . . . until the miners and Indians become accustomed to the change; it not being possible to send a gunboat, the best revenue vessel should be made as nearly equal to a gunboat as practicable."[91]

Ten years after its adoption, Alaska was still America's foundling, if Sitka's growth was any measure. The District capital had become, as one government official described it, "Goldsmith's Deserted Village."[92] Although it was not then appreciated, the business retreat of the early seventies had been paralleled by scattered and diverse economic consolidation across the Great Land. Indeed, by 1877, Alaska's latent natural treasures were being transformed into kinetic resources by man at a quickened pace. The next ten years would witness not only the territory's greatly expanded utilization but also an enlarged public recognition of what had been purchased in 1867.

NOTES

1. *Alaska Herald,* January 20, 1871.
2. *Alta California,* November 14, 1867.
3. *The Sitka Post,* April 20, 1877.
4. *Sacramento Daily Union,* February 16, 1874.
5. Report of Major John C. Tidball . . . , NA, RG 98, Roll 2, A Volume Entitled, "Treaty, Reports . . . ," reveals how early the Army pay chest assumed significance to the total economy.
6. Frank A. Golder, "Mining in Alaska Before 1867," *Washington Historical Quarterly,* VII (July, 1916), 233–238; and S. B. Okun, *The Russian-American Company,* trans. by Carl Ginsburg (Cambridge, Mass., 1951), 249.
7. *Alaska Herald,* July 23, 1873.
8. *New York Times,* May 4, 1867.
9. *Alta California,* November 21 & 25, 1867.
10. "Census of Sitka Alaska [1870]," NA, RG 98, Roll 2, A Volume Entitled, "Treaty, Reports. . . ."
11. C. L. Andrews, "Biographical Sketch of Captain William Moore," *Washington Historical Quarterly,* XXI (July, 1930), 195–203; XXI (October, 1930), 271–280; XXII (January, 1931), 32–41; XXII (April, 1931), 99–111. A brief summary of the foregoing is: Will H. Chase, *Reminiscences of Captain Billie Moore* (Kansas City, 1947).
12. *Ibid.,* 83.
13. C. L. Andrews, *Wrangell and the Gold of the Cassiar: A Tale of Fur and Gold in Alaska* (Seattle, 1937), 44–52; and C. L. Andrews, "Biographical Sketch," (January, 1931), 34–37.
14. Eliza Ruhamah Scidmore, *The Guide-Book to Alaska and the Northwest Coast* (London, 1893), 70.
15. Chase, *Reminiscences,* 86–87.
16. Letter from M. P. Berry to John Sherman, Secretary of Treasury, May 14, 1877, CHR, Vol. 1877; Scidmore, *The Guide-Book,* 72.
17. S. Hall Young, *Hall Young of Alaska: An Autobiography* (New York, 1927), 162–164; *San Francisco Chronicle,* January 4, 1879.
18. Richard Mathews, *The Yukon* (New York, 1968), 75–82.
19. Leroy N. McQuesten, *Recollections of Leroy N. McQuesten of Life in the Yukon, 1871–1885* (Dawson City, Yukon Territory, Canada, 1952), 3.
20. Mathews, *The Yukon,* 85.
21. George Wardman, *A Trip to Alaska: A Narrative of What Was Seen*

and Heard during a Summer Cruise in Alaskan Waters (Boston, 1885), 189.

22. C. L. Andrews, "Alaska Whaling," *Washington Historical Quarterly,* IX (January, 1918), 4–5.

23. Benjamin F. Gilbert, "The Confederate Raider Shenandoah: The Elusive Destroyer in the Arctic and the Pacific," *Journal of the West,* IV (April, 1965), 169–182.

24. Herbert L. Aldrich, *Arctic Alaska and Siberia, or Eight Months with the Arctic Whalemen* (Chicago, 1889), 17–18.

25. *Ibid.,* 29.

26. Andrews, "Alaska Whaling," 8.

27. *Alaska Appeal* (published in San Francisco), August 30 and December 1, 1879.

28. *The West Shore,* March 8, 1890; C. L. Andrews, *The Story of Alaska* (Caldwell, Ida., 1953), 143–145.

29. Two fine studies tracing the Eskimo adjustment to western society are: Norman A. Chance, *The Eskimo of North Alaska* (New York, 1966), and James W. VanStone, *Point Hope, An Eskimo Village in Transition* (Seattle, 1962).

30. Ivan Petroff, "Population and Resources of Alaska . . . 1880," cited in: *Annual Report of the Commissioner of Education, 1904* (Washington, D.C., 1904), I, 1099.

31. Mary Charlotte Alexander, *Dr. Baldwin of Lahaina* (privately printed, 1953), 67–68, and Ralph S. Kuykendall, *The Hawaiian Kingdom 1778–1854: Foundation and Transformation* (Honolulu, 1957), 28 ff., give the problem's background, while CHR, 1870's, reveal the intensity of the clandestine traffic.

32. Wardman, *A Trip to Alaska,* 149–150.

33. Aldrich, *Arctic Alaska,* 143–146.

34. Excellent on this famous trade that linked the Americas to Asia are the scholarly articles by F. W. Howay, "A List of Trading Vessels in the Maritime Fur Trade, 1785–1825," in *Transactions of the Royal Society of Canada,* XXIV (Section II, 1930), 111–134; XXV (Section II, 1931), 117–149; XXVI (Section II, 1932), 43–86; XXVII (Section II, 1933), 119–147; XXVIII (Section II, 1934), 11–49; and Samuel Eliot Morison, *The Maritime History of Massachusetts, 1783–1860* (Boston, 1961).

35. William H. Dall, *Alaska and Its Resources* (London, 1870) has scattered references to these elusive figures, as do AHD and Henry Wood Elliott, *Our Arctic Province: Alaska and the Seal Islands* (New York, 1886).

36. Wardman, *A Trip to Alaska,* 165.

37. McQuesten, *Recollections,* 7.

38. *Weekly Astorian,* October 16, 1875; Alfred H. Brooks, *Blazing Alaska's Trails* (Caldwell, Ida., 1953), 321–322; L. D. Kitchener, *Flag over the North: The Story of the Northern Commercial Company* (Seattle, 1954), 155–156.

39. Mathews, *The Yukon,* 77 ff.

40. McQuesten, *Recollections,* 6.

41. Wardman, *A Trip to Alaska,* 49–51; Elliott, *Our Arctic Province,* 36–38; and *Alaska Appeal,* December 30, 1879.

42. *Ibid.,* July 1, 1868.

43. Ted C. Hinckley, "Ice from Seward's Icebox," *The Pacific Historian,* XI (Summer, 1967), 28–38.

44. *New York Times,* December 15, 1870.

45. *Alaska Herald,* December 27, 1873.

46. AHD, I, 312; Hubert Howe Bancroft, *History of Alaska, 1730–1885* (San Francisco, 1886), 602; Wasyl and Theodore Luciw, *Agapius Honcharenko and the Alaska Herald* (Stamford, Conn., 1963).

47. Kitchener, *Flag over the North,* 33; Richard A. Pierce, "Prince D. P. Maksutov: Last Governor of Russian America," *Journal of the West,* VI (July, 1967), 404–405.

48. Letter from General Agent Charles Hirsch, Kodiak District to Alaska Commercial Company, San Francisco, May 31, 1877, Kodiak Copybook 1868–1894, Alaska Commercial Company Collection, University of Alaska, College, Alaska. This collection is hereafter cited as: ACC.

49. *Biographical Directory of the American Congress, 1774–1961* (Washington, D.C., 1961), 1331.

50. A brief introduction to the Company is: Samuel P. Johnston, *Alaska Commercial Company 1868–1940* (San Francisco, 1940); and typed manuscript "310 Sansome Street," ACC. Useful on Company personalities are: Rudolf Glanz, *The Jews in American Alaska, 1867–1880* (New York, 1953), and Gerstle Mack, *Lewis and Hannah Gerstle* (New York, 1953).

51. Record Book, Station Tyonak File, ACC.

52. Confirmation of this may be found in the *Annual Reports of the Commissioner of Education* (Washington, D.C. 1873–).

53. AHD, I, 310.

54. The whole matter is well reviewed in Bancroft, *History of Alaska,* 645–659. See the informed opinion of an historian who had lived and worked there, C. L. Andrews, *The Story of Alaska,* 150.

55. *The Alaska Bulletin,* March 5, 1875; *Alaska Herald,* December 27, 1873 and July 1, 1875.

56. William Gouverneur Morris, *Report upon the Customs District, Public Service, and Resources of Alaska Territory,* U.S., Senate, 45th Cong., 3d Sess., Exec. Doc. No. 59, 13.

57. For example, see: Robert G. Athearn, *High Country Empire: The High Plains and the Rockies* (New York, 1960), 36 ff; David Lavender, *Bent's Fort* (New York, 1954), 45 ff; and in particular note the statement of Francis Paul Prucha, *The Sword of the Republic; The United States Army on the Frontier, 1783–1846* (London, 1969), 198.

58. Orders: October 8, 1878, November 23, 1878, August 19, 1882, and October 13, 1882, Letterpress, Vol. I, The John Callbreath Collection, University of Washington, Seattle, Washington.

59. A useful sociological study of this condition is: Edwin M. Lemert, *Alcohol and the Northwest Coast Indians* (Berkeley, 1954).

60. *Alaska Times,* June 25, 1869; *New York Times,* December 15, 1870.

61. Letter from Captain J. W. White to General J. C. Davis, July 18, 1868, NA, RG 98, Roll 2, Miscellaneous Records 1867 to 1878, Including Unentered Letters, Record of Liquor Cases and Discharge Book.

62. Letter from General J. C. Davis to General J. B. Fry, May 27, 1868,

NA, RG 98, Roll 1, Letters Sent, 1867–70; Letter from George P. Mc-Night to General J. C. Davis, May 21, 1870; Letter from John A. Webster to William Kapus, December 27, 1871; Letter from J. T. Hartley to William Kapus, March 8, 1872; Letter from E. F. Thompson to W. Chapman, Collector, November 26, 1873, all CHR.

63. Letter from George Boutwell, Secretary of the Treasury, to William Kapus, Collector, March 30, 1870, CHR, Vol. V.

64. For an understanding of the liquor problem on the frontier, see: Joseph Peter Donnelly, S.J., "The Liquor Traffic Among the Aborigines of the New Northwest 1800–1860," (unpublished doctoral dissertation, St. Louis University, 1940). To appreciate the U.S. Army and Revenue Marine's Alaska charge, see: U.S., Congress, House, *Jurisdiction of the War Department over the Territory of Alaska,* 44th Cong., 1st Sess., Exec. Doc. No. 135, February 29, 1876; and Stephen H. Evans, *The United States Coast Guard, 1790–1915: A Definitive History* (Annapolis, 1949).

65. *Alaska Herald,* December 5, 1875; *Alta California,* January 2, 1876.

66. *The West Shore,* June, 1876, 2.

67. Morris, *Report upon the Customs District,* 84.

68. H. W. Elliott, "Ten Years' Acquaintance with Alaska, 1867–1877," *Harper's,* LV (November, 1877), 806.

69. *The West Shore,* June, 1876, 3.

70. AHD, II, 43.

71. Summaries of the protracted and complex post-Civil War soldier-Indian relationship are to be found in: Ray Allen Billington, *Westward Expansion: A History of the American Frontier* (New York, 1960), Chap. 32; Thomas D. Clark, *Frontier America: The Story of the Westward Movement* (New York, 1959), Chap. 30; LeRoy R. Hafen and Carl Coke Rister, *Western America: The Exploration, Settlement, and Development of the Region Beyond the Mississippi* (Englewood Cliffs, N.J., 1941), Chaps. 28 and 29; and John A. Hawgood, *America's Western Frontiers: The Exploration and Settlement of the Trans-Mississippi West* (New York, 1967), Chap. 9.

72. *Alaska Herald,* July 24, 1873.

73. *Ibid.,* August 3, 1875; and *Jurisdiction of the War Department.*

74. *Ibid.,* 14.

75. Abe Laufe (Ed.), *An Army Doctor's Wife on the Frontier: Letters from Alaska and the Far West, 1874–1878* (Pittsburgh, 1962), 109.

76. *Portland Standard,* March 19, 1879; Bancroft Scrapbooks, Vol. 81. This volume of the H. H. Bancroft collection at the Bancroft Library, University of California, Berkeley, is filled with West Coast newspaper clippings on Alaskan affairs.

77. *Alaska Times,* June 4, 1869.

78. Ellis Paxson Oberholtzer, *A History of the United States Since the Civil War,* I (5 vols.; New York, 1917), 542.

79. *Alta California,* November 15, 1867.

80. Davis called it Kou Island. For explanation, see: Donald J. Orth, *Dictionary of Alaska Place Names* (Washington, D.C., 1967), 549.

81. *New York Times,* April 25, 1869.

82. Eliza Ruhamah Scidmore, *Alaska: Its Southern Coast and the Sitkan Archipelago* (Boston, 1885), 254–255. Richard Worsam Meade's letter-press volume, New York Historical Society, New York City, supplies additional data on these destructive raids.

83. Letter from General J. C. Davis to General J. B. Fry, February 9, 1869, NA, RG 98, Roll 1, Letters Sent, 1867–70.

84. Report of Major John Tidball, NA, RG 98, Roll 2, A Volume Entitled Treaty, Reports. . . .

85. *Alaska Herald*, July 13, 1874.

86. *The Sitka Post*, February 20, 1877.

87. *Ibid.*, February 5, 1877; C. Delavan Bloodgood, "Eight Months at Sitka," *The Overland Monthly*, II (February, 1869), 183.

88. *The West Shore*, June, 1878, 142.

89. *The Sitka Post*, April 20, 1877 and June 5, 1877; *Chicago Tribune*, April 30, 1877; *Alta California*, March 31, 1877.

90. Every imaginable charge was hurled at the Army. For a sampling, see: U.S., Congress, House, *A Resolution . . . Relative to the Alleged Suffering of United States Soldiers in Alaska*, 40th Cong., 2d Sess., Exec. Doc. No. 117, January 27, 1868; *The Alaska Times*, July 23, 1869; and U.S., Congress, Senate, *In Answer to . . . Military Arrests in Alaska*, 44th Cong., 1st Sess., Exec. Doc. No. 33, Pt. 3, January 7, 1876.

91. *New York Times*, April 13, 1877.

92. Morris, *Report upon the Customs District*, 13.

☆ ☆ ☆ ☆ ☆ ☆ ☆ ☆ ☆ ☆ ☆ ☆ ☆ ☆ ☆ ☆ ☆ ☆

CHAPTER FOUR

Utilization 1877-1887

Here, then, is a land, not too difficult of access, containing in itself materials for food, fuel, lights, shelter and much of the clothing of men, abounding in sources of wealth — a land in climate suited to human life and human activity. . . . It waits for its inhabitants, for the alphabet and the ten commandments, for the Church, the common school, and civil law. — Julie McNair Wright, Among the Alaskans.

THE YEAR 1877 is memorable to American historians for it marked the "end" of Reconstruction. When President Rutherford B. Hayes withdrew Federal troops from the South that year, certain profound questions underlying America's climactic war remained unsolved. Concurrently, a far less conspicuous evacuation of the Army from Alaska marked an even more ambiguous turning point. The government's police arm, it was hoped, would no longer be required on the Far North frontier. This was the nineteenth century, and the paramountcy of civilian rule, be it in South Carolina or Sitka, was incontrovertible.

If post-Civil War Americans were ignorant and apathetic as to the reconstruction of Southern society, they were immeasurably more so in dealing with their gigantic North Pacific acquisition. Could a comprehensive development policy have been determined for a region so huge, so contrasting in climate, people, and resources, when even the experts confounded each other's testimony? It might have been possible, but the Americanization of Alaska proceeded midst confusion and controversy. Indeed, Alaska reflected the United States in its prodigious natural wealth and difficult-to-fathom diversity. Just as there was no lack of public and private leadership to specify what, when, and how to solve the multitude of national challenges, so did Alaska's enormity spark creative and discerning advocates. But the United States had *evolved* from thirteen tiny political entities, and the westward-moving frontier had cushioned many of the shocks incurred from individual and regional blunders. Although harsh and conspicuously wasteful, the Americanization of the contiguous West had been a profound trial-and-error human laboratory. Alaska, like Minerva, had been born full-grown. As of October 18, 1867, from Fort Tongass to Point Barrow to Attu the colossus was entirely American. Furthermore, the whistle scream of ocean and river steamers, the cries of technology's onrush, forewarned that exploitation throughout the Far North might be precipitous. The Great Land was not quite a *terra incognita* when purchased, but its peculiar circumstances demanded prudent development. Possibly it would have been better had it been a *terra incognita* like the moon frontier a century later. Americans then might have approached it with more humility, and instead of the traditional hasty eclecticism, long-range, District-wide plans could have been formulated.

A decade after Alaska's purchase, any educated American who sought to inform himself on the noncontiguous territory would have encountered two emerging, variant positions on what the Great Land was worth and how it should be treated. On one hand were men who, for mixed reasons, soft-pedaled its resources and insisted that Alaska's uniqueness made a go-slow policy in the northland imperative. Opposed to this conservative view were people like the ebullient Panhandle frontiersmen as well as more restrained types such as the McQuesten breed. Enunciating these divergent opinions were two highly intelligent Americans, both of whom were outdoorsmen and able writers. Henry Wood

Elliott and William Healey Dall first came to Alaska in 1865 when it was still Russian America. They had been employed as members of the Scientific Corps attached to the Western Union expedition, an abortive undertaking which had sought to run a telegraph line across North America and the Bering Strait to Asia and thence to Europe. By the time Cyrus Field successfully laid his Atlantic cable and cut short their Far North labors, Elliott and Dall had become bewitched by wilderness Alaska. Elliott ultimately came to be known as "Fur Seal Elliott" for his monomaniac conservation efforts on behalf of the Pribilof Islands' fur seals; and in time Dall's scientific work on Alaska matters (and mollusks) gained him international renown. Professor Morgan Sherwood has called him the "Dean of Alaska Experts," an honor to which he is certainly entitled.[1]

Notwithstanding Dall's scientific prestige and his presence in the nearby Smithsonian Institution, Congressmen too long accorded his opinions less credence than those of Elliott. There was substance to both men's arguments, but Elliott's were simply too unprogressive, too unrealistic. With the Sitka business retreat in mind, Elliott wrote in 1877:

We have learned enough of the country and climate by this time to know that the lands and fishing waters now occupied by the natives of Alaska will never be objects for the cupidity of our people; therefore it is plainly to be seen that as the Indians there are undisturbed, they in turn are not going to disturb us, and the subject of maintaining law and order there thus becomes a very simple one indeed, and inexpensive. In order that the natives may continue self-supporting, it is the duty of the government to suppress all agencies which tend to debauch and ruin them and their hunting industries.[2]

Congressmen, already baffled and deeply annoyed by a plethora of Far West land scandals, Indian wars, and "the ceaseless badgering of pettyfogging Western politicians," gladly accepted the "inexpensive" part of Elliott's argument while overlooking its corollary. Alaska was poor, opined Elliott. It would "never be objects for the cupidity of our people." Fine. Solons interpreted this to mean delayed Americanization within the Great Land, and thus no fraudulent homesteads, no aboriginal tensions and expensive Army heroes, and no more pesky politicos from out West irresponsibly demanding this and that in Capitol Hill cloakrooms. Elliott knew, and notwithstanding their self-imposed blinders, so did many Representatives and Senators, that while Alaska might remain relatively undeveloped, it was not and never could be a socio-economic vacuum. "It is the duty of the government to suppress all agencies which tend to debauch and ruin [Alaska's indigenes] and their hunting industries," Elliott had insisted. How ineffectual Congressmen had been in meeting this charge was patently obvious by 1877. What hope was there for Alaskans when a penurious Congress could not even pay its soldiers that year!

A few months after the United States Army withdrew its troops from Alaska, there arrived at Wrangell a Presbyterian home mission organizer, ostensibly a man of "peace and goodwill." Fortunately for Alaska, Dr. Sheldon Jackson was no patient, long-suffering Vicar of Wakefield. Only a little over five feet tall, with a personality and philosophy that matched those of John Calvin himself, Sheldon Jackson hated sin and loved work.[3] A product of the same hell-fire New York matrix that had shaped Joseph Smith and Charles Finney, Jackson had wanted to serve the Lord ever since he first heard Scripture. Education at Union College and Princeton Theological Seminary, followed by Indian school labor in Kansas, a chaplain's tasks in the Civil War, and parish duties in Minnesota only challenged him to widen his religious responsibilities. Throughout the 1870's, Jackson blazed a record of home mission work, that is church founding, over an eleven-state area from the Canadian boundary to the Rio Grande.[4] As if this were not empire enough, the "Rocky Mountain Superintendent," as the never modest clergyman liked to be called, longed for new lands to conquer. Jackson's organizational and promotional fire, sometimes carelessly handled, intimidated his New York chiefs.

His cousin urged him to retire to a senior pastorate—"He had earned it." But not until nine years after the century's turn when another apostle of the strenuous life, President Theodore Roosevelt, was stepping down from the presidency, would Jackson withdraw from his self-appointed Alaska labor. No one realized it in 1877, certainly Jackson didn't, but pioneer Alaska had found her most influential protagonist.[5]

Years afterward Jackson gave various reasons why he escorted Widow Amanda McFarland to a missionary assignment in distant Alaska: his 1877 action "established the Protestant church in Alaska"; church superiors favored such a step; the printed pleas of a Wrangell native compelled him to act. Only the latter claim holds up. The pre-purchase Lutheran church qualified as Protestant, and Jackson's Home Board headquarters already had their hands full supporting and managing a vast western outreach. It was a soldier of the Alaska command who had first observed the worship of Wrangell's Christian natives. In a letter which Jackson promptly had published in the *Chicago Tribune*, the soldier poignantly relayed the Indians' fervent wish for a missionary teacher.[6]

Jackson may have envisioned himself an Alaskan Marcus Whitman, his famous denominational forebear, one of those who ultimately had responded to the Nez Perce visit to St. Louis in 1831. As with Whitman in Oregon, Jackson would never again behold a land so exciting, so challenging as the Far North frontier. No Whitman, Jackson eschewed any root-bound mission station role. In 1883 the Rocky Mountain Superintendent sold his Denver home and moved to Washington, D.C. It was not fear of meeting the bloody death accorded Whitman that impelled Jackson to travel annually from Alaska to the District of Columbia for the rest of his career. His action was hard-headed, business-age, common sense. Without a ceaseless pressing of political buttons at the nation's capital, the territory could never hope to communicate its peculiarities and needs to Congress. Once this was accomplished, he reasoned, financial and legislative enlightenment would follow.

What, precisely, did Jackson conceive as his Far North charge, and how did he propose to carry it out? Initially he seems to have been interested merely in erecting another mission, trusting that in time a duly constituted church would emerge. A Presbyterian cross on the map of Alaska would please his fellow churchmen in the United States and add to the list of his missionary successes. However, to deny the man his religious conviction and the fact that he always envisioned himself as "doing the Lord's work" is to overlook his intense, hour-by-hour, religious commitment and the humane labors it spurred. Before long he saw the Wrangell mission as only a means to an end: the Christian elevation of Alaska's population. Because the great bulk of the District's residents were aboriginals, this meant primarily evangelization of the natives.[7]

In company with thousands of other nineteenth-century Christian field workers, Jackson had come to realize that unless native peoples could acquire a rudimentary grasp of the white man's civilization, Christianization must fail. Sanitary living habits, the mutual obligations of wedlock, the dignity of the individual—these and other elemental social concepts were complicated and blurred by aboriginal societies. For this reason, in Alaska as in Africa, the Far West, and Polynesia, primary education had usually preceded, or at least accompanied, Protestant conversion.[8]

As any modern anthropologist knows, uncontrolled acculturation magnifies the inevitable agony of harsh and rapid social change. The Rev. William Duncan of British Columbia offered Jackson a fascinating model of rigidly regulated Indian acculturation. At his baronial reserve of Metlakatla approximately twenty miles south of Alaska, the Yorkshire-born missionary had performed social wizardry. Beginning in the early 1860's, Duncan had transformed a warlike, sometimes cannibalistic group of British Columbia Tsimshian Indians into a Christian community with a vir-

tually self-contained economy. By 1878 the German anthropologist Aurel Krause could report:

. . . Metlakahtla possessed its own schooner which made regular
commercial trips to Victoria, a community warehouse, a merchandise store for alien Indians, a soap factory, a smithy, a sawmill, a
schoolhouse which cost about four thousand dollars; a large building for public assemblies, courts and the care of strangers; a mission house, a church, a woolen mill, a rope and cord factory, a
tanning establishment, shoe factory and much else.[9]

*This late 1880's view of the interior of a Northwest Coast Indian home re-
veals a great deal about native acculturation. (Smithsonian Office of
Anthropology, Bureau of American Ethnology Collection)*

Here natives lived in Victorian bungalows with manicured lawns surrounded by white picket fences. Every child attended school. Interlopers, particularly those with hoochinoo, found themselves in the custody of Duncan's native Tsimshian police and guests of the Metlakatla jail. "He has done this work with voluntary aid and contributions of the Indians," noted one American visitor in 1875, "and is by their help rendered independent of any outside support to carry on the mission work. There are no paid officials, no annuities, no treaties, and no thieving Indian agents, but the whole is managed just as any community of white people manage their town affairs. . . ."[10]

Duncan's was an extraordinary achievement, but could Alaska's diverse native peoples be expected to gather into similar isolated reserves? Would the American citizens accept the enormous expense thus incurred, and how could they be aroused to this humanitarian need? Above all, where would the nation find citizens willing to sacrifice themselves in a saga like that of William Duncan?

In the years after the Civil War, much of the Christian community, Catholic and Protestant, had participated in what came to be called Grant's Peace Policy. A major part of this well-intended effort had been a refurbishing of educational programs on the Indian reservations that stretched from Texas to the Dakotas.[11] Helen Hunt Jackson and other reformers stridently denounced the Peace Policy's shortcomings. The "reservation folly," pauper-forming annuity goods, and careless, sometimes corrupt civil servants — Sheldon Jackson was all too familiar with the plight of the "Vanishing Red Man." He dedicated himself to preventing another national disgrace on the Alaskan frontier. Although Jackson visited Metlakatla, and later applied a number of Duncan's lessons, the Presbyterian leader proved to be astonishingly innovative in his Alaska work.

Jackson's campaign to educate and convert Indian, Aleut, and Eskimo eventually forced him to link together a chain of questions and answers. A "mission girl" was eminently more attractive than her unschooled counterpart. How was she to be protected from the frontier flotsam that wished to exploit her? A "mission boy" who apprenticed as a cobbler was easy to bilk. Could the mission teacher praise the virtues of the white man's world and still guard his charge from the guile of certain Caucasian traders? The old saying about "merchants and missionaries mixing about as well as oil and water" was painfully true. And what would happen when the girl and boy wished to get married? Would the race-conscious Caucasian accept them? Above all, could the aboriginal people hope for any certain legal safety when even the white population possessed no District law, and the territory had no Governor, not to mention a judge? In time Jackson would advocate reasonable solutions for each of these quandaries. Fortunately he did not have to supply them all at once.

To begin with, he had to awaken Americans to Alaska's needs. In the space of a decade Jackson not only bound his denomination inextricably to the Great Land but also convinced thousands of his countrymen how great that land really was.[12] His first Far North field worker, Widow Amanda McFarland, soon won an audience that none could have predicted. Denied the radio waves which in the 1930's would rivet John Doe's attention to the South Pole isolation of Admiral Richard Byrd, Jackson employed Victorian sentiment emblazoned by both printer's ink and platform histrionics. Mrs. McFarland's toils to impart Christian teaching to a group of Indian girls in the midst of lascivious Wrangell prospectors took on heroic proportions. Jackson described her privations before women's auxiliaries from Iowa to Boston. It was not only Alaska's native pagans who challenged Americans but their white brethren as well. The night before the Wrangell miner John Boyd was "jerked to Jesus," he heard about "his savior" from a robust and ever so earnest Christian lady. As the Presbyterian missionary, Mrs. Amanda McFarland, later recalled, "Twice in the night . . . he sent for me. He was then in great distress . . . he had not heard a prayer for twenty years until I prayed with him."[13]

Sunday School children formed Alaska bands, their mothers packed missionary barrels for the "Land of the Midnight Sun," and families forewent a new parlor whatnot in order to support an "Alaskan seeking Christ." Preachers, professors, and particularly politicians were importuned on Alaska's behalf. Jackson utilized a wide variety of periodical outlets, among them *The Occident, The Chautauquan, The Truth, Goldthwaite's Geographical Magazine,* and his own journal, the *Rocky Mountain Presbyterian.*[14] His book, *Alaska and Missions on the North Pacific Coast,* published in 1880, although veneered with statistics and authoritative quotations, was essentially propaganda. Jackson delivered five-, ten-, twenty-minute, or two-hour talks on Alaska all over the northeastern quarter of the United States.

Jackson appeared before hundreds of groups, but he probably gained the deepest satisfaction when lecturing to educational societies. At the first and second National Education Assemblies, held in 1882 and 1883, both at Ocean Grove, New Jersey, Sheldon Jackson was a major speaker. In company with such addresses as "The Negro in America" by Frederick Douglass and "Indian Civilization a Success" by Captain Richard H. Pratt of the well-known Carlisle Indian School, was his discourse on "Education in Alaska" (1882) and "The Indians of Alaska" (1883). In March, 1882, he discussed "The Neglect of Education in Alaska" with the Departments of Superintendents of the National Education Association.[15]

As he warmed to his cause, and as he really began to understand his adopted land, Jackson discovered that the McFarland melodrama symbolized something immensely greater. The real melodrama was Alaska. In his eyes the region combined hero and heroine. Bulging with muscular resources, shimmering in a natural loveliness, the land had been cruelly shunned by a cold-hearted Uncle Sam. What was worse, Uncle Sam's apathy had invited the advances of avaricious villains. Jackson was all too familiar with bunko artists, prostitutes, saloon-keepers, and the class of merchants who were more pirate than pioneer. In his opinion, they were social lepers. Clearly, the long-range answer was resident home-builders.

To alert Americans to Alaska's problems, Jackson resorted to arguments both crude and sophisticated. Embellishing the truth became a standard practice of his. Tales of witchcraft and female slavery ignited sparks among his lady audiences. One became so aroused that she exploded in righteous anger. "In all that country there is no law—there can be no restraint—and the lowest animal passions of the rough miners, trappers, hunters, soldiers, and sailors rage unchecked. The Indian woman is considered the lawful spoil of those men."[16] To a generation engrossed by manufacturing and markets, Jackson painted word pictures of potential dollars and cents. On the subject of Alaska's marine and mineral resources he was most eloquent, and if neither humanitarian nor mercenary wedges succeeded in prying open closed minds, he resorted to patriotism. By employing half-truths and exaggerations, he made a compelling argument that Russian America had been progressive, but now, under the Stars and Stripes, it had fallen into somnolence. What power did Alaska's Calvinist Prince Charming believe would awaken this Sleeping Beauty? Philanthropic Christians, congressional appropriations, and commercial enterprise, all spurred on by a sympathetic citizenry, would supply the magic touch. This is an over-simplification. Alaska had found her knight, all right, and his lance would prick the bubble of public complacency, but without the Great Land's fabulous dowry, Jackson's self-assumed errantry would have been in vain. For most assuredly there was nothing quixotic about Alaska's resources. What Jackson could not at first have appreciated was that the accelerated utilization of Alaska's treasures would occur during the 1880's, precisely when he embarked upon his quest.

Immigrant George E. Pilz was spurred by a far different quest. He had arrived in the United States the year that

Russian America changed its name. Equipped with a mining engineer's education, part of which he had obtained from the University of Berlin, Pilz had gladly cut Old World bonds to tie himself to the New. Like so many of his fellow Alaskans, he had first pursued his mining post-graduate study in Nevada and California gravel pits. Pilz seems to have landed at Sitka with not only more money than most, but also a far better grasp of how to invest it. He quickly discerned that the District's future lay with her fisheries and mineral wealth. Engineer Pilz, like his capital neighbor, Ames Whitford, was flexible and not easily discouraged.[17]

By 1878 the Cassiar rush had stabilized. There was talk about erecting a small five-stamp mill ten miles from Sitka, and up and down the Panhandle, prospectors continued to scratch away at likely bonanza sites. From far-off Unga Island a shipment of coal was dispatched to San Francisco. Less glamorous than gold, it was, nevertheless, an indication of the territory's mineral diversity.[18] But 1878 is particularly memorable in Alaska as the date when the salmon-canning industry really got its start.

Before Alaska's purchase, United States fishermen had found it profitable to operate along Russia's sweeping North Pacific littoral from Asia to North America. To America's West Coast these seamen returned with halibut, herring, and especially cod. In 1866, Captain J. W. Keen unloaded a cargo of northern halibut in San Francisco. "The fish sold at 25 cents per pound in the hold, but so many had spoiled that the venture was a failure."[19] The preceding year marked what would become a more successful venture when the brig *Timandra* and the schooner *Alert* sailed from San Francisco for codfishing off Siberia's Okhotsk coast. Inevitably, grounds closer to home were sought, and in 1865, Captain Matthew Turner returned from Russian America's Shumagin Islands (south of the Alaska Peninsula) with a profitable cod catch. By 1867 three schooners were fishing Alaska's Shumagin waters, and the sight of curing cod at Sausalito, in San Francisco Bay, made its appearance.[20] By 1870, San Francisco's cod fleet had ballooned to some nineteen vessels, and three years later the *Alaska Herald* could boast:

The cod taken at the Shumagin grounds is superior to that caught in the Ochotsk Sea, being thicker, fatter, and of better taste, and it brings one-half cent more per pound. This consideration, in conjunction with the fact that the trip to the Ochotsk is nearly twice as long as that to the Alaskan coast, renders the Shumagin fisheries especially profitable. . . . For the first season or two, all was haphazard and the market was overstocked, but now the demand exceeds the catch.[21]

In 1891 the schooner *Moonlight*, handled by twelve men using hooks and lines, caught 50,000 cod in a six-month season. More than a million cod were being hauled in annually by that date.[22]

Other fish, which had been taken in quantity before the American occupation and which proved increasingly remunerative after 1867, were the Alaska herring and the eulachon, or candle-fish. The demand by Oregon and California tanneries for oil resulted in the formation of the Northwest Trading Company, headquartered at Portland. Like most other West Coast firms doing business in Alaska, the Company was forced to diversify its activities. John M. Vanderbilt, the Company's field superintendent, at first located at Killisnoo (Admiralty Island, Southeastern Alaska), became a general trader, and for a while managed the steam tugs *Favorite* and *Louise* operating throughout the Alexander Archipelago. The Northwest Trading Company also killed quite a number of hump and finback whales in 1881, as many as ten in one week. Because the whalers' rocket projectiles had no lines, the wounded beasts often sank to the bottom. All but one were lost. Nevertheless, a confidential report that year to Company stockholders listed a 20 percent return on the invested capital. In the opinion of President Paul Schulze, the District was badly underrated. Vanderbilt was just as optimistic.[23] Justification for their sanguine belief came within that decade when the Killisnoo reduction plant of the Alaska Oil and Guano Company annually packed tens of thousands of barrels of herring and eulachon oil. A portion of the oil was carried to English processors to remove its "fishy odor," after which it was marketed in the United States as salad oil. Hundreds of tons of the fish residue from the Killisnoo works came to be used as fertilizer by Hawaiian and Southern California farmers.[24]

No source of Alaska marine wealth could match that of her superabundant salmon. Despite the limitations of a shorter run than that which existed throughout the Pacific Northwest salmon grounds, the sheer magnitude of numbers made it inevitable that this natural treasure would be exploited on an increasing scale. As with Alaska's halibut and cod, the salting of salmon for southern markets had preceded the American occupation. Because the closer Oregon and Washington salmon were already being exploited, the Great Land's vast resources were not immediately sought after.[25] Nevertheless, few visitors to Alaska remained silent on this aquatic surfeit. In 1869 the *Alta California's* Sitka reporter noted, "Salmon fishing is carried on extensively by all the Russians and Indians, the salmon, dried, being a staple winter food with them. . . . Less than a quarter of a mile from where we are now writing [a Russian] drew in at one haul fourteen hundred and twenty-seven salmon." A large one "freshly caught," weighing twenty pounds could be bought "for two bits." Another observer told how in just one sweep, boat-handled seines trapped "two tons of salmon, weighing five to twenty pounds each.[26] Even the cautious Henry Wood Elliott was moved to write, "it may be said that the salmon which run up its rivers every spring and summer will yet be utilized as a source of productive industry." Elliott became ecstatic about the Yukon salmon: "the raw material is there, of the largest size, the finest flavor, and in the greatest number known to any stream in the world."[27]

By the mid-seventies there were eighteen salmon canneries in operation along the lower reaches of the Columbia River, putting up more than 400,000 cases containing one-

The Klawock cannery during the 1890's. Among the oldest in the District, it included Indians in its labor force. At one end of the sheltered dock is a native canoe, and at the other a steam launch used for hauling fish, moving nets, transporting trade goods, lumber, workers.

to two-and-a-half-pound tin cans. It was a profitable business, and its expansion into the Far North frontier was predictable. A few years after the purchase, Indian trader
George Hamilton established a salmon saltery at Klawock on
Prince of Wales Island (Alexander Archipelago). By 1875
he was annually salting more than 830 barrels of salmon and
dreaming of building a cannery. Lacking the necessary
capital, Hamilton sold his Klawock plant to a newly incorporated San Francisco firm, the North Pacific and Trading
Company.[28] In 1878 the founding of two small canneries
initiated what would soon become one of the major pillars
supporting the Great Land's economy. By May of that year
the North Pacific and Trading Company had "entirely reno-
vated" Hamilton's old facilities, and "put in new machinery
of every kind, and every appliance for the curing, salting,
boiling and canning of the fish . . . they had 350,000 tin
cans made." Concurrently, another cannery was being
erected five miles north of Sitka by Cutting and Company of
San Francisco. Although Cutting's field superintendent
began late in the season and without any previous plant to
build on, his men somehow succeeded in hammering together a structure, placing the machinery, and preparing the
cans and crates in time to process some of the 1878 catch.
The combined first-year pack of the two canneries was
8,159 cases.[29] Public taste, technology, and the relatively
cheap price of Alaska's salmon had dictated these investments. Washington Territory competition and a variety of
unpredictable difficulties cut the profits of these pioneer
enterprises. Ironically, so great was the 1879 salmon run and
so limited were their facilities, that Cutting was forced to
return many fish to the sea, and after only two annual packs,
the Company closed its Sitka plant.[30]

Another likely reason why Cutting and Company abandoned the field at the conclusion of 1879 was the near ex-
plosion caused by the importation of Chinese laborers from
San Francisco. "The Indians themselves wanted to catch
the fish and do the canning, and what money there was to

spend in wages," the *New York Herald* reported. One chief angrily informed the Cutting superintendent, "If an Indian can make a hoochinoo still he can make a can to hold a fish."[31] The infuriated natives were pacified only after their chiefs had been promised that the Chinese transported north were there merely to instruct them. Labor problems and marketing and financial difficulties created a slow take-off for the salmon-canning industry. But from 1882 on it bounded forward, at almost a geometric increase for the remainder of the decade. For the initial period 1878–1881, the industry remained confined to Southeastern Alaska, and the pack total did not appreciably increase. In 1882 the business was commenced in Cook Inlet (with Cutting's old equipment) and the Kodiak region; two years later, canning entrepreneurs reached the Bering Sea Coast and by 1889 were within Prince William Sound. The cases packed reveal how spectacular the actual increase was: 1881, 8,977; 1884, 60,886; 1887, 206,677; 1888, 412,115; and the last year of the eighties, 714,196.[32]

It was a breathless growth. Like much of America's late nineteenth-century industrialization, fish canning (*and* enriched consumer menus) were too frequently accompanied by severe competition, exploited labor, and prodigal waste. The pros and cons of man's technological power were not lost upon contemporaries. In the late eighties, author Maturin Ballou evoked a rhapsodic image of a changing Alaska:

In spite of government neglect, commerce is steadily increasing and developing Alaska; it invades all zones, proving the greatest of civilizing agencies. Not only is it the equalizer of the wealth, but also of the intelligence, of nations, and this one branch alone is gradually populating whole districts. When the active packing season is over there is still profitable employment for all. Some are occupied in making the tin cans to hold one pound each; others are taught to become coopers, furnishing the casks for shipping such fish as are split, salted, and exported in that form; while others are occupied in making pine wood boxes to contain two dozen each of the filled cans. Thus a well conducted fishpacking establishment employs many people, and presents a busy scene all the year round.[33]

Regrettably, Ballou had made a sweeping generalization based on one vicinity, the Klawock area in the Panhandle. It was only in the Southeastern region that canneries had such a healthy impact on the local economy. And even here the discerning travelogue writer, Eliza Scidmore, saw things quite differently than did Ballou:

The Alaska canners are not held to any restrictions as in British Columbia, not taxed nor hindered in any way. . . . There is no tax upon cannery boats, no limit to the size of netmeshes, no closed season. . . . The canneries drain the country of their natural wealth; make no permanent settlements, nor any improvements; spend almost nothing of their profits in the Territory; and are a fruitful source of trouble and corruption among the native people.[34]

Throughout the 1880's as the canneries spread north-westward, the indigenes, always difficult to regiment, lost out. Excepting for the Klawock plant (and minor mission canneries), the packing force soon became predominantly Chinese. The passive, extremely diligent orientals were "very satisfactory labor . . . are ready to work at any and all hours, and apply themselves strictly to the work for which they are paid."[35] Even where the actual salmon fishing was involved, the natives proved unreliable. Originally, Indians had transported salmon to the canneries, or at least been critical in their catch. But before long, small steam barges or tugs went to the villages because the native proved "improvident, knowing that nature has provided for them without much labor." The Indian was not reluctant to boast, "white men and Chinese must work to get something to eat, while the waters and the forests furnish the Indians with all they want." The aboriginals, not seduced by modern advertising, were confident that a "small amount of money will supply them with the few necessaries which money alone will purchase."[36] This free, season-regulated way of life had no place in a society increasingly dominated by assembly line speed-up:

In the skillful manipulation of the cans and machines within doors, neither [the Indian] nor the whiteman can approach the automatic dexterity of the Chinese, who, being paid by the piece, take no account of a day's working hours, and keep the machinery moving as long as there are fish in the cannery. The fish are thrown from the arriving scows to a latticed floor, or loaded directly into the trucks and rolled into the cannery. The cleaner seizes a fish and in two seconds trims and cleans it — beheading, detailing, and rending it with so many strokes of his long, thin knife. It is mashed, scraped, cut in sections the length of a can, packed, soldered, steamed, tested, vented, steamed again, resoldered, lacquered, labelled, and boxed. The tin is taken up in sheets, and an ingenious machine punches, rolls, and fits the covers to the cans, which roll down an inclined gutter of melted solder which closes the edges. The experts can tell by the tap of a finger, if each can is air-tight.[37]

The assault on Nature's abundance was unbelievable. Crowded about the inconspicuous mouth of the Karluk River on the northwest shore of Kodiak Island, competing firms worked feverishly to stay abreast of each other. Tarleton H. Bean, government ichthyologist, was awed by the harvest. "The number of salmon actually caught in Karluk Bay," he wrote, "is so large as to make a true statement concerning them seem incredible. In 1888 the [Karluk] canneries put up over 200,000 cases, . . . or more than 2,500,000 fish." The next year in excess of three million were canned.[38]

It was incredible, no doubt, and the 1880's would witness other spectacular economic advances within the Great Land. Alaskan publicist Jackson rejoiced at this wealth, as did resident businessmen like Whitford and Pilz. They were happy to supply the cannery workers with necessary sundries and wage-eroding luxuries. Their disgust at the Chinese importation of opium and the Indian workers' penchant for alcohol may even on occasion have matched Jackson's. For the Sitka merchants these clandestine goods presented troublesome legal annoyances. In Jackson's eyes the traffic had raised ominous moral and sociological questions.

At the very heart of Jackson's promotional endeavors was

native salvation, socio-economic and spiritual. Across the Far West the white man had constructed forts to protect his commerce against the attack of savages. Jackson now methodically set about inaugurating Protestant forts, Christian missions to protect native Alaskans against what too often was an imported temporal savagery. His support of Amanda McFarland's efforts crystallized into a school for girls. To reinforce her sacrifices in 1878 and 1879, he introduced two able young Presbyterian ministers to the territory, the Rev. John Green Brady and the Rev. S. Hall Young.[39] Although both were ministerial novices, Jackson could not have chosen better. They were tough physically and extremely resourceful. Because they were professionally inexperienced, the embers of their youthful idealism still glowed. Upon these coals the Far North bellows blew its challenge. The resultant blaze lighted two distinguished careers of public service; indeed, until death extinguished their flames long after the turn of the century, the Hall-Brady devotion for Alaska never dimmed.

Both men arrived in the Panhandle at a time when even the residents were not certain who was responsible for District matters. After the Army's withdrawal, the highest territorial official was the Collector of Customs.[40] Supposedly he had recourse to Revenue Marine vessels in time of emergency. One week after the Army's departure, Sitka's segregated Indians acted to claim their civil rights. While horrified whites looked on, a large portion of the stockade was torn down. Once this was accomplished, the Indians occupied all of the empty buildings and removed doors, windows, and partitions. Chief Annahootz addressed the community:

The Russians have stolen this country from us and after they have gotten most of the furs out of the country they have sold it to the Boston Men for a big sum of money, and now the Americans are mad because they have found that the Russians had deceived them, and have abandoned the country, and we are glad to say that after so many years hard fight we get our country back again.[41]

Chief Annahootz in the 1880's. To the summer tourists he was pointed out as "the Indian who had saved Sitka from a massacre."

Annahootz was a bit premature. However, for a society in which too many would have agreed with Fred M. Smith of Unalaska, who wrote, "I am of the opinion . . . that an Indian is a good Indian when he is a dead Indian" — well, one can imagine the consternation.[42] The Collector appealed to John Sherman, Secretary of the Treasury, *"The Indians indulge in threats which no doubt they will put in practice when they find that no gunboat of any kind appears on the scene."*[43] It was rank exaggeration, and of course a gunboat finally did appear. The Indians did not get Alaska back, but they enjoyed a victory of sorts. The stockade was never rebuilt, and henceforth some occupied houses whose facades matched those of the white Sitkans.

Again in February of 1879, fear of an Indian massacre swept Sitka, and again there was a genuine basis for the hysteria. In both the red and white communities, hard types got drunk and threatened to precipitate serious trouble. "Prospectors (often another name for loafers) hang about the place," one visitor noted. With time hanging on their hands, they were frequently drunk. One "gang of such rowdies and bummers" succeeded in getting an Indian woman intoxicated and then burned her up in her home.[44] Street fights and random killings mounted. Afterward Annahootz claimed it was only his bared bosom, he had scars to prove it, that averted an "indiscriminate butchery of the few whites." Before matters quieted down, an English warship, the H.M.S. *Osprey,* had to be called in.[45] John Brady got all of Sitka's merchants to sign a pledge to import no more liquor. It lasted until the ink was dry. Whether or not there was an imminent threat, the *Osprey* affair was humiliating. Thereafter, until the territory obtained its Organic Act, the United States Navy was given the task of maintaining law and order in the District.[46]

Alaska's pioneers later held that the naval commanders displayed more alacrity than their soldier predecessors. But the aristocrat of the services is usually more popular. Not only is the Navy more glamorous, but sailors sail away, and on this lonely frontier, absence inevitably made the heart grow fonder. Of all the Navy's commanding officers in the Far North, none exceeded the energy and affection for the task exhibited by Commander L. A. Beardslee. Understandably, the officer promptly repaired Sitka's wharf, surveyed the harbor, and set out buoys. After he launched a community clean-up campaign, the *Alaska Appeal* exclaimed, "in his supressing of the illicit stills he has struck at the root of all the evils from which we suffered. He has made the Indian clean up the village, and made him keep it clean."[47]

When the Commander turned to Sitka's chaotic white citizens, it was another story entirely. Courageously unmindful of what had occurred in the early seventies, Beardslee, assisted by Brady and a handful of other capital residents, created a new "civil authority in Alaska." On July 25, 1879, a town meeting resulted in the election of a Chief Magistrate and five selectmen. This "provisional council" was ostensibly granted authority "to try civil and criminal cases and take charge of estates." The Chief Magistrate, Mottrom D. Ball, the District Collector, conceded that their organization was only "a compact for their temporary peace and protection . . . and in no sense a legal government." Despite this, not three months passed before Ball had to admit it was "utterly impracticable."[48] At Wrangell, S. Hall Young was delighted when both Beardslee and the local Indians assisted him in waging a Carrie Nation campaign against local bootleggers.[49] During a boating trip with naturalist John Muir, Young had seen the rotgut whiskey from native stills devastating an entire village. Muir described the saturnalia,

While we were yet half a mile or more away, we heard sounds I had never before heard—a storm of strange howls, yells, and screams rising from a base of gasping, bellowing grunts and groans. Had I been alone, I should have fled as from a pack of fiends, but our Indians quickly recognized this awful sound . . . as the "whiskey howl" . . . . The whole village was afire with bad whiskey.[50]

Brady had his work cut out for him in the vicinity of Sitka, while Young concentrated his humanitarian labors about Wrangell.

Commander Henry Glass, Beardslee's successor, was also a source of community strength. Brady had initiated an Industrial School for native teenagers at Sitka, a school that is today Sheldon Jackson College, but the Indian boys soon found playing hookey more exciting than becoming proficient carpenters. At this point Glass rounded up the truants, decorated them with name tags, and until regularity of attendance was established, held a "morning muster." Glass subdued a dangerously obstructionist shaman by publicly cutting off his prized locks and having him rigorously scrubbed from head to toe to remove his "supernatural powers."[51] For the whites the sight was comical; for the aboriginal, it was the abasement of progress.

We can only guess when it was that Ames Whitford first mentioned his need for a business partner in young Brady's presence. No doubt Whitford reasoned that Brady's education and missionary connections would be good for business. Furthermore, his sawmill needed to be rebuilt, and Brady was an experienced millwright. It had not taken Brady long to discover that a missionary career was not in harmony with his personality. Like his mentor, Jackson, he was cut out for action. The formation of the Whitford-Brady partnership did not seriously diffuse his opportunity for Christian service in Alaska. After all, the wise use of God's blessings never frightened a Calvinist. Judging from the success of their partnership, Sitkans agreed with the Lord. Brady had also studied law prior to coming north. Before long he was honored as clergyman, sawyer, merchant, and lawyer. In a few years it would be Judge Brady, and in time, Governor Brady.

In 1880, George Pilz could hardly have predicted that his energetic fellow townsman John Brady would ever become anything but a good preacher. Certainly when the Sitka mining engineer helped grubstake prospectors Joe Juneau and Richard Harris, he had no guarantee that their gravel-grubbing would lead them to Gold Creek and the birth of boom-town Juneau. Here, during October of 1880, Juneau and Harris struck pay dirt, and the usual rush began. The boom town spawned on the Gastineau Channel opposite Douglas Island was variously labeled Pilztown, Harrisburg, Fliptown, and Rockwell.[52] Fliptown was a miners' joke, while the last name was chosen in honor of Navy Lieutenant C. H. Rockwell. The officer appreciated the prospectors' cordiality, particularly since he was in a lawman's role, but he rejected the honor. Juneau and Harris, like California's James Marshall, enjoy more fame as dead historical figures than any sizable wealth which their 1880 discovery provided them during their lives. In later years Pilz muttered that the two prospectors had given him a raw deal. Pilz's near-imprisonment in San Quentin on a forgery conviction rather weakens his veracity. But he never lacked tenacity. Pilz returned to Alaska and was still hunting an Eldorado when he finally cashed in his chips in the 1920's.[53]

If scheming and sweat produce riches, Pilz, Harris, and Juneau should have retired wealthy. But the rules of western mining had changed. The placer diggings about Gold Creek and Silver Bow Basin demonstrated that a few good cards and a little cash were not enough. After two years the easily accessible placer pickings had been superseded by hard-rock quartz mining. Ultimately the mineral wealth that surrounded Juneau would prove to be enormous, but as in the territory's fisheries, it took money to make money—large-scale investment would supplant the capital-short individual operator. To be sure, western mining had always been a gamble. However, given the low-grade ore of Juneau's neighboring Douglas Island, the man who lacked a large poke might as well stay out of the game.

In the twelve years before he came to Alaska, John Treadwell had mastered the skills of both quartz and hydraulic mining in Nevada and California. Intrigued by one of the endless rumors of a fabulous deposit in the vicinity of Gold Creek, San Francisco businessmen John D. Fry and James Freeborn sent Treadwell north to evaluate a particular claim. The vein turned out to be unprofitable. Mining historian T. A. Rickard has offered one version of what happened then:

While waiting for a steamer at Juneau . . . [Treadwell] first met French Pete (otherwise Pierre Erussard), who had opened a store in that town. Pierre happened to need ready money to pay for freight on stores that had just arrived from the south; he wanted $500, and was willing to accept that sum for an interest in his mine on Douglas island. Without going to see the claim, Treadwell "took a flyer," and advanced $500. . . . Then he went across the water to see what Pierre possessed. . . . Treadwell stated that the Paris lode was too low-grade and suggested that if Pierre would give him a quit-claim deed for $5 he would try to sell the mine in San Francisco, and would undertake to trade at Pierre's store if the sale were effected. The deal was made.[54]

The Californian had picked up the Paris Lode for a few chips; he was in the game, but would Treadwell's San Francisco backers ante up the large kitty? They did, and by May, 1882, he had returned to Douglas Island with a five-stamp mill. How Treadwell forced Vulcan to relinquish his thinly speckled gold quartz by battering him with the most modern mining technology has become a North Country legend. The five-stamp operation became a 120-stamp mill by 1885 and then doubled in the next two years; dividends in 1885 were $75,000, two years later $125,000, and in 1889, $300,000.[55]

The spiral had just begun. The low-grade ore could return a profit only if the most modern mining technology was employed. An 1886 visitor to Treadwell's mushrooming Douglas Island operation has left a description that harks more of twentieth-century automation than nineteenth-century individuality.

The mill is designed for the reduction of gold ore sulphurets and free gold, and has one hundred and twenty stamps of nine hundred pounds each, with a crushing capacity of three hundred and sixty tons per day. The ore when it comes to the mill goes through the grizzles and rock-breakers into the ore bins, from which it is drawn out directly into the feeders, which feed it into the batteries, where it is crushed wet and amalgamated for free gold. From the mortars the pulp is taken over copper plates, where any free gold which may escape is amalgamated. Then from the copper plates it is taken to and passed over the free concentrators, which save the sulphurets and the tailings, and sluiced off. From the concentrator room the sulphurets are taken to chlorination works where they are treated for the gold which they contain by the chlorine gas, and the gold comes out in fifteen thousand dollar and eighteen thousand dollar bricks, which are shipped monthly by steamer to the mint in San Francisco. About one hundred thousand dollars a month is the product.[56]

This swelling enterprise quickly eclipsed the "poor-pickings," that is, the miners who still tossed earth in the nearby mountains. Likewise, the business the Treadwell Mine fed into the Douglas Island-Juneau complex soon far surpassed earlier financial gains won at either Wrangell or Sitka. Pollution accompanied the profits. Within a few years the "heavy plume of smoke from the Treadwell's chlorination works" killed off the "vegetation for a mile up and down the Island's edge." On Douglas Island and across Gastineau Channel, Juneau's timber demands rapidly leveled the forest cover.[57]

Fearful that miners would be no less destructive of the region's Indians, Jackson located a missionary among them. In this instance it turned out to have been a case of casting bread upon waters. Mrs. Sara Dickinson, a full-blooded Tongass Indian who had worked for two years as Amanda McFarland's interpreter at Wrangell, came north. Supported by her white trader husband, Sara Dickinson established a mission-trading station at Chilkat Inlet up Lynn Canal, north of Juneau. It was Chilkat country and still dangerous. Luckily, Indian males warmed to the immediacy of the Northwest Trading Company's barter goods. Their wives and children, equally pleased, came to see the Indian woman who spoke and dressed like a white woman. The next year missionaries Eugene Willard and his wife Carrie arrived, and Mrs. Dickinson became their interpreter. Don-a-wauk, a tough old chief who had laughed at Sara's entreaties to cast off his lecherous habits, now freed his slaves — not, however, without suffering acute humiliation before his friends. Needless to say, the slaves were stunned and thankful.[58]

About Douglas Island a new kind of slavery appeared. Though natives tried mill work, the snorting, smashing machines repelled them. For a people raised in a wilderness, the mill was a prison, and they wandered off. When too many of Juneau's unemployed Yankee prospectors also refused to surrender themselves to this roaring, foul-smelling inferno, Chinese were imported.[59]

For all its blowsy appearance, Juneau hosted Alaska's first really consequential territorial political gathering. Actually, years before in October, 1869, Sitka had held a "People's Convention." John H. Kinkead had been elected president, "speeches, resolutions and all" filled the air, but to no avail. Congress turned a deaf ear to Sitka's request for "some simple form of civil government." Now Juneau would have its try. In one sense her August 1881 convention mirrored political reality, whereas the aspirations of the 1869 gathering had been wildly improbable. Kinkead seems to have presided over a convention in which were present delegates "from Kadiak, Unalaska, Cook's Inlet, Stikine and Tongass."[60] The 1881 Juneau convention was strictly a Panhandle affair. Eighteen delegates were provided for, but only fifteen arrived, five each from Juneau (at that time still called Harrisburg), Sitka, and Wrangell. Mottrom Ball was there from Sitka and S. Hall Young from Wrangell. Young served as the convention's secretary. Juneau's delegates included Edmund Bean, another of the "old-time miners," that is, another Far West veteran goldseeker. The preceding year Bean had led one of the first party of miners to surmount Chilkoot Pass. The men had then proceeded some distance down the headwaters of the Yukon River.[61]

The Juneau convention was reasonably representative of that part of Alaska occupied by immigrant white settlers, that is, men of the Brady-Vanderbilt-Whitford stamp, citizens who had some appreciation and understanding of representative government. The delegates voiced the usual plea for an Organic Act and the necessity of civilian rule. To insure that their collective declaration was heard, provision was made for a territorial delegate to Congress, this spokesman to be elected by Panhandle pioneers. In September, Southeastern Alaskans cast a total of 294 write-in ballots. The fact that delegate candidate Ball had been a Confederate Colonel proved no liability; his constituency gave him an overwhelming majority of 236 votes.[62]

What is especially intriguing about this historic meeting is how these men identified themselves. Their petition was entitled, "Memorial of the people of Southeastern Alaska to the President and Congress of the United States." Here was hard-headed political pragmatism. Not an amorphous Alaska speaking but "the people of Southeastern Alaska," the only distinct zone in 1881 that *was* being rapidly Americanized. This region possessed a geographic unity, a common aboriginal culture, and a shared historic past. Furthermore, and despite the water barrier, the Alexander Archipelago and its nearby coast had become, like the older sister commonwealths to the south, economically tied to dynamic centers on the Pacific Slope. What if the Panhandle's leadership had then been encouraged to move toward statehood? What if a few powerful Republican giants had come out for an eventual State of Lincoln, a political entity to embrace the region between Chilkoot Pass and the Panhandle's southern tip? Had Congress carved out such a state, the subsequent history of the Great Land would have been radically changed. It was a fateful opportunity, but Congress missed it.

NOTES

1. Morgan B. Sherwood, *Exploration of Alaska, 1865–1900* (New Haven, 1965), 37.

2. H. W. Elliott, "Ten Years' Acquaintance with Alaska 1867–1877," *Harper's*, LV (November, 1877), 803.

3. Still the best biography of Sheldon Jackson is the uncritical summary by his associate, Robert Laird Stewart, *Sheldon Jackson: Pathfinder and Prospector of the Missionary Vanguard in Rocky Mountains and Alaska* (New York, 1908). To judge his relative import in Far West history, see:

Colin B. Goodykoontz, *Home Missions on the American Frontier* (Caldwell, Ida., 1939), 319–322.

4. Alvin K. Bailey, "Sheldon Jackson, Planter of Churches," *Journal of the Presbyterian Historical Society,* XXVI (September and December, 1948), 129–148, 193–214, XXVII (March, 1949), 21–40; Andrew E. Murray, "Presbyterian History in Colorado," *Journal of the Presbyterian Historical Society,* XXVIII (March, June, September, 1950), 1–20, 79–103, and 147–165.

5. Ted C. Hinckley, "The Presbyterian Leadership in Pioneer Alaska," *Journal of American History,* LII (March, 1966), 742–743.

6. Sheldon Jackson, *Alaska and Missions on the North Pacific Coast* (New York, 1880), 135–138. On Jackson's Home Board, see: Clifford Merrill Drury, *Presbyterian Panorama: One Hundred and Fifty Years of National Missions History* (Philadelphia, 1952).

7. Some pamphlets and booklets by Jackson that convey his view of his commitment are: *Alaska and Its Inhabitants* (n.p., n.d.); *Facts About Alaska: Its People, Villages, Missions, Schools* (New York, 1903); and *The Presbyterian Church in Alaska: An Official Sketch of Its Rise and Progress, 1877–1884, with the Minutes of the First Meeting of the Presbytery of Alaska* (Washington, D.C., 1886). Also insightful is his letter to Miss E. Singleton, October 18, 1887, Sheldon Jackson Correspondence Collection, Vol. 26, p. 193, Presbyterian Historical Society, Philadelphia. Hereafter this correspondence collection is cited as: JCorr.

8. Too many historians stumble on the missionary. Nineteenth-century authors made him bigger than life, and twentieth-century social scientists either underestimate or confuse his very real humanitarian achievements. Helpful in reaching something of a balance are: Kenneth Scott Latourette, *The Great Century in Europe and the United States of America, A.D. 1800–A.D. 1814*, Vol. IV, *A History of the Expansion of Christianity* (New York, 1941); and Stephen Neill, *Christian Missions* (Baltimore, 1964).

9. Aurel Krause, *The Tlingit Indians,* trans. by Erna Gunther (Seattle, 1956), 226.

10. Sheldon Jackson, *Report of the Commissioner of Education, 1877* (Washington, D.C., 1878), 12. Useful on Duncan's work are: John W. Arctander, *The Apostle of Alaska: The Story of William Duncan of Metlakahtla* (New York, 1909); Frederick Webb Hodge (Ed.), *Handbook of American Indians North of Mexico,* Part I (Washington, D.C., 1907), 905–906; and William H. Collison, *In the Wake of the War Canoe* (London, 1915), 24 ff.

11. The standard source for Grant's Peace Policy is: Loring B. Priest, *Uncle Sam's Step-Children: The Reformation of United States Indian Policy, 1865–1887* (New Brunswick, N.J., 1942). For fresh insights on church involvement in this program, see: R. Pierce Beaver, *Church, State and the American Indians* (St. Louis, Mo., 1966); and Henry E. Fritz, *The Movement for Indian Assimilation, 1860–1890* (Philadelphia, 1963).

12. Details of his Alaska advertising campaign may be traced in: Ted C. Hinckley, "Publicist of the Forgotten Frontier," *Journal of the West,* IV (January, 1965), 27–40.

13. Charles A. Anderson (Ed.), "Letters of Amanda R. McFarland," *Journal of the Presbyterian Historical Society*, XXXIV (June and December, 1956), 83–102 and 226–244, and (March, 1957), 33–56.

14. *The Occident*, September 26, 1877; *The Chautauquan*, November, 1880; *The Truth*, January 30, 1880; and *Goldthwaite's Geographical Magazine*, February, 1892.

15. Convention programs found in Sheldon Jackson Scrapbooks: Vol. 5, p. 77; Vol. 2, p. 21; and Vol. 64, p. 123. These valuable scrapbooks are located in the Sheldon Jackson Collection, Presbyterian Historical Society, Philadelphia. Hereafter these scrapbooks are cited as JScrap.

16. Hinckley, "Publicist," 33.

17. George E. Pilz, "Reminiscences: Pioneer Days in Alaska," (unpublished MS, University of Alaska Library, College, Alaska).

18. Theodore C. and Caryl Hinckley (Eds.), "Ivan Petroff's Journal of a Trip to Alaska in 1878," *Journal of the West*, V (January, 1966), 49; *Alaska Appeal*, March 6, 1879.

19. *The Alaskan*, April 9, 1892.

20. Gordon P. Jones, "Cod Bangers to Alaska," *Alaska Sportsman*, XXXII (March, 1966), 8 ff.; *Alaska Herald*, January 1, 1870.

21. *Alaska Herald*, July 9, 1873.

22. *The Alaskan*, October 31, 1891 and December 19, 1891.

23. Ivan Petroff, "Alaska As It Is," *The International Review*, XII (February, 1882), 118; Letter from John C. Drew to Sitka Collector, October 26, 1882, Vol. XXII, CHR; *Alaska Appeal*, April 15, 1880; "Confidential Report to Stockholders," Vol. 7, p. 36, JScrap; "Excerpts . . . Report," December 13, 1887, Vol. I, p. 334, AHD.

24. Henry Wood Elliott, *Our Arctic Province: Alaska and the Seal Islands* (New York, 1886), 57; F. C. Sessions, "Alaska," *Magazine of Western History*, V (December, 1886), 270 ff.; Hubert Howe Bancroft, *History of Alaska, 1730–1885* (San Francisco, 1886), 744; *The Alaskan*, December 19, 1891.

25. Good for obtaining an overview of the early salmon story are: C. L. Andrews, "The Salmon of Alaska," *Washington Historical Quarterly*, IX (October, 1918), 243–254; Howard M. Kutchin, *Report on the Salmon Fisheries of Alaska* (Washington, D.C., 1899); and Jefferson F. Moser, *The Salmon and Salmon Fisheries of Alaska* (Washington, D.C., 1899). To appreciate how one major canner linked up his Oregon and Alaska salmon enterprises, see: Gordon B. Dodds, *The Salmon King of Oregon: R. D. Hume and the Pacific Fisheries* (Chapel Hill, N.C., 1959).

26. *Alta California*, August 10, 1869; and Charles Hallock, *Our New Alaska: or Seward Purchase Vindicated* (New York, 1886), 132.

27. William Gouverneur Morris, *Report upon the Customs District, Public Service and Resources of Alaska Territory*, U.S., Senate, 45th Cong., 3d Sess., Exec. Doc. No. 59, 114.

28. *The Sitka Post*, January 5, 1877; *Alta California*, October 6, 1875; *Alaska Appeal*, March 6, 1879; and Morris, *Report upon the Customs District*, 114–115. The North Pacific and Trading Company was in large part the old San Francisco firm of Sisson, Wallace and Company.

29. *Ibid.*, 115; Moser, *The Salmon,* 49; and Captain George Bailey, *Report Upon Alaska and Its People* (Washington, D.C., 1880), 7.

30. *Ibid.*, 16; *Alaska Appeal,* September 30, 1879.

31. *New York Herald,* April 17, 1879; JScrap, Vol. 8, p. 131; and Eliza Ruhamah Scidmore, *Alaska: Its Southern Coast and the Sitkan Archipelago* (Boston, 1885), 194–195.

32. Moser, *The Salmon,* 49.

33. Maturin M. Ballou, *The New Eldorado: A Summer Journey to Alaska* (Boston, 1890), 192.

34. Eliza Ruhamah Scidmore, *The Guide-Book to Alaska and the Northwest Coast* (London, 1893), 58.

35. James W. VanStone, *Eskimos of the Nushagak River: An Ethnographic History* (Seattle, 1967), 74–77; Moser, *The Salmon,* 24.

36. Carter H. Harrison, *Summer's Outing and the Old Man's Story* (Chicago, 1891), 136–137; and Moser, *The Salmon,* 25.

37. Scidmore, *The Guide-Book,* 57–58.

38. Tarleton H. Bean, *Report on the Salmon and Salmon Rivers of Alaska, with Notes on the Conditions, Methods and Needs of the Salmon Fisheries* (Washington, D.C., 1890), 181–182.

39. S. Hall Young left his own story, *Hall Young of Alaska: An Autobiography* (New York, 1927). For his first years in the Great Land, see: Ted C. Hinckley, "The Early Alaskan Ministry of S. Hall Young, 1878–1888," *Journal of Presbyterian History,* XLVI (September, 1968), 175–196.

40. One newly appointed Collector of the Customs came to Sitka, and, after seeing the Indians at first hand and without any immediate police power to check them, departed by the same steamer. C. L. Andrews, *The Story of Alaska* (Caldwell, Ida., 1953), 152.

41. Letter from Edward G. Harvey, Special Deputy Collector, to John Sherman, Secretary of Treasury, October 15, 1877, CHR; *The Alaskan,* February 12, 1898.

42. Letter from Fred M. Smith, Jr., to Colonel [Crittenden?], November 8, 1879, Vol. 18, CHR.

43. Letter from M. P. Berry, Collector, to John Sherman, Secretary of Treasury, July 10, 1877, CHR.

44. *The Alaskan,* June 12, 1886; Hinckley and Hinckley, "Ivan Petroff's Journal," 14; Bancroft, *Alaska,* 623–624.

45. Madge Wolfenden and J. H. Hamilton, "The Sitka Affair," *The Beaver,* Outfit 286 (Winter, 1955–56), 3–7; Clippings, March, 1879, Bancroft Scrapbooks, Vol. 81; *Alaska Appeal,* March 22, 1879; Letter from M. D. Ball, Collector, to Capt. George Brown, USN, April 11, 1879, CHR; Clipping, *New York Herald,* JScrap, Vol. 8, p. 129; *Rocky Mountain Presbyterian,* February, 1879.

46. On the Navy in Alaska, see: Mel Crain, "When the Navy Ruled Alaska," *United States Naval Institute Proceedings,* LXXXI, (February, 1955), 198–203; Ted C. Hinckley, "Punitive Action at Angoon," *Alaska Sportsman,* XXIX (January, 1963), 8 ff. and (February, 1963), 14 ff.; U.S., Congress, House, *Report of United States Naval Officers Cruising in Alaska*

Waters, 47th Cong., 1st Sess., House Exec. Doc. No. 81; and the micro-filmed letters of the Navy's commanding officers in Alaska that are now available, National Archives and Records Service, Washington, D.C.

47. *Alaska Appeal,* August 30, 1879.

48. L. A. Beardslee, *Report of Commander L. A. Beardslee . . . June 15, 1879 to June 22, 1880,* 46th Cong., 2d Sess., Senate Exec. Doc. 105, Vol. 4; *Alaska Appeal,* August 30, 1879; Letter from M. D. Ball, Collector, to John Sherman, Secretary of Treasury, October 1, 1879, CHR.

49. Young, *Hall Young,* 116 and 226.

50. John Muir, *Travels in Alaska* (Boston, 1915), 131–132.

51. Jackson, *Alaska and Missions,* 391–395; Henry Glass, "Naval Administration in Alaska," *Proceedings, United States Naval Institute,* XVI (January, 1890), 1–19.

52. R. N. De Armond, *Some Names Around Juneau* (Sitka, 1957), 26–27, and *The Founding of Juneau* (Juneau, 1967), are both required sources for those tracing the history of Alaska's twentieth-century capital.

53. *The Alaskan,* November 20, 1886; Pilz, "Reminiscences," well evidences his bitterness and unreliability in regard to the truth.

54. T. A. Rickard, *Through the Yukon and Alaska* (San Francisco, 1909), 26. Billie Barnes Jensen, "Alaska's Pre-Klondike Mining: The Men, the Methods and the Minerals," *Journal of the West,* VI (July, 1967), 417–431, surveys the pioneer prospector.

55. Lyman Knapp, *Governor's Annual Report, 1890* (Washington, D.C., 1890), 15; George F. Forrest, "Juneau the Capital of Alaska," *Alaska-Yukon Magazine,* Special Gastinau Number (September, 1907), 13–15.

56. Sessions, "Alaska," 273. The monthly output was probably closer to $80,000. Miner W. Bruce, *Alaska, Its History and Resources, Gold Fields, Routes and Scenery* (Seattle, 1895), 32.

57. Scidmore, *The Guide-Book,* 86.

58. Jackson, *Alaska and Missions,* 368–371; *Proceedings of the Alaska Boundary Tribunal* (Washington, D.C., 1904), I, 89; Young, *Hall Young,* 77 ff.; and Julia McNair Wright, *Among the Alaskans* (Philadelphia, 1883), 208 ff.

59. Ted C. Hinckley, "Prospectors, Profits and Prejudice," *The American West,* II (Spring, 1965), 58–65.

60. *Alaska Herald,* July 9, 1873.

61. Jeannette Paddock Nichols, *Alaska: A History of Its Administration . . .* (Cleveland, 1924), 66. Young, *Hall Young,* 258; and De Armond, *The Founding of Juneau,* 118–121.

62. *Ibid.,* 121 and 137.

CHAPTER FIVE

And Recognition
1877-1887

Let the Congress of the United States provide Alaska with a government and a system of common and industrial schools. Let the Christian churches hasten to send in missionaries, and a brighter day will dawn upon that long and sadly neglected portion of our common country. — Sheldon Jackson, Alaska, and Missions on the North Pacific Coast.

UNOFFICIAL DELEGATE Mottrom Ball arrived at the national capital in December of 1881. Here he joined the nation's eight official territorial delegates already seated in the House of Representatives. Obviously the 294 Panhandle voters (some of whom were not United States citizens) who had cast ballots in the September, 1881 election were not enough to convince Washington that Alaska was rushing toward statehood. To no one's surprise, a congressional committee soon shelved the "Memorial of the people of Southeastern Alaska." Ball was treated respectfully, and, as Alaska historian Robert De Armond has written, "was voted $4,665 for 'expenses and compensation as delegate or agent of the people of Alaska,' which means that he probably made at least as much as he would have done working a placer claim in Gold Creek Valley for the same length of time."[1]

Ball might secure little more than congressional respect, but public recognition of the District was clearly growing. Washington Territory's Governor William Augustus Newell had felt the Juneau convention important enough to journey

north for the proceedings.[2] Oregon backers of the Northwest Trading Company directed their field superintendent
John Vanderbilt to speed up his construction of the Juneau
branch store. Wasting no time, Vanderbilt beached a large
covered barge at the foot of Seward Street until a more substantial structure could be erected. Vanderbilt's clerk, boy-
ish Edward De Groff, became the community's first postmaster. Hard-working, imaginative, positive in outlook, De
Groff was the kind of enthusiastic frontiersman whose spirit
not even an Archipelago mist could dampen. In December
of 1881, he was among those who officially changed Harrisburg's name to Juneau.[3]

Alaska's stateside image was also changing. Although the
1881 Panhandle petition formed only a ripple in the activities
of the Forty-seventh Congress, it combined with similar
Alaska waves steadily slapping away at legislative apathy. At
the national capital Ball joined an expanding group of allies
unafraid to drop rocks into the pond of congressional in-
difference. Gone were the days when a man like Congressman and one-time Confederate Vice-President Alexander
Stephens could, without any challenge, snort, "That snow-
bound wilderness — not enough white men there to make a
decent county — never will be."[4] Too many Senators and
Representatives still held such an erroneous opinion, but
should they mouth it publicly, they were certain to be cor-
rected. Foremost in setting the record straight was Sheldon
Jackson.

Jackson's admonitions and communications took many
forms. A born lobbyist, he sought to influence government
policy at its highest levels.[5] In 1881 the assassination and
lingering death of James A. Garfield thrust the one-time
New York spoilsman, Vice-President Chester Arthur, into
the White House. Jackson, and no doubt Ball, reached the
new president. In his first State of the Union Address, President Arthur reminded his countrymen, "I regret to state
that the people of Alaska have reason to complain that they
are as yet unprovided with any form of government . . .

Sheldon Jackson was appointed General Agent for Education in Alaska in 1885. A self-appointed lobbyist, he became Alaska's chief advocate in Washington, D.C.

there is immediate necessity for . . . the education of the people and [to] secure the administration of justice."[6] Among those pleasantly surprised at the manner in which President Arthur addressed himself to Alaska was the prominent Indiana attorney John W. Foster. To his fellow Presbyterian he volunteered some sound advice about Jackson's campaign for an Organic Act for Alaska. "The acts of Congress organizing the territories of the Union will by no means

145

fit Alaska. . . . Let some godless broken down whiskey drinking political hack be sent there as governor and three boon companions as judges and . . . another as territorial secretary . . . it will turn back the hands on the dial plate of the clock of Christian progress in Alaska a quarter of a century."[7] Foster thought that Jackson had "done much for Alaska letting daylight in upon it." So much in fact that the lobbyist had "earned the right to say who shall hold its offices and lay the foundations of its future institutions."[8]

Throughout the 1880's other part-time residents of the national capital joined with Jackson in drawing attention to the Great Land's needs. Among them were California's Senator John F. Miller, past president of the Alaska Commercial Company, and government investigators like artist-author Henry Wood Elliott and Alaska census-taker Ivan Petroff. In the early eighties, as District Census Agent, Petroff had compiled a comprehensive and extremely readable report.[9] Petroff, like Elliott, was a peripatetic Alaska advocate. Each would become increasingly bizarre in behavior. Time would show that the land's brutal, ambivalent beauty had affected their rationality. Still, the land gripped them, and despite their heterodoxy, they voiced her cause.

A latecomer in the Alaska chorus, one whose penchant for publicizing Alaska in print and lecture hall occasionally approached even Jackson's effusiveness, was Lieutenant Frederick Schwatka. Here was a West Pointer whose vocational talents embraced law, medicine, and journalism. A cultivated mind, coupled with a rugged physique, ideally fitted him to be an explorer. Schwatka first gained the public eye for his reports on the lost Sir John Franklin expedition. His 1883 Yukon River explorations and his subsequent books and articles focused official attention on a gigantic segment of Alaska as yet but dimly understood.[10]

John Muir was still another American that Alaska bewitched. On a canoe trip with missionary S. Hall Young, the famed Pacific Coast naturalist discovered Glacier Bay. Then, as the two of them scrambled over the vast network of rock

and ice, missionary Young almost joined the angels. En-
thralled by the utter massiveness of their find, he took a false
step and fell against a chasm wall. Both his arms were in-
stantly dislocated. Worse, he found himself slowly slipping
toward a ledge with a thousand-foot drop-off. Young's story
of how Muir rescued him is a classic in high adventure. Both
of them were able writers, and their descriptions and tales
of life in America's northern holding helped initiate Alaska's
tourist industry.[11]

In 1881, Henry Villard directed the first large excursion
party northward. It numbered eighty, and included General
Nelson Miles, then in command on the Pacific Coast, and a
military band. Their route traced the Inside Passage. Long
since famous among mariners, the Villard party's cruise
through the Alexander Archipelago invited the creation of
yet another Far West "scenic tour."[12] The well-equipped
passenger steamer *Idaho*, plus the promotional virtuosity of
Villard, commenced what has today become the West's most
popular coastal marine tour. Henry Villard will forever be
remembered as the extraordinary corporate leader who
drove through to success the Northern Pacific Railroad,
the line which linked the Midwest to the Pacific Northwest.
Villard loved to excite the imagination. Everything he did
was calculated to build up a land-sea transportation network over America's Northwest. In 1880 his steamer
Columbia, equipped with four blazing 60-lamp Edison dyna-
mos, had dazzled Portland's citizenry.[13] Quite as flamboyant,
Villard's 1881 Alaska excursion lighted the way north for
the nation's burgeoning tourist business. Twelve years
earlier, Samuel Bowles, editor of the *Springfield Republican*,
had written that Alaska "alarms the love of comfort."[14]
Villard eliminated any alarm over loss of comfort. In 1883
he completed the second transcontinental railroad. He then
united this Northern Pacific Railroad to his Oregon Railway
and Navigation Company. Now an East Coast American,
tired of Europe's spas and scenes, could take the railroad
west and a passenger steamer north.

Here again the push of Sheldon Jackson intrudes itself. The Northern Pacific Railroad was but a year old when Jackson organized a memorable National Education Association summer excursion from the Midwest to Alaska. Encouraged by Villard, Jackson's tour railed west on the Northern Pacific and then steamed north along the Inland, or more correctly the Inside Passage, route. "All were enthusiastic over the scenes and experiences which your zeal and generalship brought within our observations and enjoyment," wrote the NEA president.[15] Later, Alaskan newspapers would complain about the sightseers who, "like the blind man who caught hold of the elephant's tail, thinking they have seen everything, proceed to write up Alaska as a barren waste. . . ."[16] Most tourists definitely did not return home convinced it was a "barren waste"; quite the contrary, in fact. They came, they saw, and thereafter Alaska had conquered a few more allies. The Archipelago's natural magnificence inspired prophecy. "May not these islands be the sanatorium of the North Pacific," speculated one traveler, "to which thousands, worn out with labor and care, shall resort to inhale the fresh air of the sea, and grow strong again? . . . In another generation it may be the fashion to have a seaside cottage in Alaska! Then it will be the resort of yachtsmen, whose launches will skim these inland waters. . . ."[17] Tourists' accolades ranged from "the most heavenly peace, the richest coloring, the daintiest beauty" to "a trip that will lie in memory as a perpetual joy." Muir was more than exuberant.

To the lover of pure wilderness Alaska is one of the most wonderful countries in the world. No excursion that I know of may be made into any other American wilderness where so marvelous an abundance of noble newborn scenery is so charmingly brought to view as on the trip . . . to Fort Wrangell and Sitka.[18]

If anything, the tourists over-rated the District's immediate economic prospects. An 1886 visitor forecast that "Alaska will prove when developed, as valuable a country as Norway, and far superior to Russia." An Englishman soberly predicted, "In the future it will be one of the richest, if not the richest portion of the union."[19] Such prognostications were based primarily on the humming fish canneries which excursionists toured, as well as the rapidly expanding Alaska Mill and Mining Company operation on Douglas Island. Superintendent John Treadwell was intensely proud of his creation and, until their numbers became a hazard, enjoyed directing excursionists through his works.[20] Some goggle-eyed visitors affirmed that the extraordinary modernization "in extracting the precious metal will soon make gold over-abundant, reduce its value so as to make it inconvenient to carry." Possibly this explains the hasty confusion that motivated one dear lady to sin. Mistaking pyrite for free gold, she "carried at great trouble," reported one of her traveling companions, "a large piece on board the steamer, thinking she had a 'find' rich enough to pay all the expenses of the Alaskan journey, and she looked so happy over it that no one had the heart to undeceive her."[21]

Navy Commander Beardslee and the ever-curious Schwatka, as well as other uniformed travelers, had great fun recounting their Alaska hunting and fishing experiences.[22] Late nineteenth-century American sportsmen still found gratification midst an abundance of wild life in the fields and streams of the contiguous Far West.[23] Nevertheless, during the 1880's, as the Far North tourist tide began to swell, a few daring sportsmen penetrated Alaska's primitive central mass in quest of game. In 1886–1887, H. W. Seton-Karr claimed to be the "first modern traveller" to circuit the Alpine coastline from Cape Spencer to the Kenai Peninsula. Bears, seals, salmon, trout, ducks, geese, grouse, ptarmigan, and much else titillated his rod and gun.[24] But these men were precursors. "Inexhaustible" was the way many Americans viewed their more accessible Far West hunting and fishing resources. Decades would pass before the harsh facts of ecology would compel America's Nimrods and Izaak Waltons to turn north.[25] Who of the pioneer generation could have predicted the transportation revolution that would abet this shift?

One of the major features of an Inside Passage vacation was the sea voyage itself. Because the travelers were surrounded on every hand by mountaineous islands, they were usually free of seasickness. Villard had two giant iron sidewheelers built for the Alaska run. During the 1880's, his Oregon Railway and Navigation Company's *Alaskan* and its near twin, the *Olympian*, offered the passenger heavily carpeted, 200-foot grand saloons aglow with crystal chandeliers. Travelers' staterooms boasted running water and genuine brass beds. And for those who felt so inclined, a seaborne prostitute was usually about to keep one company for the voyage.[26] Accommodations aboard the Pacific Coast Steamship Company vessels were likewise comfortable, but its crews were salty. At one moment Captain James C. Carroll could play the genial host, and the next, an ear-scorching shipmaster. His free use of nautical obscenities shocked many of his passengers. One resentful young woman, angered by the news that he was not going to spend what she believed was sufficient time at a particular point of interest, got up a passenger petition demanding he lengthen the stay. Carroll gallantly but firmly informed her, "My dear madam, I regret very much to disappoint you and your friends, but this steamship is not run by petitions."[27] Whenever possible, Carroll entered Glacier Bay so that his passengers could frolic on the ice. In 1884 there were 1,650 sightseers; two years later, 2,753; and by the end of the summer season in 1890, more than 5,000 tourists had seen the territory.[28] The trip had become fashionable and the summertime presence of Western nabobs and Eastern elite proved it.

Pioneers strove to impress the growing number of junketing Congressmen like Thomas B. Reed, Joseph N. Dolph, and Henry L. Dawes. "We think the society of Sitka is highly cultivated," declared one visitor, "judging from what we saw of it at their homes and at the grand ball given by the Sitkans in honor of our passengers." Between festivities, Panhandle residents sandwiched in expressions of need. No group exhibited more imagination in combining the soft sell with the felt need than the missionaries. At Juneau, Doctor W. H. R. Corlies distributed attractive handbills among the ships' passengers that welcomed them to the mining center and reviewed his mission's deficiencies. The Sitka Indian Industrial School band blared out a noisy greeting when the excursion steamer came to rest alongside the capital's dock, and at Wrangell one missionary after another served as an unpaid tour leader.[29]

Sheldon Jackson exerted himself to keep the tourist traffic growing. Surely there was no better way to publicize the Great Land. To reinforce his cajoling letters urging busy Congressmen to come north, he often sent along samples of native craftsmanship.[30] Embarrassed by Sitka's Lincoln Street crones who unctuously peddled poorly wrought wares to steamer passengers, Jackson collected for public exhibit at the District capital the artistic masterpieces carved by Alaska's proud forebears. The miner riffraff held the native culture in contempt. Jackson's zealous collecting proved otherwise, and not for some far-off stateside exhibition, but right in the indigenes' homeland where his museum displayed tangible reminders of what once had been. Among the esteemed scholars who aided Jackson and lauded his work were his good friend Alice Fletcher of the Bureau of Indian Affairs, William H. Dall and Spencer W. Baird at the Smithsonian Institution, geographer Marcus Baker, and educators Nicholas Murray Butler and Daniel C. Gilman. To preserve Sitka's priceless heritage of native artifacts, Jackson erected Alaska's first concrete structure at his own expense.[31]

The Presbyterian leader realized that although the means for transmuting the Alaskan frontier into a Christian commonwealth must necessarily be unique, the District's long-range aspirations were fundamentally the same as those pursued since the western march began. Far North maturation and domestic prosperity could be diagramed by a three-legged stool. The development of her vast economic prospects composed one leg. A second leg was an effective in-

The Indian village at Sitka as it appeared in the late 1880's. Not a genuine Tlingit structure or a totemic figure appears.

ternal government. The third indispensable support was Alaska's cultural and humanitarian growth. Here was where Jackson would have preferred to devote all his energy. But until the other two props were in place, there was little to guarantee a law-abiding society, one that would both protect and educate the native inhabitants. Let the economy take care of itself. Jackson would concentrate his efforts on preparing the aboriginal for the white society, that is, educating him and at the same time campaigning for the enactment of territorial law to help shield the native within the cloak of an ordered white society.

In the early eighties Jackson obligated the major Protestant churches to a far-sighted ecumenical blueprint in Alaska. His fellow churchmen did not always appreciate what he was about. Afterwards, some realized they "had bitten off more than they could chew," but one and all, none discounted Jackson's driving organizational quest to protect the Far North aboriginals. Within ten years the Presbyterian missionaries in Southeastern Alaska could rejoice in the presence (or promise) of Baptists at Cook Inlet, Kodiak, and Prince William Sound, Friends (Quakers) at Douglas Island, Methodists on the Alaskan Peninsula and Aleutian Islands, Moravians in the Kuskokwim Valley, Episcopalians along the Yukon River, and Congregationalists on the Bering Sea Coast. And finally, in 1890, because no one else would accept the job, Jackson tricked his own Presbyterian board, already straitened financially, into undertaking the Point Barrow mission on the remote Arctic Coast.[32] All of this had been initiated within a period of twelve years. At the outset Commander Beardslee had presaged the vital role of the Alaska missionary.

Missionaries had been sent by the Presbyterian Board of Home Missions, and their work soon became apparent upon the Indians. Businessmen, and miners who had been deterred from bringing their families to Sitka on account of the absence of all law, became satisfied that it was safe to send for them, and a church for whites, another for Indians, and Sunday-Schools sprang into existence.[33]

These Christian workers quickly discovered that their ministry to Alaska included men of every color. The Rev. S. Hall Young encountered a New Englander, and college graduate, living among the Kake Indians. He could communicate only with "grunts and monosyllables," a man "filthy, degraded and hopelessly lost."[34] Mrs. Edith Kilbuck, a Moravian missionary laboring in the Kuskokwim region, noted, "The natives say 'nearly all the white men we see are rough and carry revolvers as though we were wild animals to be afraid of. Why don't you first Christianize those of your own kind, and then their example would help us to do right.'"[35] The awful solitude of the Great Land's mid-continent interior affected men in unpredictable ways. In some instances it caused grizzled miners to become altruistic and even chivalrous. At other times the lack of a pay streak and the lonely, moor-like terrain blanketed by the prolonged Arctic night might snap a weak mind. Temporary madness in Alaska's gigantic Yukon Valley proved as dangerous as temperatures of 60 below zero. The good Roman Catholic Archbishop Charles J. Seghers wanted only to bring a message of love to the people of Central Alaska. He never knew why his wilderness companion suddenly became his killer.[36]

Roman Catholics, like their Protestant brothers, had first sought to establish missions in the Far North during the 1870's. Notwithstanding the historic Protestant-Catholic rivalry, Roman Catholic missionaries proximated the methods and humanitarian goals of the Protestants. Regrettably, the centuries-old distrust was carried north. Although cooperation between the two bodies was not what it might have been, the Protestant-Catholic feud was cooling. By century's end, particularly in so isolated a region as the Yukon Valley, there were numerous proofs of a quickening reconciliation.

Bishop Seghers' martyrdom only spurred his brother Jesuits to crystallize his dream. At the close of the 1880's the Catholics had established missions at Nulato and Holy Cross on the Yukon.[37] Tanunak mission on the shore of the

Bering Sea soon followed. The three Sisters of St. Ann who arrived at Holy Cross quickly became legends, not only in Boston and Baltimore but up and down the great river. Swarms of mosquitos and mice, inside and outside of their cabin, could not run them off. The Sisters' garden, surely one of the first in this part of the Yukon Valley, caused considerable stir among the natives. Sister Mary Calasanctius later recalled, "The eyes of the Indians were not round enough to observe this marvelous achievement of civilized man. They would pull up a turnip — they had never seen this vegetable before — examine it carefully — and just as carefully return it to the soil."[38] Like the Congregationalists to the north and the Moravians to the south, these dedicated Christian men and women did their best to minister to mind, body, and spirit — and to both native and nonnative Alaskans.

The manner in which Jackson electrified Christian opinion and magnetized East Coast humanitarians to his cause is a superb illustration of pressure politics. To transform public influence into law, he allied himself with his fellow Presbyterian, Senator Benjamin Harrison of Indiana. During October of 1883, Jackson established his permanent residence in Washington, D.C. Here he could immediately fortify Senator Harrison's drive for Alaskan legislation. From the spring of 1883 to May of 1884 the degree of national consciousness awakened toward Alaska reached a peak not evidenced since its purchase. The volatile Jackson drove himself to maneuver this force into the political arena. Presbyterian, Baptist, Methodist, and Episcopalian bodies bombarded Congress. The young but vigorous National Education Assembly and National Education Association gave special attention to Alaska's educational deficiencies. The State Teachers' Associations of such states as Connecticut, Vermont, New Hampshire, and Massachusetts called upon Congress "for an appropriation for an industrial school at Sitka and common schools at the chief centers of population in Alaska."[39]

Jackson had more than 100,000 circulars printed and sent

out to American teachers. They urged the "friends of education to rally and flood their Congressmen with petitions asking special attention to the claims of Alaska." Such distinguished professors as W. S. Tyler and Julius H. Seeley of Amherst and William Graham Sumner, Cyrus Northrop, and Noah Porter of Yale volunteered their signatures. Wendell Phillips, the old warhorse of humanitarian causes, promised Jackson his active assistance.[40] Ultimately, the Forty-eighth Congress, which first met in December of 1883, was engulfed in a torrent of petitions. They descended on Capitol Hill from more than 25 states. From New York alone there were forwarded some twenty memorials from cities as scattered as Catskill, Rochester, and Fredonia.[41]

Jackson hoped to couple his proposals for Alaska education and civil government legislation into a single act. Obviously Alaska needed both. The Jackson-Harrison legislative achievement was Alaska's Organic Act of May 17, 1884. The law created a Governor, a District Court with Judge and District Attorney, a Marshal, four deputies, and a Clerk, as well as four commissioners to handle minor legal matters. Particularly comforting to Jackson was Section 13. It required the Secretary of the Interior to make "needful and proper provision for the education of children of school age in the Territory of Alaska, without reference to race, until such time as permanent provision shall be made for the same." To finance this generous action, the hardly munificent sum of $25,000 was extended. Further, the mission schools were each assured 640 acres, and "that the Indians . . . shall not be disturbed in the possession of any lands . . . now claimed by them."[42]

To no one's surprise, John Brady was selected as one of the commissioners. Political experience, Republican party loyalty, and a halo of pioneer status dictated President Chester Arthur's gubernatorial appointment on July 4, 1884. Nevada's third governor and Alaska's first, John H. Kinkead, packed his grip and began the trip northward. He was to regret it.

The feud that erupted between Jackson's Alaska workers and Governor Kinkead's administration started with petty misunderstandings. In a much wider sense, their friction posed a venerable frontier dilemma: how to reconcile the immediate physical needs of a community with long-range civil and esthetic goals. The transient seaman, barkeeper, and miner carried north an essentially exploitive attitude. Among too many of them there was but slight concern over the cultural enrichment of the region in which they found employment. They aimed "to git thar poke" and go home. Traditionally, it was the West's agrarian settlers, and the village people who served them, who were concerned about their youngsters' tomorrow. These were the citizens who promoted law and order, knitted local government into a state government, built a schoolhouse and a "little brown church."[43] In time the towns that thrived became permanent fonts of culture. Men and women who labored to achieve these same ends within a boom-town environment never harbored any illusions about the basically parasitical society which they supplanted: Americanization should promise human edification; at the hands of the miner-prostitute crowd, Americanization could become retrogression. But Alaska had no farmers. Were her settlers, her constructive Americanizers, to be essentially town-dwellers, residents of Panhandle communities like Wrangell, Sitka, and Juneau?

America's Alaskan frontier, and in the nineteenth century this would remain primarily the Panhandle, was hardly a case of "root hog or die." Southeastern Alaska's climate was too equable, its flora and fauna too abundant. Nevertheless, the immigrant white population confronted discouraging hardships in becoming secure economically. Sitka's near-eclipse, and particularly the small businesses that blinked out, only spotlighted the unrewarding nature of the region for the home-builder type of settler. By the mid-eighties grass grew on Wrangell's streets and placer mining in the vicinity of Juneau had played out. Miners wandered

Governor John H. Kinkead, 1884–1885, was Alaska's first Governor after the Organic Act of 1884 created a District government. Petty misunderstandings between the missionary-teacher faction and the miner-Orthodox Church elements helped precipitate his early removal. (Alaska State Historical Library)

off or grudgingly became mill employees in the rapidly spreading Douglas Island works. Territorial isolation, the damp atmosphere, and a shortage of such essential amenities as white women compounded the Far North's socio-economic inhospitality. Generally, the brand of American who would involve himself in such a society cared little about cultural horizons.

The rough-and-tumble environment attracted an inordinate number of "hard cases." In the late seventies, William Gouverneur Morris had stated, "Many of those who go there are adventurers in the fullest sense of the word." A few years later, in a letter to his chief, the Secretary of the Treasury, he was more blunt: "There are in this country as God-abandoned, God-for-saken, desperate, and rascally a set of wretches as can be found on earth. Their whole life is made up of fraud, deceit, lying and thieving, and selling liquor to Indians which they manufacture themselves."[44] In 1882, California's Senator John Miller became so revolted at the scale of lawlessness that he proposed a joint resolution "to authorize the President to declare martial law in the territory." Certainly Juneau's tourists got an eyeful! Prospector D. A. Murphy recalled how a "properly convicted" Indian was strung up as the monthly steamer came in, and later as the *Idaho* pulled away from the wharf, another native was hanged.[45]

Given such conditions as these, one can hardly resist speculating as to what it was that once again drew John Kinkead to Alaska. When Alaska's territorial administrators steamed north in September of 1884, Jackson's promotional and humanitarian campaigns had gained considerable headway, so much so, that the following April Congress appointed him as the District's first General Agent of Education.[46] Both the Governor and the General Agent served under the Secretary of the Interior, but unlike Alaska's territorial administration tucked away off at Sitka, Jackson's office was in Washington, D.C. Why didn't the Kinkead men appreciate his very real power? Possibly the clerical collar produced a misleading image of weakness. It was a fatal miscalculation.

At first glance it would appear that Kinkead and Jackson should have been reasonably harmonious co-workers. They were Christians and Republicans. Both had a practical knowledge of the three-legged stool (economic development, law and order, and cultural civility), without which the territory could never support itself. Each man dreamed of an Alaska that combined the best facets of an Ohio, Nevada, and Oregon. Their goals did not diverge widely; neither did their specific means to achieve these goals. What tended to separate them was their different popular constituencies. Kinkead wanted to build on a miner-merchant base similar to that on which the states of Nevada and California had been founded. But Jackson distrusted these frontiersmen, particularly when they came into association with the native people. Although he had more confidence in the merchants, for they had a proprietary commitment and, frequently, families, Jackson correctly sensed that for all the transient miner's widely heralded independence, he was hardly the clay from which to mold a unique Far North state.

There was another ramification to the Jackson-Kinkead split. This was the contradiction between long-range goals and immediate development, between building citizens out of an ill-equipped aboriginal population and encouraging Alaska's largely mobile white minority to stay in Alaska by bending to their demands. Moralist Jackson suspected the miner population. Politician Kinkead had to work with it. Kinkead put top priority on economics, Jackson on guiding the territory's socio-cultural transformation. For the gigantic land to prosper, Alaska required both.

On September 15, 1884, the United States Navy's administration of Alaska came to an end. Commander Henry R. Nichols formalized the affair by having the cannon of the U.S.S. *Pinta* bark an appropriate Governor's salute. After commending the naval officers for their work, Governor

Kinkead set about preparing his first annual report. The Organic Act stipulated that such a report be compiled annually and completed by October 1. Understandably, Alaska's first Governor submitted a brief statement. Kinkead's 1884 *Report* lauded the territory's mining and fishing industries. It included the perceptive sociological note that fur production had fallen off because "the natives prefer the employment offered them by the white canneries, fisheries, mines and various other industries where the pay is sure, and they are comfortably housed, clothed and fed." With an eye on the quickening tourist traffic, he urged that "Baranov's Castle" be repaired.[47] Baranov in fact had never seen the rectangular wood structure that dominated the Sitka waterfront, but it had seen a lot of capital history and merited preservation. Kinkead had been Alaska's first postmaster, and he was acutely conscious of the District-wide communication-transportation inadequacies.

Our mail facilities must be increased. We should have at least semimonthly communications with Port Townsend. A monthly mail service should be established between this post [Sitka] and Ounalaska touching at several important points *en route*. Ounalaska, under the terms of the present organic act, is made a judicial point, with resident commissioner . . . is 1200 miles to the westward of Sitka, with no authorized or direct communication between them. A prisoner or litigant, to avail himself of the District court tribunal, must go by way of San Francisco. . . .[48]

The Governor praised the work thus far accomplished by the Presbyterian Board of Home Missions, but it distressed him that there was not a single school for white children in the territory. On the question of controlling the illicit liquor flow that washed over Alaska, he began what became a gubernatorial chant, prolonged and futile. "I can see no good reason why saloon-keepers, merchants, traders, and others should not contribute their mite in the way of license. . . ."[49] "High license," as it came to be called, was intended to protect the stable village merchant while hurting the vagabond trader who sold liquor to the native, that is, to separate the two classes of liquor dealers and leave those who pandered to the aboriginals' avidity for alcohol open to prosecution. Unfortunately, the missionary element saw every reason why the territory should remain absolutely "dry." And therefore the sensible adoption of "high license" was delayed until the harsh realities of the Klondike rush forced its acceptance.

If President Arthur had appointed Jackson and Kinkead at the same time and compelled them to remain together at the same office, the unfortunate 1885 clash might have been avoided, their elementary policy differences notwithstanding. But they did not talk things out. Inevitably, the misunderstandings inherent in inaugurating a pioneer government in a complex territory (immeasurably more so than most appreciated) "a million miles from Washington, D.C." became exaggerated. Jackson's acclaim as an Alaska authority had puffed his self-importance. He presumed that the new Governor would seek him out and became resentful when he didn't. This pique was soon clouded by darker differences, some small, some serious.

Governor Kinkead was entirely correct when he requested that Jackson's substitution of Presbyterian names for the native geographic place-names be reversed.[50] The implacable missionary opposition to high license was also infuriating. However, on matters affecting the Sitka Industrial School, the Governor and his co-workers should have been far more circumspect. This school was the emotional and physical heart of Jackson's Far North mission system. To it he hoped to channel the best of the District's aboriginal students. After becoming proficient in the skills of a white society, sewing, carpentry, mechanics, and so on, the native would be employable, not an object of scorn. Most important, reasoned Jackson and the missionaries, the young man or woman could not be shorn of his self-respect.[51]

Even before the new Governor arrived at Sitka, a *St. Louis Globe-Democrat* reporter caught Kinkead short. The Governor appeared to depreciate Jackson's educational work.[52] Unfortunately, the Governor's 1884 *Annual Report* had not yet appeared in print. Despite the fact that he had not yet read Kinkead's favorable observation on the Christians' labors, Jackson should have discounted the newsman's comments. After all, Kinkead had promoted religious education in Alaska ten years before Jackson landed there. Further on in the interview, the Governor declared that the missionaries were "not liked by the white people" in Alaska. This was an accurate statement only if one particularized what segments of the white population disliked the Christian field workers. As on the Hawaiian frontier, what wandering, adventure-seeking Yankee appreciated being told to treat a native belle like a girl back home? From the first the Russian Orthodox Church leadership had been intimidated by the energetic missionaries. Although neither as vocal nor as vituperative as the miner crowd, the priests could also be captious.[53]

By the mid-eighties, Sitka's Russian American element had regained something of its cultural self-confidence. Understandably, the lengthening path of Protestant missions being hacked out by Jackson and his allies rankled the Russian Orthodox Church hierarchy. Not so long ago this had been their exclusive domain. Priest Nicholas Metropolsky was surely guilty of envy, even if there was some justice to his plaintive objections. "We were here first and taught many American children . . . to read, write, and speak Russian. . . . We have not received a single penny from the Government for our educational work in Alaska."[54] Until 1884 every penny of the financial aid for Presbyterian mission schools had come from private donors. Metropolsky, later to become Sitka's Bishop, did not flaunt the fact that until the First World War his own establishment continued to receive a significant degree of monetary support from Russia.[55] Probably the most exasperating of Metropolsky's grievances was the number of native enrollments his Calvinist competitors had gained, especially at the capital.

Governor Kinkead's task, the cross every politician must bear, was to reconcile squabbling factions. A public official's first instinct is to bend to the wishes of the larger and more demonstrative bloc of citizens. No doubt these factors caused Kinkead to over-commit himself to the miners and Russian Americans. Other conditions magnified his blunder. The zealousness of his co-workers, Alaska's first judge and its first district attorney, caused the Governor to align himself with this segment of Alaska's population. Concurrently, Kinkead's ignorance of native acculturation made him under-value the role of Jackson's Industrial School and the missions it served.

Ward McAllister, Jr., was Alaska's first District Judge. Although he had passed the bar, he was a *cheechako*, that is, an Alaska tenderfoot. McAllister must have known he was ignorant of the native peoples. In all likelihood the brash 30-year-old judge may have looked upon his responsibility as a major league player might view an engagement in the bush leagues. After all, his uncle was New York City's society arbiter. Had "Judge" McAllister asked more questions before he departed from his San Francisco law office, he would have discovered that if there was anyone in the District upon whom he should not sharpen Dame Justice's sword, Dr. Jackson was that man. McAllister's co-worker, Alaska's first United States District Attorney, E. W. Haskett, was not so much callow as dreary. The Iowa Republican was inadequately educated, banal, and often boorish.[56]

Governor Kinkead viewed the elevation of the territory's Indians as one of his important tasks. The missionaries' campaign to convince Sitka's Ranche inhabitants to abandon their ghetto and build white men's cottages met his approval. It distressed Kinkead when townsmen protested this action. He noted that while the "whites have no absolute title to the land . . . [they] feel that the missionary people are rather aggressive and are taking possession of the best part of the would be town. . . ."[57] On the Indians' behalf the Christian educators were more than "aggressive"; they were downright authoritarian. To indelibly acculturate the native young people admitted to the Industrial School, the staff required their parents to sign papers virtually giving them over to the institution for a period of five years. It was highly questionable from a legal as well as a pedagogical standpoint; however, uncontrolled acculturation, particularly of a people set in the midst of a society which is itself aggressively competitive, can prove devastating for the group struggling to accommodate socially. Jackson and his co-workers sought in part to emulate William Duncan's sociological shield. The Industrial School arrangement was not without its flaws, but the burden of developing a better system lay on its critics.

In April of 1885, at approximately the same time he secured his General Agent of Education appointment, Jackson was shocked to receive the following report from A. J. Davis, Superintendent of the Industrial School:

You will be surprised and grieved to learn that we have lost more than half of our children. A spirit of persecution seems to have seized some of the people including several of the officials of the civil government. . . . The District Attorney has been violent and will continue to cause us further trouble if he remains. They have enjoined us from doing any work and have instilled among the Indians a spirit of distrust and even of dislike. . . .[58]

Furious at this assault by McAllister and Haskett, Jackson and his Alaska lieutenants launched a counter-attack. Its violence was soon to rock the White House.

Governor Kinkead, who had recently praised the spreading network of mission schools in a letter to the Secretary of the Interior, found himself caught in the angry blast. The civil administrators were attacked as: "drunks," which Haskett was; as "dandy dudes," which McAllister was; and men intent on wrecking the school in order to provide the lecherous miner riffraff with nice, clean mission girls. This was a wild exaggeration. For all the hyperbole, it was a blast certain to enflame Victorian ears.[59]

Why, in fact, had the Judge and the District Attorney commenced hostilities with the Presbyterian establishment by opening fire on their five-year contractual system? The pair's motives were mixed. They had unquestionably succumbed to the blandishments of a jealous priest and the racist, Christian-baiting miner crowd. What easier way to win territorial popularity than to vanquish the killjoy missionary? Publicly they insisted that they were defenders of American liberty. And in truth McAllister and Haskett had for the last few months been applying telling legal blows to the hard-to-kill institution of native slavery. Now, if they were to be consistent, they convinced themselves, the five-year contract must go. Naval and Revenue Marine officers had been fighting Northwest Coast Indian slavery for years, but never had they done anything directly to injure the Sitka school; quite the opposite, in fact. Certainly none of them had ever confused a shaman with a college-educated missionary. To spin legal theory when an ashamed nation was at last demanding action to redress the plight of the Indians was all very foolish.

McAllister clearly revealed his ineptitude for public office with the trap he used to subdue Jackson. When Jackson came north, the District Attorney had him thrown into jail on trumped-up charges. Martyrdom promised magnificent publicity in the missionary press. Jackson made the most of it.[60] There was a roar of protest from Los Angeles to Cape Cod. Even busy Congressmen stopped and asked, "What's going on up there?" Jackson took no chances and applied the *coup de grace*. President Grover Cleveland's brother, William Cleveland, a Presbyterian minister, and the Commissioner of Education, Presbyterian John Eaton, both solid Jackson men, visited the White House.[61] Democrat Cleveland did not need to be reminded that Kinkead and company wore the Republican label. On May 7, 1885, President Cleveland appointed Alaska's second Governor, Democrat Alfred P. Swineford. As for the outgoing administration, the long-time Western politico, Kinkead, accepted his ejection as a part of the time-honored spoils system. Youthful Ward McAllister was extremely bitter. He made an attempt to be reinstated and suffered the added humiliation of being snubbed by his former audience in Sitka. Haskett got drunk—so drunk, in fact, that he accidentally killed himself.[62]

Contention over the operation of Alaskan schools did not

die in 1885. Indeed, Jackson charged ahead. By the year's end he had initiated an organizational pattern that fused federal and philanthropic monies and created common (or "day" or "public") schools in conjunction with the mission institutions. Some Alaskans believed these day schools were intended primarily for the white children living in the District's population centers. Certainly the General Agent did not want them to become either exclusively Caucasian or native. But after some Juneauites threatened a preview of the twentieth century's Prince Edward County tragedy, where the public schools were closed to halt integration, Jackson retreated and set up a separate common school for the natives. Unquestionably, the manner in which the General Agent openly criss-crossed mission school personnel with public school teachers was unconstitutional. He justified his action on three grounds: Grant's Peace Policy reservation schools had unblushingly mixed federal funds and denominational revenues; the major Protestant churches had tacitly accepted his coordinate role in the District; and Alaska's social needs cried out for action.[63]

Like Alaska's first Governor, her second arrived at his post late. Alfred P. Swineford did not realize the appropriateness of a Christian leader as a General Agent of Education. In fact, the District's two-sided school system still received substantially more denominational aid than federal funds. Unfortunately, the Kinkead conflict had left Jackson unnecessarily sensitive to criticism by "spoilsmen." Swineford was a blatant Negrophobe; he had long made merry jest of temperance advocates; and during the Civil War he had been a Michigan Copperhead, three facts that were grave liabilities in Jackson's eyes. On the other hand, President Cleveland's appointee did have much to recommend him. He was a mining authority. The man's own political metal had been tempered by experience in the Michigan legislature and as Marquette's Mayor, and his communicative qualities had been sharpened by years of newspaper management. Swineford knew the value of getting the truth and

Governor Alfred P. Swineford, 1885–1889. A one-time Michigan Copperhead and confirmed negrophobe, Swineford had little sympathy for the missionary faction and feuded bitterly with Sheldon Jackson. His political experience in Michigan combined with his journalistic talents made him a formidable opponent. (Alaska State Historical Library)

was not afraid to espouse it when he believed he possessed it.[64]

Once again Alaska's chief executive officer sought to build a political house on the sandy foundation of a miner electorate. Garrulous and convivial, they doubtless seemed sound enough. Before long the men demonstrated their instability. In 1886, Juneau's white rabble imitated their "southside" brethren and resorted to mob rule. The object of their wrath was Treadwell's Chinese workers. Throughout the early 1880's, westerners had brutally expelled Chinese from a number of Far West mining communities.[65] Although they justified their violent acts by claims that the Asians were immoral, it was more often a case of their economic competition and old-fashioned xenophobia. During June of 1885, Richard Harris wrote Sheldon Jackson, "The people here seem to be kind of demoralized. They are commencing the dynamite business here against the Chinese. . . . It is a serious affair that a civilized community should resort to such cowardly actions. . . ." Swineford was appalled and wrote to his Washington superior urging soldiers be sent north to restrain the "rough element."[66] After more dynamite did not move the Chinese out of Treadwell's Douglas Island works, "rum sellers and bummers" took direct action. When the orientals asked their employer for arms with which to defend themselves against the mob, Treadwell wisely refused their request. Had he given them arms, the outnumbered Chinese might have been massacred.[67]

By the time Governor Swineford arrived, the Chinese had been herded aboard two schooners and dispatched southward. Swineford's exertions to secure justice met with sullen contempt. Fortunately, Juneau's bully boys received the same treatment from Treadwell when they applied for his recent laborers' positions. As for the Chinese, after eight days with hardly room to lie down and "nearly starved," they arrived at Wrangell. Some of them actually accepted Captain Carroll's offer of protection and returned to

Douglas Island aboard his steamer *Ancon*.[68] But for most Chinese, the Pacific Slope message was clear, "Chinese go home."

One year after "the majesty of the mob" had exiled Juneau's Chinese, another scene of humanity in flight shook Southeastern Alaska. This body, however, sought sanctuary *in* Alaska. Why did Father William Duncan and his devoted Tsimshians abandon their remarkable British Columbia settlement at Metlakatla? Why, indeed, when Canadians boasted a better record of white-Indian relations than did America? Essentially the 1887 exodus resulted from Duncan's stubborn refusal to accept the dictates of the Church Missionary Society. Duncan believed that to introduce the communion service among a people who had not too long before practiced cannibalism could cause great and harmful misunderstanding. His superiors were just as adamant, declaring that eating the mystical elements, the bread and wine — Christ's body and blood — was a symbolic act that the sensitive Tsimshians would quickly appreciate. Both parties were too obdurate, and time would show that Duncan suffered from a dangerous case of megalomania. However, in 1887, Americans cheered his courageous decision.[69]

After a dramatic and sometimes dangerous ocean crossing, Duncan and approximately a thousand Indians found shelter on Annette Island. Here at the Panhandle's southern tip on an insular wilderness, the redoubtable patriarch commenced his second saga. Duncan wasted no time in getting the support of such powerful senators as Henry L. Dawes and Henry Teller. Keenly conscious of public relations, he promptly erected "a large guest house" and commenced a newspaper to explain his needs. Within a year "upwards of 130 long huts and board shanties were scattered along the shore"; a "good sized building" served as temporary school and church. Before many years passed, "New" Metlakatla would boast bungalows and handsome public structures duplicating the delightful Victorian village that lay deserted to the south.[70]

Without the dawn of bright prosperity that broke across Alaska in the 1880's, Duncan probably could never have played both Moses and Joshua to his Indian Israelites. And although his Tsimshian Indians had moved farthest down the white man's path, all of Alaska's aboriginals felt some pressure of accelerated change. Schwatka told how the Athabascans of the interior had discarded their "uncouth and rude cooking utensils" while tea and tobacco had become "the articles most sought after."[71] Panhandle Indian police were now handling numerous minor native squabbles. Visitors to the capital were astonished to find the once-fearsome Annahootz on the public payroll and keeping law and order. Americanized clothes, homes, and even boats manufactured by the Industrial School invariably produced approving nods. But there were losses as well as gains. Governor Swineford's 1887 *Annual Report* chronicled the other side of the ledger: "The mortality rate as compared to the number of births furnished me by the authorities of the Greco-Russian Church indicates the gradual extinction of the native people. . . ."[72] If the Presbyterians at Sitka were any judge, haste must be made or even the indigenes' record would be lost. Accordingly, in 1887, Sitkans formed the Society of Natural History and Ethnology.[73]

In that year an ambitious proposal was made to tap the Great Land's interior: open a southeastern land gate and thus compete with the distant and expensive western gateway where the Yukon River debouched into Bering Sea. Peripatetic Edmund Bean sought nothing less than a charter to construct "a practical pack trail" linking Alaska's Lynn Canal with Canada's Lake Bennett. Bean's suggested route would help to break down the mountain barrier separating the Panhandle from the upper reaches of Canada's Yukon.[74] This stretch of that exceedingly lengthy river, a water highway that united the Great Land and Yukon Territory, had some strangely named tributaries. One of them carried the appelation Klondike. In 1887 it was only a place-name on Canada's Yukon Territory maps.

Despite the fact that a segment of public opinion still persisted in visualizing one-sixth of the nation as a site for a penal colony, Alaska had at last won a healthy degree of recognition and utilization from informed Americans.[75] Fishing, mining, tourism, improvements in territorial law, and permanent patches of American settlement—the Alaska of 1887 formed quite a contrast to the listless District twelve years earlier. Yet, the Far North frontier still lacked a satisfactory degree of national acceptance. How ironic that in nine years a gold discovery outside of Alaska by a vagabond prospector would provide not merely acceptance but notoriety.

NOTES

1. R. N. De Armond, *The Founding of Juneau* (Juneau, 1967), 122.

2. S. Hall Young, *Hall Young of Alaska: An Autobiography* (New York, 1927), 258.

3. De Armond, *The Founding of Juneau*, 151–152.

4. Young, *Hall Young*, 274.

5. Ted C. Hinckley, "Sheldon Jackson and Benjamin Harrison," *Pacific Northwest Quarterly*, LIV (April, 1963), 66–74.

6. James D. Richardson (Ed.), *A Compilation of the Messages and Papers of the Presidents*, (22 vols; New York, 1911), X, 4651.

7. Letter from John Foster to Sheldon Jackson, October 31, 1881, JCorr., Vol. 11, p. 284.

8. Letter from John Foster to Sheldon Jackson, April 29, 1882, JCorr., Vol. 12, p. 169; and John Foster to Sheldon Jackson, May 5, 1882, JCorr., Vol. 12, p. 174.

9. Ivan Petroff, *Report on the Population, Industries and Resources of Alaska* (Washington, D.C., 1884) in *10th Census*, VIII (Washington, D.C., 1884).

10. *New York Times*, November 3, 1892; U.S. Military Academy, West Point Association of Graduates, *Twenty-Fourth Annual Reunion* (New York, 1893), 67–70; and Morgan B. Sherwood, *Exploration of Alaska, 1865–1900* (New Haven, 1965), 77 ff.

11. S. Hall Young, *Alaska Days with John Muir* (New York, 1915), Chap. IV; L. M. Wolfe, *Son of the Wilderness: The Life of John Muir* (New York, 1951), 210; and John Muir, *Travels in Alaska* (Boston, 1915).

12. Henry Villard, *A Journey to Alaska* (New York, 1899), 35.

13. Oscar Osburn Winther, *The Great Northwest: A History* (New York, 1956).

14. Samuel Bowles, *Our New West* (Hartford, Conn., 1869), 499; Ted C. Hinckley, "The Inside Passage: A Popular Gilded Age Tour," *Pacific Northwest Quarterly*, LVI (April, 1965), 67–74.

15. Letter from T. W. Bicknell to Sheldon Jackson, October 7, 1884, JCorr., Vol. 13, p. 422. For a resumé of the tour, see: JScrap, Vol. 11, p. 72.

16. *Alaska Journal*, April 1, 1893.

17. Henry W. Field, *Our Western Archipelago* (New York, 1895), 101.

18. Alice W. Rollins, *From Palm to Glacier* (New York, 1892), 106; Letter from A. L. Frisbe to Sheldon Jackson, September 9, 1884, JCorr., Vol. 13, p. 403; and Muir, *Travels*, 13.

19. William Gray, *Musings by Campfire and Wayside* (Chicago, 1902), 255; Francis C. Sessions, *From Yellowstone Park to Alaska* (New York, 1890), 53; Sara King Wiley and William H. Wiley, *The Yosemite, Alaska, and the Yellowstone* (New York, 1893), 153.

20. Eliza Ruhamah Scidmore, *The Guide-Book to Alaska and the Northwest Coast* (London, 1893), 86.

21. Wiley and Wiley, *The Yosemite*, 153.

22. James Wickersham, *A Bibliography of Alaskan Literature, 1724–1924* (Cordova, Alaska, 1927), 125 and 58 ff.

23. Earl Pomeroy, *In Search of the Golden West: The Tourist in Western America* (New York, 1957).

24. H. W. Seton-Karr, "A Fresh Field for the Sportsman," *Fortune*, XLVII (March, 1887), 394–406.

25. Roderick Nash, *Wilderness and the American Mind* (New Haven, 1967); and Leo Marx, *The Machine in the Garden: Technology and the Pastoral Ideal* (New York, 1964), trace this painful public awakening.

26. Gordon Newell, *Pacific Steamboats* (New York, 1958), 18–20.

27. Pacific Coast Steamship Company, *All About Alaska* (n.p., 1890) features complete data on the comfortable tourist accommodations. E. W. Wright (Ed.), *Lewis and Dryden's Marine History of the Pacific Northwest* (New York, 1961), 150; Matilda Barnes Lukens, *The Inland Passage: A Journal of a Trip to Alaska* (n.p., 1889), 9–10.

28. *The Alaskan*, June 30, 1888; *Eleventh Census of the United States*, VIII, 250–251.

29. Sessions, *From Yellowstone*, 111; Letter from Carrie Willard to Sheldon Jackson, August 4, 1895, JCorr., Vol. 10, p. 6. Both *The North Star* and *The Alaskan*, each of which was published at Sitka, listed notable visitors to the capital. Illustrated Circular, Juneau, 1887, JScrap, Vol. 18, p. 77; Horatio G. Broke, *With Sack and Stock in Alaska* (London, 1891).

30. Letters from John G. Ames to Sheldon Jackson, March, 1880, JCorr., Vol. 10, p. 97; Henry L. Dawes to Sheldon Jackson, January 18, 1885, JCorr., Vol. 24, p. 3.

31. This is related in detail in the author's "Sheldon Jackson as Preserver of Alaska's Native Culture," *Pacific Historical Review*, XXXIII (November, 1964), 411–424.

32. This astonishing expansion is best detailed in Jackson's section of the *Annual Reports* of the Commissioner of Education for the eighties and nineties. Each of the religious denominations and its workers have published various documents dealing with phases of their specific northern ministry. For example, see: J. Taylor Hamilton, *The Beginning of the Moravian Mission in Alaska* (Bethlehem, Pa., 1890); Hudson Stuck, *The*

Alaska Missions of the Episcopal Church (New York, 1920); Mrs. James Mc-
Whinnie, *History of Kadiak Orphanage, Wood Island, Alaska: 1892–1906*
(n.p., n.d.): and Tollef Larson Brevig, *Apaurak in Alaska*, trans. by J. W.
Johnshoy (Philadelphia, 1944). Jackson notes the first pivotal inter-
church planning meeting in: "What Missionaries Have Done for Alaska,"
The Missionary Review of the World (July, 1903), 497–504.

The manner in which Jackson manipulated his superiors into a position
where they were forced to accept the Point Barrow assignment may in
part be traced in: Letter from Sheldon Jackson to Henry Kendall, Feb-
ruary 27, 1890, Letterpress Volume, "Sheldon Jackson Letters," Vol.
1, p. 295, Speer Library, Princeton Theological Seminary, Princeton,
N.J. (hereafter this material is cited as: PUTS); Letter from William Irwin,
Presbyterian Board of Home Missions, to W. T. Harris, Commissioner of
Education, March 24, 1890, Alaska Schools, Unfiled, National Archives,
Washington, D.C.; Letter from Rev. Henry Booth to Sheldon Jackson,
April 10, 1890, JCorr., Vol. 15, p. 269; and Letter from O. D. Eaton to
Sheldon Jackson, April 24, 1890, JCorr., Vol. 24, 319.

33. L. A. Beardslee, *Reports of Captain L. A. Beardslee Relative to Affairs
in Alaska . . . 1882*, 47th Cong., 1st Sess., Senate Exec. Doc. 71, Vol. 4,
Part I. A recent and useful summary of the missionary in Alaska is: Tay
Thomas, *Cry in the Wilderness: "Hear Ye the Voice of the Lord,"* (Anchorage,
1967).

34. Young, *Alaska Days*, 76–77.

35. Extract from Mrs. Edith Kilbuck's Diary, JScrap, Vol. 15, p. 140.

36. Gerald G. Steckler, "The Case of Frank Fuller: The Killer of Alaska
Missionary Charles Seghers," *Pacific Northwest Quarterly*, LIX (October,
1968), 190–202; Capt. M. A. Healy to Secretary of the Treasury, November 26, 1887, Miscellaneous Letter Collection, Sheldon Jackson Museum, Sitka, Alaska.

37. For background material on the Roman Catholic achievement in
Alaska, see: Francis Barnum, "A Compendium of the History of the
Catholic Missions in Alaska from their Foundation until 1900," JCorr.,
Vol. 22, p. 419–429; and Joseph M. Piet, *The Land of the Midnight Sun—
Alaska: The Missions of Alaska* (Spokane, 1925). Wilfred P. Schoenberg,
A Chronicle of the Catholic History of the Pacific Northwest: 1743–1960 (Ore.,
1962), is a splendid achievement but largely overlooks Alaska.

38. Mary Joseph Calasanctius, *The Voice of Alaska: A Missioner's Memories* (Lachine, Quebec, 1935), 125.

39. Endorsement of Churches, JCorr., Vol. 23, p. 245; Resolutions of a
Special Committee of Presbyterian General Assembly . . . May 1883,
JScrap, Vol. 8, p. 142, letter entered in the *Congressional Record*, 48th
Cong., 1st Sess., January 23, 1884, Vol. 15, pp. 597–598; Second National
Education Assembly, JScrap, Vol. 11, p. 21; Report of the National Edu-
cation Association, JScrap, Vol. 5, p. 71; letter from Thomas W. Bicknell
to Secretary of the Interior, Henry M. Teller, JCorr., Vol. 13, p. 170;
and Alaska Education, JCorr., Vol. 23, p. 246.

40. Circular Issued to Teachers of the United States, 1883, JCorr.,
Vol. 13, p. 268; Memorials to Congress of U.S. for Education in Alaska,
December, 1883, JCorr., Vol. 23, pp. 199–205; Letter from Wendell

Phillips to Sheldon Jackson, December 29, 1883, JCorr., Vol. 13, p. 266.

41. *Congressional Record*, 48th Cong., 1st Sess., Index to Vol. 15, 8.

42. Ted C. Hinckley, "Sheldon Jackson, Presbyterian Lobbyist for the Great Land of Alaska," *Journal of Presbyterian History*, XL (March, 1962), 3–23, discusses this lobbying triumph in considerable detail. For discussion of the Organic Act, see: Jeannette Paddock Nichols, *Alaska: A History of Its Administration* . . . (Cleveland, 1924), 49 ff. For the text of the Organic Act, see: Thomas H. Carter, *The Laws of Alaska* . . . (Chicago, 1900), 439–444.

43. Page Smith, *As a City upon a Hill: The Town in American History* (New York, 1966), develops this social thrust admirably.

44. U.S., Senate, *Report of a Special Agent on the Territory of Alaska and the Collection of the Customs-Revenue Therein*, 44th Cong., 1st Sess., Exec. Doc. No. 37, March 20, 1876; Letter from W. G. Morris to William Windom, Secretary of the Treasury, November 7, 1881, CHR.

45. Senator Miller, May 22, 1882, JScrap, Vol. 9, p. 96; Herbert L. Heller (Ed.), *Sourdough Sagas: The Journals, Memoirs, Tales and Recollections of the Earliest Alaskan Gold Miners, 1883–1923* (Cleveland, 1967), 24–25.

46. Appointment as General Agent of Education, JCorr., Vol. 14, p. 34; JScrap, Vol. 64, p. 139.

47. John H. Kinkead, *Governor's Annual Report, 1884* (Washington, D.C., 1884), 2.

48. *Ibid.*, 5.

49. *Ibid.*, 7.

50. Letter from Gov. John Kinkead to Postmaster General, July 16, 1885, Alaska Governors' Papers, Letterpress Vol. I, Federal Records Center, Seattle, Washington. Hereafter this collection is cited as: AGP. Letter from Sheldon Jackson to Hon. W. F. Vilas, July 29, 1886, PUTS, Alaska Schools, Vol. 4, p. 160. The commander of a U.S. Coast Survey steamer referred to the scrapping of Indian place names as "an act of vandalism." Eliza Ruhamah Scidmore, *Alaska Its Southern Coast and the Sitkan Archipelago* (Boston, 1885), 272.

51. Genevieve Mayberry, *Sheldon Jackson Junior College: An Intimate History* (New York, 1953), 7–20.

52. *St. Louis Globe-Democrat*, December 19, 1884, JScrap, Vol. 23, p. 32.

53. Letter from Sheldon Jackson to President Grover Cleveland, April 3, 1885, JCorr., Vol. 14, p. 50C; and Sworn Statement of Missionaries, April 10, 1886, JCorr., Vol. 25, p. 132.

54. Russian Orthodox Church Report, Sitka, AHD, II, 14; Report of Nicholas Metropolsky to Alaska Ecclesiastical Consistory, May 21, 1885, AHD, III, 133–134.

55. Lester D. Henderson, "The Development of Education in Alaska, 1867–1931" (unpublished Ed.D. dissertation, Stanford University, 1934–1935).

56. Letter from H. L. Johnson to Sheldon Jackson, August 4, 1885, JCorr., Vol. 14, p. 92; Letter from A. L. Frisbie to Sheldon Jackson, September 9, 1884, JCorr., Vol. 13, p. 403.

57. John H. Kinkead, "Notes on Alaska," 1885, JCorr., Vol. 24, p. 15.

58. Letter from A. J. Davis to Sheldon Jackson, April 10, 1885, JCorr., Vol. 14, p. 35.

59. Letter from John Kinkead to Secretary of the Interior, March 23, 1885, AGP, Letterpress Vol. I; Sheldon Jackson, *A Statement of Facts Concerning the Difficulties at Sitka, Alaska, in 1885* (Washington, D.C., 1886), gives the General Agent's side of the controversy.

60. J. Arthur Lazell, *Alaskan Apostle: The Life Story of Sheldon Jackson* (New York, 1960), 11–22. Young, *Hall Young*, 275–277. For further details of the imbroglio, see: JCorr., Vol. 14, and PUTS, Alaska Schools, Vol. I.

61. Letter from A. J. Davis to Sheldon Jackson, July 27, 1885, JCorr., Vol. 14, p. 91; Letter from Sheldon Jackson to President Grover Cleveland, April 3, 1885, JCorr., Vol. 14, p. 50C; Letter from Sheldon Jackson to Miss R. E. Cleveland, June 17, 1885, JCorr., Vol. 26, p. 1; Letter from Sheldon Jackson to President Grover Cleveland, June 17, 1885, JCorr., Vol. 26, p. 4.

62. *The Alaskan,* November 21, 1885, December 19, 1885, and March 6, 1886.

63. The distinction between these two types of schools was vague both because of Jackson's Protestant assumptions and because sparse public funds forced him to economize. For example, he had no qualms about putting a missionary's spouse on the public payroll. By hiring someone already in Alaska, the General Agent eliminated transportation expense. He also aided a poorly paid missionary teacher and assured himself of hiring someone with, as he put it, "a missionary spirit." Letter from Sheldon Jackson to Benjamin Harrison, December 8, 1888, JCorr., Vol. 25, p. 180. As late as 1957, the feeling persisted that the "only suitable administrators for American dependencies must have something of the patriot and missionary in their make-up. . . ." John Wesley Coulter, *The Pacific Dependencies of the United States* (New York, 1957), 11. Jackson was quite aware that he walked a thin wire between church and state, and thus he continually tried to explain his program. Letter from Sheldon Jackson to L. Q. C. Lamar, Secretary of the Interior, July 20, 1885, PUTS, Vol. I, p. 251.

64. Interviews by author with Mrs. Agnes Shattuck (daughter of Gov. A. P. Swineford), August 4, 1962, Juneau, Alaska. The Governor's letters, his Michigan newspapers, etc., in his daughter's possession, were of considerable aid in this evaluation. Swineford's *Annual Reports* and *Alaska: Its History, Climate and Natural Resources* (Chicago, 1898) also reveal something of the man.

65. Various studies detail the history of the Chinese on the Pacific Slope. A standard account is: Mary R. Coolidge, *Chinese Immigration* (New York, 1909). Newer are those by: Gunther Barth, *Bitter Strength: A History of the Chinese in the United States, 1850–1870* (Cambridge, Mass., 1964); and Ping Chiu, *Chinese Labor in California, 1850–1880: An Economic Study* (Madison, 1963).

66. Letter from R. T. Harris to Sheldon Jackson, June 10, 1885, JCorr., Vol. 14, p. 48; Letter from Gov. A. P. Swineford to L. Q. C. Lamar, Secretary of the Interior, February 19, 1886, National Archives,

RG-430, U.S. Interior Department Territorial Papers Alaska, Roll I. Hereafter this is cited as: TAP.

67. Ted C. Hinckley, "Prospectors, Profits and Prejudice," *The American West,* II (Spring, 1965), 58–65, relates the episode.

68. *Alta California,* August 28, 1886, and other clippings, JScrap, Vol. 17, pp. 51–52.

69. Rev. Thomas Crosby, *Up and Down the North Pacific Coast by Canoe and Mission Ship* (Toronto, 1914), 402; H. A. Cody, *An Apostle of the North: Memoirs of the Right Reverend William Carpenter Bompas, D.D.* (New York, 1908), 190–191; Stuck, *The Alaska Missions,* 6 ff. Letter from Henry Kendall to Sheldon Jackson, December 20, 1886, JCorr., Vol. 13, p. 249, and January 14, 1887, JCorr., Vol. 14, p. 261; Henry S. Wellcome, *The Story of Metlakahtla* (London, 1887), 348–350.

70. *The Metlakahtlan* (New Metlakahtla), I (November, 1888); "From Alaska. Mr. T. N. Strong's Impressions of the Metlakahtlas," Michael Healy Scrapbook, M. A. Healy Collection, Huntington Library, San Marino, California; *The North Star,* December, 1887 and September 1888; *The Alaskan,* March 12, 1887 and September 22, 1888. Strangely enough, this dramatic exodus then produced little if any serious United States–Canada diplomatic attention. Peter Buzanski, "Alaska and Nineteenth Century American Diplomacy," *Journal of the West,* VI (July, 1967), 451–467.

71. Frederick Schwatka, *Report of a Military Reconnaissance in Alaska, Made in 1883* (Washington, D.C., 1885), 101.

72. William T. Hagan, *American Indians* (Chicago, 1961), 137–138, and especially Hagan's, *Indian Police & Judges: Experiments in Acculturation & Control* (New Haven, 1966) provides a scholarly review of how the Far West's Indian police developed at this same period. Salary Receipt signed by Gov. John Kinkead, June 3, 1885, TAP, Roll I; *The Alaskan,* November 14, 1885; Letter from Gov. A. P. Swineford to Secretary of the Interior, October 12, 1885, AGP, Letterpress Vol. 1; Abby J. Woodman, *Picturesque Alaska: A Journal of a Tour Among the Mountains, Seas and Islands of the Northwest from San Francisco to Sitka* (Boston, 1889), 170; Alfred P. Swineford, *Governor's Annual Report, 1887* (Washington, D.C., 1887), 32; Julia McNair Wright, *Among the Alaskans* (Philadelphia, 1883), 196.

73. Letter from Sheldon Jackson to Nicholas Murray Butler, September 6, 1887, JCorr., Vol. 26, p. 157; Letter from D. C. Gilman to Sheldon Jackson, December 4, 1887, JCorr., Vol. 14, p. 180. *Constitution and By-laws of the Society of Alaska Natural History and Ethnology,* pamphlet, PUTS.

74. Letter from Gov. A. P. Swineford to L. Q. C. Lamar, Secretary of the Interior, February 12, 1887, TAP, Roll 1; Letter from Edmund Bean to A. P. Swineford, January 24, 1886 enclosed in above, *Ibid.* Bean's offer was rejected. H. Muldrow to Gov. of Alaska, February 16, 1887, CHR.

75. *The Alaskan,* February 20, 1886; U.S., Congress, House, *Report 1685,* 49th Cong., 1st Sess., April 15, 1886.

CHAPTER SIX

Acceptance Without
1887-1897

On the shores of the inside channels which the Russians twenty-five years ago dared not navigate without an armed guard, shotted guns, and boarding nettings, we are met today by the busy hum of the thriving mining towns, with sidewalked streets, enlivened by rumble of wheels and clatter of hoofs, with hotels and boarding houses, large stores, steam laundries, saloons and churches, steam ferries puffing from shore to shore, the muffled roar of blasts and the glare of electric lights. —Ivan Petroff, "Twenty-Five Years of Alaska," North American Review, *1892.*

PRESENT AT THE 1888 Democratic National Convention were two Alaska representatives. Here was yet another feeble, unofficial effort to gain wider recognition for the territory. The action aroused little comment but marked a distinct advance from the political apathy exhibited twelve years earlier. "The Presidential election," the *Sitka Post*'s editor had written in 1876, "has somewhat had the effect of arousing the lethargic enthusiasm of our local politicians, but the cosmopolitan nature of the population renders it a difficult matter to arrive at any conclusion as to which party the majority inclines to."[1]

As the territory's economy quickened during the eighties, so did its awareness of the quadrennial presidential elections. John G. Brady polled his fellow Sitkans during the 1884 Blaine-Cleveland battle. Except for a jester who marked his ballot for the feminist attorney Mrs. Belva Lockwood, the results testified to the Republican party's traditional grip on post-Civil War America.[2] But the GOP ascendancy had ended. James G. Blaine lost the 1884 election as the voters finally put a Democrat in the White House. Four years later Grover Cleveland was again the people's choice, but owing to the Electoral College, he was defeated, and the Republican Benjamin Harrison became President. Accordingly, Governor Swineford lost his Far North sinecure, and a Vermont Republican, Lyman Knapp, became Alaska's third Governor.

Like his predecessors, Governor Knapp was a reasonably honest, if plodding, public servant. He lacked Swineford's journalistic competence as well as his executive gusto. But when it came to the martial touch, Knapp had no peers. A Civil War veteran who had been seriously wounded as a combat officer with the Army of the Potomac, the Governor relished the functions that provided him an excuse to don his militia uniform and preen before the District's light-opera militiamen. Unfriendly newspapers laughed at this posturing.[3] Regrettably, Knapp was symptomatic of a nation that had begun to strut.

Imperialism was a form of patriotic intoxication. Industrialized countries had taken to gulping down the rankest kind of chauvinism. Sometimes a dose of imperialism was prescribed for domestic ills, on other occasions as a cure for a nation's ego. A decade before the United States joined in the imperialist binge and commenced the Spanish-American War, the North Pacific fur seal dilemma foreshadowed what lay ahead. The diplomatic hassle between Canada and the United States over pelagic hunting caused some Americans to declare that "Alaska was worth fighting for."

The Alaska Commercial Company's 20-year monopoly had proved quite profitable for San Francisco businessmen. Therefore it came as no surprise when in the mid-eighties the Company's Pribilof Islands fur monopoly came under renewed pressure. It was not a fresh assault by the embittered group of California competitors who had lost out in 1870. Now the Company was threatened by a diversified

Governor Lyman E. Knapp, 1889–1893. A veteran of the Civil War, Knapp had a weakness for military pomp which made him the butt of many jokes in Sitka. (Alaska State Historical Library)

collection of fishermen and one-time whalers. A surprising number of these pelagic, or ocean, hunters had once worked the Grand Banks; some of them had sailed their vessels all the way from Gloucester, Boston, and Halifax. As historian Ellis P. Oberholtzer has written:

A sudden and marked increase in demand for [seal] fur had led to a rise in its price and the sea was scoured by seal hunters of many nationalities. . . . It had become a profitable pursuit. Fashion in dress had made it so. Seal skin, like silks and satins and diamonds and pearls, was the hall mark of wealth and elegance. Capes, muffs and tippets were made of it. A woman who might be coated from neck to heels in this soft fur was the envy of beholders.[4]

The pelagic hunters killed fur seals at sea, outside the cloistered waters surrounding the Pribilofs. Before long, their success produced howls of protest from the Alaska Commercial Company. And to the independent seamen's astonishment, some newspapers began to call them "poachers," or worse, "fur seal pirates," and picture them as desperate men. Because the Alaska Commercial Company was an American-owned organization and a number of the pelagic hunters were Canadian, America's national honor was quickly involved.[5]

In 1886 the revenue steamer *Corwin* seized one American and three Canadian vessels engaged in pelagic hunting. Notwithstanding the fact that the ships were clearly in international waters, they were escorted to Unalaska and stripped of their rigging to prevent flight. Their protesting skippers were hauled to Sitka, fined, and consigned to a month in jail. Understandably, the British press reacted in anger. The next year more than a dozen sealing ships were caught. Fewer than half of them were American. Unfortunately, during the post-Civil War years, "truculence characterized many of our newspapers; a like spirit with reference to Canada and Great Britain generally, marked our Presidential campaigns."[6] A few wildly jingoistic Americans insisted that as a result of the 1867 purchase, the United States had inherited a *mare clausum*. English diplomats, on far more sensible grounds, replied that national jurisdiction ended at the three-mile limit. Fortunately, war talk did not pass the sputtering point. Public sentiment still favored arbitration instead of armaments.

While the two North American powers waited for the verdict of an international tribunal, Commander Robley D. Evans, the United States Navy's "Fighting Bob," was given sixteen warships and told to clean out the "fur seal pirates." Commander Evans snared the pelagic hunters' major supply

The Revenue Marine and the Navy combined to protect both Alaskans and their resources. This British Columbia seal hunter, skipper of the Thornton, *had his vessel beached on Unalaska. Shaking his fist in frustration, he was helpless until his rigging was returned.*

ship, the Canadian vessel *Coquitlam*, but to sweep the North Pacific clear of sealers was definitely not a task to be accomplished in a season. It was just as well. The next year the international tribunal ruled against the United States, requesting payment of $473,151 in damages to Canada for the unwarranted seizure of the Canadian vessels. "We got the hot end of the stick," was "Fighting Bob's" laconic comment. Not until 1911 would a reasonable settlement be adjudicated.[7]

The seal imbroglio's significance has been noted by historians. Too frequently its diplomatic aspects have overshadowed the controversy's other implications. Economically, the squabble between the Alaska Commercial Company and the independent pelagic hunters was comparable to a feud between a big open-range cattle baron and a group of individual homesteaders. Robert De Armond has succinctly stated that the Alaska Commercial Company "got Uncle Sam and Uncle Sam's Navy, plus most of the public press and a considerable part of the Congress to help them. If the cattle barons had been as successful as the Alaska Commercial Company, there wouldn't be a farmer west of the Mississippi."[8] The fur seals' habits and the jargon of the pelt harvest complement the cattle industry analogy. Male seals were known as bulls, females as cows. Instead of being called dogies, their offspring were known as pups. For an autumnal and winter range the seals swam southward, where, in lieu of grass, they subsisted on sea food. As spring approached, the sleek fur animals commenced their trek to the Pribilofs. There was no range roundup, for the seals came ashore of their own accord. Seal branding was attempted and then abandoned. Alaska Commercial Company employees, like Wyoming cowboys cutting out a fully developed steer, separated the choice seals from the herd on the rocky Pribilof shore. Also like the cattle industry, sealing had paid well, and it possessed a certain romantic aura.

The fur seal business also posed one of the great dilemmas faced by modern society: how to permit a number of competing capitalists to exploit a rich natural resource and at the same time enforce intelligent conservation. In 1870 the government had evaded the question and given the Alaska Commercial Company a legal monopoly on the Pribilofs. The Company had carefully observed the agreed-upon pelt ceiling in its annual slaughter. Accordingly, the Pribilof herd proliferated. Deplorably, however, the poachers of the mid-eighties threatened to wreck this balance. Especially revolting was the pelagic hunters' wastefulness. Many a mortally wounded seal slipped beneath the waves before it could be gaffed. And because females only mothered their own pups, the killing of a cow usually assured the death of her progeny. After the expiration of the 20-year lease in 1890, the North American Commercial Company succeeded to the grant. The Alaska Commercial Company continued to maintain its profitable shipping and mercantile network. Because the sea hunters had considerably reduced the number of Pribilof pelts available, the new managers' profits suffered.[9]

As a recognized expert on the Pribilof wealth, Henry Wood Elliott was dispatched northward to investigate. Elliott had married an Aleut girl, learned one of the native tongues, and truly loved the amorphous Great Land. His report on the seals' destruction was scathing. Much of his denunciation rang with the righteous anger of a nature devotee shaken by the ecological mayhem. Rudyard Kipling had neatly summed it up, in his "Rhyme of the Three Sealers": "There's never a law of God or man runs north of Fifty-Three." It was too bad that Elliott's artistic fervor outran his reportorial veracity. Before he cooled off, he not only hotly condemned the large corporations as well as the poachers, but the federal civil servants in the Far North, and even the United States Secretary of State. "Fur Seal" Elliott was superseded by Stanford University's President, and recognized ichthyologist, David Starr Jordan. Luckily for the Pribilofs' animal inhabitants, Elliott remained their outspoken, if intemperate, advocate.[10]

At the expiration of the second 20-year lease in 1910,

the fur seal herd that had numbered an estimated three million in 1867 had been reduced to one of but thousands. What could the people's elected representatives do to prevent the fur seal from being eliminated like the sea otter? Congressmen became socialists and turned the administration of the islands over to the federal government. What about the pelagic hunters, some of whom deserve to be called Alaska pioneers and whose earnings often benefited Alaska? In 1897, Congress approved an act that forbade Americans, both individuals and vessels, to engage in pelagic sealing. By the North Pacific Sealing Convention of 1911, Great Britain (for Canada), Japan, and Russia agreed to prevent their nationals from marine hunting inimical to the Pribilof seals.[11]

The exploitation of Alaska's fur seal by external interests, and the corollary drain-off of profits to outside investors, had its counterpart in commerce, mining, and canning. Here again the petty capitalist was submerged by the large corporation. With the century drawing to a close, Alaskans protested that the District had become a colonial banquet table for voracious corporate giants, primarily the North American Commercial Company, the Alaska Commercial Company, the North American Trading and Transportation Company, the "Treadwell Group of Mines," and the Alaska Packers' Association. The Alaskans' charge that these businesses "made their money up north and spent it down south" was the truth but not the whole truth.

Historians have long known that late nineteenth-century America witnessed a rapid acceleration of business consolidation. The economies of large-scale operation dictated such concentration and swelling urbanization became its corollary. Only in recent years have historians begun to probe the concomitant rise in public apprehension and the socio-psychological by-products created by this ineluctable movement. As Robert H. Wiebe has discerned:

Countless citizens in towns and cities across the land sensed that something fundamental was happening to their lives, something they had not willed and did not want, and they responded by striking out at whatever enemies their view of the world allowed them to see. They fought . . . to preserve the society that had given their lives meaning. But it had already slipped beyond their grasp.[12]

Alaska's pioneers not only had to adjust to this vast cultural change but to a radically different environment as well. If the Great Plains isolation sometimes caused Populists to mouth irresponsible denunciations of big business during the 1890's, imagine how irrational were some of the lonely Alaskans' condemnations.

Indisputably, the Alaska Commercial Company, its Yukon River competitor, the North American Trading and Transportation Company, and the Pacific Coast Steamship Company were large firms, and the bulk of their profits were channeled outside of the District. Yet lacking their capital, their vessels, and trained employees, the Great Land's development would have been substantially slowed. And the complaint that they ruthlessly crushed competition totally overlooks Alaska's enormity. In such an arena as this, it was difficult to crush anyone indefinitely. As the Alaska Commercial Company's Kodiak agent complained in 1878, "This is a hard place to make anything as the Ice Co. and J. Shirpser and Co. do business hand in hand and try to make it hard for us by all in their power."[13] Certainly, after 1893 the Yukon River commercial rivalry between the Alaska Commercial Company and upstart John J. Healy's North American Trading and Transportation Company was severe enough. And it did not stop with freight-rate competition. "Back of the contests to make the best time loading and unloading on an upriver run, or to be the latest boat down river through murderous ice, there was many an individual contest ashore in saloon or street."[14]

No different than the mercantile-transportation companies, the Treadwell Mines had operated to return a profit to outside investors. And just as those firms had employed many resident Alaskans and boosted the District's economy, so had the famous Juneau mines. By century's end, three companies in fact had grown into what was collectively referred to as the Treadwell Group. They were the Alaska United Gold Mining Company, the Alaska Mexican Gold Mining Company, and the Alaska Treadwell Gold Mining Company. Altogether they united 880 roaring, crashing ore stamps. To obtain two dollars worth of gold — that is, a pea-sized piece of bullion — the mills had to move and refine one ton of ore. Visitors might shake in disbelief at the gigantic man-made Glory Hole and a company boarding house that could feed 480 men at one sitting, but without this massive investment in men and machines, the gold quartz could never have been extracted from Douglas Island.[15]

Of all the business groups damned for exploiting the territory and tending toward monopoly, the salmon-canning industry most easily fitted the condemnation. Ironically, however, fishing had become what historian Clarence Hulley called the "backbone of the territory's economy with regard to permanent value."[16] Writing in 1897, government inspector Howard M. Kutchin gauged this wealth from a national perspective. "The salmon fishing industry of Alaska represents more capital, employs more men, adds more to our foreign trade, and contributes more to the food supply of the world than any and all interests there. . . ."[17]

Mention has already been made of the seemingly inexhaustible mass of salmon that were taken at Karluk River, Kodiak Island, during the 1880's. This sublime example of nature's munificence continued into the next decade. Indeed, all along Alaska's littoral, the salmon pack was abundant, so abundant, in fact, that by the 1890's the supply had outrun the demand. The result was predictable and prompt.

In September, 1891, the Alaska Packers' Association was formed to dispose of the unsold salmon of that season's pack (some 363,000 cases), and five trustees were appointed to manage the business. This association was not incorporated and expired after the salmon were sold. The successful operation of these arrangements led, in 1892, to an arrangement in which nearly all (thirty-one) of

Tourists brave enough to crawl along its edge were taken out to Douglas Island to see "Treadwell's Glory Hole." A later generation would be less impressed by the mastery of nature that man's gold-mining machinery had given him.

the canneries joined, entering under the name of the Alaska Packing (not Packers') Association, for the purpose of leasing and operating and therefore controlling the canneries and reducing the Alaska pack for that year it being found too great for the market's demands.[18]

These actions were suspect. "It is claimed this consolidation is not for the purpose of raising the price of salmon," editorialized the *West Shore*, "but expressly to reduce the cost of taking, so that these canneries can compete with the other thirty canneries of the territory and make money. However, it is looked upon generally as the first step in organizing a huge salmon trust."[19]

With almost a boastful tone, the *Alaska Journal* declared, "The salmon industry, now reaching enormous proportions, has prospered so well that it has been merged into a trust."[20] By 1893 the Alaska Packing Association of 1892 had reorganized into the Alaska Packers' Association. The A.P.A. became a duly incorporated body, issued stock, and provided for a yearly distribution of the Association's profits. Headquartered in San Francisco, the "combine," as it was thereafter frequently labeled, was able to dispatch a fleet of steamers, schooners, and square-riggers for processing the annual pack. Of the 29 canneries operated in 1897, 17 belonged to the Association. Its total pack that year was 669,-464 cases, or well over 70 percent of the District's entire output.[21]

Earlier fears that a salmon trust would soon raise prices were put to rest. Because other large canneries, like the Pacific Steam Whaling Company, did not join the "combine" and expanded their own operations, a healthy degree of price competition was maintained. The threat of a market glut had produced some intelligent self-regulation. But self-regulation was desperately needed for another and even more ominous reason: the probable elimination of the salmon itself.

In January of 1889, San Franciscan John T. Brisbane wrote to Secretary of the Interior William F. Vilas:

I beg to call your attention to a great wrong being done to the Salmon Fisheries of Alaska which if not checked at once will at an early date destroy that great industry. . . . Now most of the streams in Alaska on the Pacific Coast are of the same nature and susceptible of being stopped by slight dams. The great success of the canneries on Karluk River and the enormous profits of the past season has created a perfect furor amongst capitalists both here and [on the] Columbia River and not less than twenty canneries of the largest magnitude are now preparing to seek these small streams and by not allowing the fish to pass up to the lakes will as can be readily seen only be a question of a few years that Alaska rivers will become as the Columbia and Sacramento — depleted — . . . . This industry is far more valuable than the seal fisheries and should be protected.[22]

That year Congress passed its first legislation to regulate salmon fishing. The Act of 1889 prohibited the use of barricades, both to protect the Indians and to sustain the salmon. Because no money was appropriated to inspect and enforce the law, it was dormant until 1892. Congress then supplied funds for one inspector and an assistant — for all of Alaska. And their usefulness was seriously compromised because these men could visit many of the canneries only on the very vessels they were sent north to check.[23]

Fortunately, as America's legislative gears were beginning to mesh so slowly, a number of the leading salmon canners themselves grew fearful, and searched for a means to prevent ecological disaster. In 1892, Alaska pioneer John C. Callbreath commenced a fish hatchery on Kuiu Island in the Panhandle. Callbreath's effort was crude, and for all his enthusiasm, he had little scientific evidence to confirm that what he had embarked upon did much good. Happily, the Alaska Packers' Association followed suit. It is noteworthy that all this was done well before the federal government created hatcheries.[24]

Further proof that the cannery owners were genuinely fearful that they might kill the goose that had laid the golden egg was seen in the support that some gave to a proposed government tax — revenue to pay for effective cannery regulation. Veteran Rogue River operator and successful Far North salmon canner R. D. Hume had been painful witness to what modern technology could do. He openly supported expanded regulation "for protection of salmon in Alaska."[25] Hume and his fellow canners had never heard of eco-systems, nor had any of them probably ever read George Perkins Marsh's *The Earth as Modified by Human Action.* However, men like Hume and Callbreath had within their lifetimes seen alterations along the eastern shores of the North Pacific that only a fool could dismiss. But seeing was not always believing, or at least acting. Many "fools" could be found among a generation nurtured on a philosophy that held America's resources to be virtually limitless. One Treasury Department Special Agent summed up the harsh dilemma, "Paradoxically though it may appear, it is nevertheless true, that none are more anxious to save and perpetuate the salmon than the canners themselves, and yet their methods are such as if continued, will very soon destroy them."[26]

Doubly paradoxical in all of this was the role of the smaller canners. They listed a whole series of grievances: price-cutting by the Alaska Packers' Association in order to ruin them; being refused passage on Association boats; charging exorbitant freight and passenger rates; and actual interference with their fishing. For all his petulance, the small operator's real grievance was that he could not enjoy what he supposed was the corporate security of the large canner. Investigations revealed that he not only often exaggerated the wrongs done him by the "combine," or the Pacific Steam Whaling Company, but also often was considerably less conservation-minded than they were.[27] Like his fellow entrepreneurs scattered across nineteenth-century America, he had inherited the anomalous golden rule of the *laissez faire* capitalist: business freedom to do what he damned well pleased, and protection to prevent other businessmen from doing what they damned well pleased against him.

With such a tradition as this to guide them, is it any won-

Heat from the canning-packing process has condensed the air over the Loring salmon cannery into steam. At the dock, a San Francisco three-master waits with infinite patience to reclaim the toehold profit-seeking man has won on its tree-blanketed shore.

der that United States Congressmen only haltingly moved to protect natural resources in the Far North? In 1896, legislation was enacted "toward termination of fishing activities in the mouths of streams (where even mobile gear is quite capable of exterminating individual runs) by prohibiting fishing above tidewater in streams less than 500 feet in width." Again it was largely unenforced. Alaska's Governor called it a "farce."[28] Belated, stumbling steps to be sure, but at least the cries of the conservationists were being heard.

Native Alaskans' protests got even less attention. As the salmon processing spiraled, the proportion of indigenous labor fell. In 1893, Hume and Thomas reported that their cannery employed "47 Italians, 20 white men and 80 Chinamen."[29] Each season the bulk of the laborers were imported from San Francisco. Cannery work was done primarily by Chinese, while "among the fisherman may be found Americans, Norwegians, Swedes, Germans, Sicilians and Negroes." Ichthyologist Tarleton H. Bean was satisfied that "the presence of the Canneries has not diminished the fish supply of the natives . . . it is really easier for them to obtain what they need for winter use than it was before the opening of the canneries." What he meant was that their acceptance of certain aspects of non-aboriginal culture was continuing. Bean noted that their historic curse still pursued them. "One great source of trouble with the natives is caused by the illegal sale of intoxicants by the Chinese and occasionally some Americans. This traffic is . . . destroying the usefulness of the people and . . . [making them] liable to pulmonary diseases."[30]

The "usefulness of the people" would not be permanently destroyed, but their acculturation struggle certainly had entered another phase as a result of the canneries' presence. Because the Panhandle Indian continued to absorb the greatest impact from the invading culture, his adjustment remained the most agonizing. By the 1890's it had dawned on the Tlingit leaders that they were in terrible trouble. At Juneau a group of them met with the District Governor to plead for protection and justice. Chief Kah-du-shan from Wrangell cut to the heart of their distress:

Long, long time ago before white people came to this country our people lived here at certain places where they went hunting and fishing. When the Russians were here, they did not have any stores in the interior, but they used to trade with our people here. . . . Then [after the purchase] the business men followed the soldiers. They commenced to trade with our people. Our people did not object, did not say any thing to them. By and by they began to build canneries and take the creeks away from us, where they make salmon and when we told them these creeks belonged to us, they would not pay any attention to us and said all this country belonged to President, the big chief at Washington. . . . We like to live like other people live. We make this complaint because we are very poor now. The time will come when we will not have anything left. The money and everything else in this country will be the property of the white man, and our people will have nothing.[31]

It was an eloquent statement, if exaggerated. Kah-du-shan would have been more accurate had he said, "The time will come when the money and everything else in this country will be the property of those who have adopted the elementary techniques and institutions of the white man." Kah-du-shan spoke with wisdom, but like all old men, he spoke nostalgically. The past was never as bright as he painted it, nor would the future be as dark as he sincerely envisioned it. Younger Indians lacked Kah-du-shan's frame of reference and therefore accepted much of what he now abhorred. Reared in a mixed red-white pioneer environment, they commonly emulated the more powerful white man's clothes, his tools, his dwelling, even his manners. (Whose manners? A miner's, a steamboat deckhand's, a cannery worker's, a missionary's?)[32] Such-minded Indians (and to lesser degrees their native counterparts in western and northern Alaska) had been exposed to white commercial village life. Yet for thousands of indigenes, the Americanization of Alaska had altered their lives only slightly. Even in the Panhandle, a surprising number of Indians continued to impose slavery on their fellows and believed in witchcraft. In 1895, Henry A. Field interviewed "two old men" at Wrangell who had but recently escaped a gruesome death because they were accused of being witches.[33]

Given such a confused and fluctuating sociological matrix, part ancient, part new, the actions and attitudes of many natives were understandably unpredictable. When the Roman Catholic Bishop from San Francisco arrived in Alaska, Indian parents greeted him with warmth. Enthusiasm also followed his offer to baptize their children. Their eagerness, no doubt, was generated by their insistence that "He would have to pay a fee for each child." Another time a mission-trained Indian, quick in computation, was employed by a cannery as "a special assistant, with good wages. Being given a note or due-bill of twenty-five dollars by his employer, he quickly saw his chance, and adroitly *raised* the figures to two hundred and fifty dollars, got the bill cashed at one of the neighboring trading establishments and suddenly disappeared. . . ."[34]

Thievery is an institution familiar to every culture. Chinese cannery workers were not paid off until they had passed within the Golden Gate, and sometimes not then. Tong Yoong and Company, one of the port city's labor contractors, skipped off with more than $40,000 and left 240 Chinese unpaid. In the midst of America's grim 1894 business depression, the *Alaskan* asked,

The men who are employed by the canning companies during the Alaska fishing season are taken back to San Francisco. . . . As soon as they have "loosened" their money in the city front saloons, they once more fall back into the army of the unemployed. Would it not, therefore, be better to pay off the men in Alaska . . . and thereby increase the working population of the territory?[35]

Would the Chinese have preferred to be "loosened" in Sitka or San Francisco?

San Francisco. What a magical name it was—and is. Its paramount role in the Americanization of Alaska certainly matches, if it does not exceed, the part San Francisco played in Nevada's early development. As the whaling fisheries could testify, easterners had underwritten investments in the Far North even before its purchase. Oregon money also went north, as did capital from various other points along the Pacific Slope. Alaska promoter Thomas Nowell of Boston reminds us that established eastern financial resources were likewise drawn upon. Yet it seems clear that the largest portion of investment capital that had flowed into Alaska between 1867 and 1897 was money originally activated by the mid-century California mining boom. Traditionally westerners have peered eastward, both to embrace and then to condemn the creditors who held them in thrall; however, in the case of pre-Klondike Alaska, it was not Wall Street but San Francisco's Montgomery Street that held the paper and collected the profits. After all, San Francisco was the largest city west of St. Louis. It cannot have been entirely coincidence that the 1880's spurt in Alaska's economy occurred only when the 1873–1878 nationwide depression had lifted, and San Francisco was itself "catching up with its ambitions."[36]

Even before the Klondike madness and publicity man Erastus Brainerd had ballooned Seattle's prominence, the location of the Puget Sound city had assured it a key place in Alaska's development. By 1894 the Brady-Whitford Sitka Trading Company had become the property of H. A. Bauer of Seattle. Two or three times each year Bauer inspected his Sitka firm. The remaining months were spent at Seattle where he could advertise, "a competent buyer on the ground we are able to offer goods at a low figure. Any article that is not in stock will be promptly sent for." It was small comfort that the twice-a-month southside mail delivery was sped up in the mid-nineties "at least twenty-four hours."[37] Capital, labor, distribution system, and markets—to Alaskans it must have seemed as though the whole economic cycle was "sent for."

Yet without the indispensable outsiders' aid, Alaska's vast natural resources might just as well have been moonscape. For the big corporations, it frequently was a case of damned if they did, damned if they didn't. Once established in an area, they were cursed by Alaskans as parasites. Should a business develop its enterprise elsewhere, it was attacked as purblind for failing to harvest the District's ungarnered wealth. And whenever a corporation poured money into the region on a large scale, it activated unpredictable social change. For example, after the Alaska Commercial Company closed out its Attu base, it was denounced for leaving the natives destitute and without a doctor. Actually, in the summer of 1889 the Company delivered $1,300 worth of provisions there to keep the Aleuts from starving.[38] But no firm could long remain where profits had ceased. Doubtless, Company managers were sympathetic with Aleuts who needed medical attention. Yet as the traders shut down their remote station all they could hope for was that somehow the natives would resume their accustomed, pre-Company existence. Attu's people could no more turn back the hands of time than could the bustling Yankee-born city of Juneau. The Alaska of the 1890's was not the Alaska of 1867.

Strangely, one group of people most harshly struck by change was among the territory's most remote. Reference has already been made to the avidity with which Bering and Arctic Coast Eskimos scrambled for guns and liquor, and the more trenchant, relentless whale hunters' pursuit of the neighboring whale and walrus. During the century's closing years the hourglass figure vogue among American women demanded huge quantities of corset stays—and until the advent of plastics that meant masses of whale baleen (slender, elastic bones arched within the whale's mouth). As early as 1872 a correspondent for the *New Bedford Standard* had penned a somber forecast:

The worst feature of the business is, that the natives of the entire Arctic shores, from Cape Thaddeus, in the Anadir Sea, to the farthest point North, a shore line of more than a thousand miles on the west coast, with the large island of St. Lawrence, the smaller ones of Diomede and King's Islands, all thickly inhabited, and our own coast of Northern Alaska, are now almost entirely dependent on the walrus for their food, clothing, boats, and dwellings. Twenty years ago whales were plenty and easily caught, but the whales have been destroyed and driven North, so that now the natives seldom get a whale. . . . Several captains lately arrived home have told me that they saw the natives thirty or forty miles from land, on the ice, trying to catch a walrus to eat, and were living on the carcasses of those that the whalemen had killed.[39]

Existence in this area of the globe was frequently precarious. In March of 1880 news broke that a schooner calling at St. Lawrence Island (Bering Sea) had come upon three mute villages. A premature break-up of the ice had denied the inhabitants both fish and walrus. They had starved to death *en masse*.[40] Throughout the eighties the natives' plight worsened. Tuberculosis and influenza joined smallpox and measles to destroy whole villages. Just as the Eskimos had created wasteful havoc among the walrus once they got their hands on modern rifles, so did the Eskimos often become their own worst enemies when whale guns and bombs came into their possession. In 1890 the *West Shore* reported that after hundreds of missiles had been fired by natives, only eight whales were caught.[41] Many of these magnificent mammals must have lumbered out to sea trailing gore, shredded by sharks, finally to sink to their deaths in depth far beyond the reach of any man. Fortunately, this ecological carnage and its dire sociological consequences had been witnessed by Alaska's man in Washington.

General Agent of Education for Alaska Sheldon Jackson had found United States Revenue Marine vessels excellent vehicles for touring his prodigious school district. In particular, he enjoyed the company of Captain Michael Healy and his cutter *Bear*. Healy, and other Revenue Marine captains before and after him, annually carried the flag to the Arctic Coast rendering assistance to whalemen and natives alike. To this day, one of the great North Country mysteries is how the hard-drinking, hard-handed, "Hell Roaring Mike" and the unbending prohibitionist Jackson ever became such close friends. Possibly Jackson saw himself as an ally in Captain Mike's futile effort to defeat John Barleycorn.[42] Whatever the basis for their comradeship, each of them had grown increasingly apprehensive at the reports of destitution among the Eskimo population. In December of 1890, Jackson informed the United States Commissioner of Education how disaster might be prevented.

Relief of course can be afforded by Congress voting an appropriation to feed them, as it has so many of the North American Indians, but I think that every one familiar with the feeding process among the Indians will devoutly wish that it may not be necessary to extend that system to the Eskimo of Alaska. It would cost hundreds of thousands of dollars annually and, worse than that, degrade, pauperize, and finally exterminate the people.

Jackson urged a two-pronged solution. The concept may have originated with his friend Healy, or elsewhere. "In connection with the system of industrial education in Alaska," Jackson wrote, "you establish an agricultural college through which you can introduce into that country the domesticated reindeer of Siberia, and train the Eskimo young men in their management, care, and propagation."[43] As usual, Jackson magnified the problem, just as he simplified the solution. But he got results. To spur Congress into action, he resorted to his standard tactic of first collecting and then planting private seed money. In 1891 the first sixteen Siberian reindeer were imported. By 1897 hundreds were to be seen in northwestern Alaska, and the federal government was paying the bill.[44] The acculturation of the Eskimo was still generations off, but at least Americanization had not meant annihilation.

When it came to native needs, Jackson could be flamboyantly bullish, and results followed. "Alaska is a very poor country . . . in which to make a fortune," he declared, "but it is a first class country in which to do missionary work for the natives."[45] Yet, whenever a chance arose to boost the white man's Alaska, he was quite objective, sometimes to the point of being bearish. Replying to a young man who had in-quired about commercial chances in the Far North, he replied, "I would not encourage you to remove there. The country is growing very slowly and opportunities for business are not good."[46] Without the infusion of practical young men still fresh enough to dream and act on faith, no Far West territory ever could have become a state. The Great Land never has had enough of this breed.

John G. Brady is a splendid example of the man who came north, raised his family there, and invested both his mind and money in and for his new land. Another genuine Alaska pioneer, and good friend of Brady's, was Edward De Groff. As noted earlier, the 20-year-old De Groff arrived in Sitka in 1880. If he had come ashore ten years earlier, the youthful easterner would probably have suffered from the business slump that was fatal to businessmen Kinkead and Murphy. De Groff was lucky. He had cast his future with Alaska at a time when canning and mining activities were infusing fresh economic blood into the territorial economy. At first a logger, De Groff was soon employed by the Northwest Trading Company at Killisnoo, later at Juneau. When not busy trading in oil and pelts, he played at photography, and on Sunday he assisted in Christian worship services among the local Indians.[47] But De Groff wanted to be his own man, and by 1886 he was.

Alaskans are inclined to commemorate the miner as their central pioneer figure. They should consider the village merchant, a man of small means and big ideas. De Groff, like Brady, Kinkead, and numerous others, was not cowed by the necessary mercantile diversification required on the Far North frontier. These men could be termed practical dilettantes. Among them De Groff was exemplary. When the Northwest Trading Company declared bankruptcy in 1886, De Groff and John Vanderbilt purchased its Sitka store. Here De Groff not only served as agent in the capital for the Alaska Commercial Company, the Pacific Coast Steamship Company, and the Alaska Oil and Guano Company, but also entered upon a direct and extensive mercantile career of his own. De Groff made certain that his purchasing agents at Portland and San Francisco were the finest available; he lured Juneau's best pharmacist into his employ. A sample of the general merchandise that he imported included cattle, fresh vegetables, fishing gear, and toilet articles. Capital residents rated his dairy products highly. After tourists began to inquire about pictures of "the land of the midnight sun," De Groff advertised himself as "Alaska's Pioneer Landscape Photographer," and what had been his hobby became another means of revenue. When the vogue for Indian masks and baskets rose, he was ready.

Sitkans never knew what to expect in Edward De Groff's store. A pet raccoon, the raffle of a Swedish meerschaum pipe, Sitka's first telephone, Baranov's coat of mail, giveaway calendars in triptych of George Washington, Abraham Lincoln, and Ulysses S. Grant, and velocipedes for the tots to ride and candy for them to munch — he missed few tricks. The *Alaskan*, the capital's major newspaper, was filled with his advertising. Sometimes it was in large type, but just as frequently it was set in single column with low-key advice to his prospective customers. "A piece of flannel dampened with Chamberlain's Pain Balm and bound on to the chest over the seat of pain will promptly relieve the pain and prevent the threatened attack of pneumonia." Naturally he had a stock of Chamberlain's cure-all on hand.[48]

De Groff built not only his business but also a better Alaska. The *Alaskan* is dotted with examples of his civic-mindedness. Among the activities he assisted in were the local school committee, an effort to obtain land for the erection of an Episcopal church, St. John's Hospital Society, the local fire brigade, and a group seeking to found a maternity hospital in the Ranche. The antithesis of the miner, he had put down his roots. He well understood that public service and profits must blossom together. While competitors had great difficulty in securing a permit "to furnish," as the *Alaskan* declared, "invalids and scientists with the ardent for medicinal, mechanical and scientific purposes

On Independence Day Sitka came alive with entertainments such as climbing a greased pole. Across the parade ground is the Governor's house, and beside it is one of the Russian watch towers. (University of Alaska Museum Photograph)

only," De Groff was trusted to sell liquor. In the same vein, it was De Groff who was asked to handle the distribution of government drugs among the Indians and to serve as custodian when the *General Siglin* was wrecked.[49] His partner, John Vanderbilt, died in 1890. Four years later De Groff married Vanderbilt's widow, and domestic success crowned his civic-commercial accomplishments.

Without the civilizing touch of women to reinforce the work of public-spirited men, the maturation of the Alaskan frontier would have been impossible. Like other earlier frontiers, the Far North became the nesting place for fallen doves, shrikes seeking a mate, and officious mother hens. Women were in high demand, and if a maid remained a miss, it was because she preferred it that way. Alaska missionaries, like their Hawaiian brethren, were enjoined to get married before they entered the field. Hardened, isolated Yukon traders, lonely for the tender touch, wore the badge of "squawman" without shame. A few, like C. H. Hamilton of Fort Cudahy, imported girls from San Francisco to do their laundry and cooking. Hamilton later fired a Swedish girl and refused to pay the young woman her back wages. Local miners forcefully reminded the trader of his agreement, and she returned to California with her pay.[50]

It was difficult for a pioneer woman not to find herself involved in school or church work. The needs were too insistent. Sitka's Benevolent Society performed the multiple functions of a modern welfare agency. Because they lived in the pre-electric kitchen age, most women spent their hours in the prosaic tasks of meal preparation, housekeeping, gardening, and, if so blessed, minding the children.

Alaska was not without her heroines. Tiny Carrie Willard was one of them.[51] The wife of a missionary, the Rev. Eugene S. Willard, Carrie had wanted to serve Christ since childhood. Youthful dreams had painted pictures of eager little pagans raptly learning about God. What an accommodation it must have been to confront dirty, black-painted faces, children whose parents too often imitated the miner rather than the missionary. Although disappointed at the careless behavior of her gold-hungry countrymen, Carrie always welcomed destitute and hungry prospectors. She almost perished during her first winter among the Chilkats. Later a devastating black measles scourge racked the Indians of Southeastern Alaska, and she and her co-workers saw the results of their labors. The casualties among aboriginals at Sitka's Ranche and at other points close to mission stations were astonishingly light.[52] In the mid-nineties, the Moravian missionaries at distant Bethel on the Kuskokwim River were not so lucky. First chickenpox and whooping cough epidemics took the lives of native children, and then in 1897 influenza attacked the population. By 1901 it was estimated that half of the Bethel region adults and all of the babies had died.[53]

Alaska's missionaries and teachers also paid a price for daring to mingle "all God's people." Some, like Peace Corps workers of the next century, came home elevated by their Far North service, but others returned embittered that they had been able to accomplish so very little. A few of Jackson's workers suffered from serious psychological inadequacies before going north, and their thankless, lonely rigors only further impaired their mental equilibrium. S. Hall Young found out that unless he got outside for a couple of years, his brain would dangerously retrogress, and Young labored at relatively civilized Wrangell. As with the case of Archbishop Seghers, it was duty in the Yukon Valley and on the Arctic Coast that posed the worst threat to mind and body.

Harrison R. Thornton was one of the first missionary-teachers at the Cape Prince of Wales area (along the eastern shore of Bering Strait). He suffered such severe culture shock and became so dispirited over the Eskimos' drunkenness and, by his standards, their uncleanliness, that his mind slipped. Paranoia set in, and his surly, suspicious behavior produced just the condition his disturbed mind had so fatally magnified. "Three Eskimo boys, aboriginal juvenile delinquents," plagued him with minor thefts and were expelled from his school. Because they also stole from their own people, they became virtual outcasts. Desperate, brooding, and possibly drunk, they killed Thornton with a whale gun, literally harpooning him. Certainly their act had symbolic overtones. Later when Captain Healy arrived on the barren coast, he had no legal problem with which to contend. Terrified at the havoc that the *Bear*'s cannon might wreak, the villagers already had executed the murderers.[54]

Dr. John B. Driggs, a pioneer medical missionary and teacher for the Episcopal Church, volunteered for Far North service in 1890, the same year as did Congregationalist Harrison Thornton. Driggs' station was at an even more distant site, Point Hope on the Arctic Coast. Whalers had committed so many outrages in the area that the Eskimo had sworn to kill any white man sent among them. How Driggs landed and first won the children by his sweetcakes made of flour and molasses, and then healed the flesh and spirit of their parents and finally hundreds of Eskimos, until his lonely death in 1918 forms an heroic story. Although he never suffered from the misanthropy that abetted Thornton's untimely end, Driggs' intellectual equipment grew lighter with each passing year. At the end he was a child but beloved by his parishioners.[55]

For all their sacrifices, the exertions of these humanitarians along the remote Arctic Coast and Alaska's vast western regions had but limited effect on the development of nineteenth-century pioneer Alaska. A permanent American society would either rise or fall as the Panhandle settlements advanced or retrogressed. No one appreciated this truth any better than did the territory's newspapers. Certainly no other institution in Alaska's embryonic towns did as much to glue together the three-legged stool of economic growth, responsible government, and social progress as did the press. Alaska's newspaper editors personified all of the courageous independence, and at times reckless shrillness, that the fourth estate was famous for on other frontiers. Almost always local politics generated far more heat than did the national presidential contests. In typical western fashion, politics was extremely personalized, frequently vituperative, yes, even physically dangerous. After one editor of Sitka's *Alaskan* had been given what the *San Francisco Chronicle* described as a "tremendous thrashing," his replacement suffered the ignominy of being "unmercifully" beaten with a bullwhip by an irate woman.[56]

In the tradition first established by ebullient Tom Murphy, Far North editors did not want their territory to remain at the pioneer level any longer than necessary. In 1891, M. E. Kenealy promised his Sitka readers that in the future "this dingy little hamlet will doubtless be the center of great mining operations."[57] Declared the *Alaskan* in 1892, "The 'wild and wooly West' a feature . . . of the Republic since 1849 . . . [this paper] does not wish to see revived here."[58] Editor E. O. Sylvester informed his readers that "capital and energy aided by good government" would "in the next quarter century" transform the territory. He predicted:

Around Juneau for miles the scene is one of bustling activity. Every mountain side trembles neath the drill and with the blast of the miners; many drills are crushing ore and the waters of every creek are discolored and heavy with the tailings they carry away. Towns have outgrown their proportions, large buildings, graded streets . . . large wharfs where great ships are coming and going daily . . . canneries appear on every favorable site; large saw mills. . . . Thousands of cattle. . . . The trading posts of the Yukon have grown to be towns where miners traders and herders reside with their families.[59]

It was heady brew he offered, but a necessary stimulant if the land was to advance. Starry-eyed prognosticating was also useful to counter the excess of what Editor C. H. Schaap called Alaska's own "grumblers, growlers and kickers."[60]

Why did the pioneer editors become so concerned with female virtue? Certainly the sparsity of womenfolk heightened their value as civilizing agents. In 1889 a furor erupted over the exploitation of native girls by miners and United States Marines. Across America women militants were insisting upon equality. News that Alaska Indian girls were being disfigured and kept locked up like wild animals by white men produced outcries from dozens of eastern female church auxiliaries. Governor Swineford damned the missionaries for their exaggeration and defended Alaska's miners. The tumult reached such proportions that Senator Henry L. Dawes came north and personally interviewed Carrie Willard to try to get the truth.[61] Four years later Editor Sylvester's *Alaska Journal* chastised Juneau citizens for their tolerance of a similar condition: "Will you allow the future of Juneau to be blighted that the dance house may run; must the center of town be given up night after night to avoid seeing sights which would bring the blush of shame. . . . Wasn't it bad enough before this new importation [of prostitutes] arrived?"[62]

Juneauites were not particularly pleased with Editor Sylvester's charges. After he denounced the community for taking harsh reprisal against members of a grand jury that had submitted an unpopular decision, his advertising suddenly vanished. The *Journal* had hardly crashed around him before Sylvester was once again praising Alaska's potentialities and indicting District immorality. This time his medium was a Sitka sheet, the *Alaska Herald*. In January of 1894, his inflammatory type exploded:

There is a terrible Monster in this country of frightful mien and sordid visage, whose grisly aspect is casting its blighting shadows throughout the length and breadth of this fair land, searing everything in its path as with a red hot iron and leaving nothing in its trail but foul disease and the ruin and desolation of the inoffensive Indian tribes. . . . This hideous monster has its origin in the lewd co-habitation of white men with native women. . . . Let every Christian man and woman who have the good of the country at heart . . . crush this hideous reptile, this Hydra-headed monster and grind him to powder.[63]

The following year Sitkans apparently decided one paper was enough for their town, and the *Herald* combined with the *Alaskan*. Sylvester, bearding the lion, returned to Juneau and commenced the weekly *Alaska Searchlight*. Was this journalistic insanity or integrity? Whichever the case, the energy of a free press made the Far North a better place in which to live.

Early in his career, Admiral Robert E. Coontz was stationed aboard the U.S.S. *Pinta* at Sitka. He recalled how valued were the stateside papers shipped north, in particular the *New York Herald*, the *Portland Oregonian*, and the *San Francisco Chronicle*.[64] Coontz enjoyed telling how in national election years when the first northbound mail steamer got within five miles of Alaska's capital, it would hoist its flag at the fore if the Republicans had won and at the main if the Democrats had triumphed. In 1892 the steamer captain placed the flag on the fore. Of course the Republicans shouted with glee and rushed to the wharf. As the vessel docked the district attorney summoned "all good Republicans" to congregate on one side of the pier, and all except a score of the entire population did so. After the steamer docked, the captain informed the stunned Republicans that Cleveland had actually won. That night the Democrats hired a hall and band and celebrated their triumph with music and speech-making. And, as Coontz capped the story, "Then, as if by some miracle, the score of Democrats increased by two hundred more."[65] With abundant problems of their own, nineteenth-century Alaskans found more fun than fury in national presidential contests.

In 1890 the District held yet another nonpartisan convention. As in 1881, the primary motive was to communicate the territory's "wrongs" to Congress. Once again a memorial and delegate, the popular steamer captain James Carroll, were dispatched southward. Carroll presented Congress his unofficial credentials and the convention's well-phrased memorial. Among its urgent demands were: a formal representative in the national capital; homestead rights in Alaska; local control of schools; improved postal service; and high license liquor regulation. Blustery Captain Carroll quickly attracted attention at Washington. Claiming the support of eastern capitalists, he offered to buy the District of Alaska![66] It was a marvelous publicity stunt, one that his coworker, Sheldon Jackson, no doubt appreciated.

Heretofore the relationship between Jackson and Captain Carroll had been strained. Carroll's notoriety as a liquor smuggler, plus his free-swinging vocabulary, had hardly endeared him to the missionaries. But Jackson had begun to reconsider his prohibitionist stand. Grudgingly he had come to recognize that Alaska was not being rapidly settled by the "stable Christian citizenry" that had typically calmed tempestuous Mississippi Valley frontier hamlets. Accordingly, in January, 1892, the General Agent of Education readjusted his liquor control blinders and cautiously endorsed high license for the Panhandle only. Although this reform was still a few years off, he was able to reorganize his District school system to allow for greater local control.[67] Pressure by Jackson and Carroll also pushed Congress into enacting land legislation, law ostensibly initiating Alaska townsites and aiding "trade and manufacture."

Alaskans would have been much happier had Congress extended America's historic homestead legislation to the Far North. The Organic Act of 1884 had confirmed that United States law referring to mining claims applied in Alaska. Yet further on, that same document had specified, "But nothing contained in this act shall be construed to put in force in said district the general land laws of the United States." This had infuriated Great Land settlers. "Why such a distinction was made," the territory's governor growled, "is past comprehension. Men may have the right to dig out ore upon lands and may obtain patents for the same, but if they dig out a cellar and build a house and improve lands for a home they cannot obtain a title." The Governor preferred to overlook the shocking land scandals that had dirtied the hands of so many trans-Missouri westerners during those years. Alaska was paying for the sins of her sisters.

The federal government proved so tight-fisted that even the 1891 land law proved useless. Writing in 1898, Alaska's Governor reported that:

> . . . a number of persons made application to purchase land under this act at $2.50 per acre; they made their deposits in national depositories and received triplicate receipts, Surveys were ordered, but when they were sent in for approval many objections were raised. . . . The General Land Office has issued one patent only under the law of March 3, 1891 for trade and manufacture.[68]

By 1892 and the second Harrison-Cleveland battle, Sitka's nominally Republican organ, the *Alaskan*, had become impatient with President Benjamin Harrison. The presence that year of two pseudo-Alaskans at the Republican National Convention had accomplished little. Harrison's party was accused of blocking "home rule" and homestead legislation. Cleveland's Democratic victory, rejoiced the *Juneau City Mining Record*, means "the downfall of a party which has lost most probably forever the confidence of the people"[69] Republican Governor Knapp knew that under the spoils system his days were numbered. "Speaking of the governorship," Captain Carroll was quoted as saying, "there is one man I would like to see get it, and he is Dr. Sheldon Jackson, a man whose whole soul is wrapped up in Alaska and a man whom all the people like."[70] Few bemoaned Knapp's departure, while a number of Alaskans were gratified by Cleveland's appointment of James Sheakley, a Wrangell resident, to the governorship. Once more the territory was to be administered by a man born east of the Mississippi, who had become a westerner following the California gold rush. Sheakley, however, had returned to his native state of Pennsylvania and ventures in merchandising, petroleum, and Democratic politics. The ex-Pennsylvania Congressman arrived in Alaska in the 1880's and as a church-going Presbyterian quickly identified himself with the Jackson camp.[71] Sheakley had been one of the District's Commissioners and had undertaken a variety of educational duties. As it tran-

Governor James Sheakley, 1893–1897. A native of Pennsylvania, Sheakley was a resident of Wrangell when Grover Cleveland appointed him Governor. Despite his experience as a Pennsylvania Congressman, a District commissioner, and an educational leader, he was only a mediocre territorial executive. (Alaska State Historical Library)

spired, Alaska's best-prepared Governor to date became a lack-luster state executive.

Throughout 1893, Sheakley, Brady, De Groff, carpenter Peter Callsen, and many of their fellow Sitkans gave of time and treasure to help restore "Baranov's Castle."[72] The belated effort by capital residents to preserve the decayed wooden structure situated on Sitka's waterfront promontory was significant. A region's history is usually honored only after its pioneers are both secure enough and sophisticated enough to do so. Equally noteworthy was the federal government's decision to expend $9,368 toward the building's restoration. Contractor C. W. Young of Juneau finished the work in September of 1893. Just six months later, on March 17, 1894, the "Pride of Sitka" went up in smoke. Amid the futile commotion to save the "Castle," the "mission boys got in and worked like beavers at the fire, but the Ranche Indians stood round and could hardly be induced by threats or persuasion to lend a hand."[73] It was a sad night. Governor Sheakley distributed coffee and cheered his dispirited neighbors. Who knows, he may even have philosophized a bit. Sitka was surely no Persepolis; was it to be a Phoenix? Neither dramatic fate awaited it. Alaska, however, had turned an historic corner. Its Panhandle had just about passed through the frontier phase.

At the close of his 1894 *Annual Report,* Governor Sheakley made note of the "mining camps in the Yukon Country. . . . A number of persons have gone into that district who have but little means and no experience in mining or other labor, and I fear that there will be much suffering for want of supplies."[74] Then he went on to urge federal action to establish mail communications and a wagon road to foster the Yukon Valley penetration. How many trans-Appalachian Governors had voiced similar contradictory pleas since the western march began?

Sheakley could have relaxed. Men had been prospecting over the Yukon River Valley since the 1870's. Some had perished, and most at one time or another had endured want, but quite a few had learned how to master the harsh wilderness. Across this vast, still vaguely defined hinterland, from the Bering Sea to the 141st meridian, the boundary line separating Alaska from Canada's Yukon Territory, moved growing numbers of men of the McQuesten breed. Most cared not one whit about the international boundary. Throughout the seventies and eighties small parties of prospectors had entered Alaska's enormous interior from both ends of the Yukon River. In 1882, Ed Schieffelin brought in a well-equipped group of goldseekers via steamboat. Their ascent of the Yukon gained a degree of public attention as Alaskans hoped for an important gold find. Previously Schieffelin had uncovered Arizona gold and helped found Tombstone. No such luck awaited his band on the Yukon. Nevertheless, Schieffelin's prospectors had publicized the convenience of the water route to the interior, at least the party returned with small quantities of gold.[75]

Moravian missionary William Weinland described Alaska's mid-continental winters as "one great big, immense, snow drift."[76] To compare the conditions there with a Sitka winter would be analogous to equating a North Dakota October with that month on the Oregon coast. After a relatively brief but intensive summer labor, most Yukon miners departed for a southside winter respite. In 1891 a newsman from the *Alaskan* interviewed some of them. "These hardy forerunners of civilization were a quite contented lot, and reported very satisfactory results in their operations. Almost without exception they intend to return next spring."[77] By 1894 improved river steamers and the competitive presence of the North American Trading and Transportation Company eased hinterland living conditions so perceptibly that miners were able to avoid the cost of going south for the winter.

January 1, 1894, found more than two hundred miners wintering in the bleak Yukon Valley settlements. Episcopal missionary J. L. Prevost united forces with prospector and townsite founder Gordon Bettles and began the eight-page

Yukon Valley frontiersman Jack McQuesten had become famous by the time this sketch was made of him in the 1890's. The artist caught something of McQuesten's strength of character and the indomitable will that enabled him to survive 50-below winters, ill-tempered Indians, and harsh isolation.

Yukon Press at St. James Mission (located where the Tanana joined the Yukon River). Its avowed purpose was "to promote man's religious, moral, and mental facilities, and to develop the great resources of the Valley." Eager readers were Yukon pioneers McQuesten, Mayo, and Harper. Meantime, to the east in the miner village of Circle City overlooking the Yukon River, a library was initiated. During 1895 impecunious Joe Juneau joined those who scrounged for gold in the vicinity of Circle City. That year Governor Sheakley estimated that 1,500 men worked placers along the Yukon Valley. For the entire region there was but a single government official: an Inspector of Customs. Inevitably, the Miners' Code ruled.[78]

Circle City, one hundred miles up river from Fort Yukon, was called the "Paris of the North" by its effusive miner inhabitants. Mrs. Schwatka warned women to stay out of the Yukon Valley. "The Virgin," "Lottie," and "Ella the Glacier" seem to have done very well at Circle City, however. For a couple of years the sparsely populated Yukon Valley mining communities seem to have exemplified the utopian trust in one's fellow man that blessed California's Mother Lode country in its first golden season. Veteran Alaska Commercial Company trader McQuesten employed such open-handed customer credit that he almost ruined himself.[79] "You might get into any cabin and see a glass or a tin or two on the shelf full of gold," one Yukon miner insisted, "and no one would think of touching it. Anyone could steal if he wanted to do so, but there were good reasons why they did not . . . there were what we called 'miners law.'" Ivan Petroff had little confidence in this kind of justice and as early as 1890 reported "shooting and stabbing affrays and murders" in the isolated mining camps.[80] It was not long before one overheard expressions that echoed the earlier castles-in-the-sky of Dodge, Murphy, and Kinkead.

The proposed Territory of Lincoln will embrace within its boundaries the valleys of the great Yukon River and its tributaries and the coast along Behring Sea. . . . The influx of population into these gold fields is so great that the residents of the interior of the present Alaska, and all who have investments there, are unanimous in their demands for such recognition from the Government as will give them protection to life and property. . . . Organization will immediately follow the territorial creation, and it is likely "the delegates from Lincoln" will soon be recognized in Congress.[81]

In 1896 Circle City claimed a citizenry of more than one thousand men and forty women, but that was before the stampede to the Klondike.[82]

Without their dreams, where would men be? Captain Bill Moore still had his. After a tour of the Upper Yukon region, he pictured "the tons of yellow dust yet to be found. . . . He decided then and there that Skagway would be the entry port to the golden fields of the Yukon. . . ." Moore, like Edmund Bean, approached the government about constructing a toll road to facilitate transportation to Lake Bennett. He got the same rejection. However, his investment guess at Skagway paid dividends, and the old man had the pleasure of rebuilding his rather tattered holdings. Years afterward, his son William Domingo evaluated his father for historian C. L. Andrews:

Father was not an educated man. Had he been so, his life would have read in a different way. He was head strong and aggressive, full of ambition, never would give up. He used to smoke when he was young. He gave it up. He did not drink to excess. He did not gamble. He was fond of his wife and children.[83]

Too often a pioneer's filial affection did not include any particular reverence for nature's munificence. Sadly, as accommodation supplanted adversity in mid-continent Alaska, respect for the environment declined. Schwatka's widow wrote that the wildlife disappeared whenever the miners appeared. Even McQuesten admitted, "Often we would get a moose in the water and all hands would grab the guns and let the steamer take care of herself, and we always killed moose on the way up."[84] Great Plains buffalo had been shot to pieces by passengers aboard steam locomotives. Now the machine devastator had taken to the water. What would happen when his owners made him airborne?

As gold-seekers dared the privations of Alaska's enormous interior, so did their comrades pick away along the coastal periphery, especially along the mainland 600 miles westward of Sitka. Here on Turnagain Arm, at the head of Cook Inlet and not far distant from the site of Alaska's dynamic twentieth-century metropolis of Anchorage, they engaged in placer mining and cleared about four or five dollars a day. During the fall of 1895, discontented with their thin pickings, the Cook Inlet prospectors trickled away. Suddenly the rumor spread that they had erred; the vicinity possessed "rich and extensive gold placers." By May of 1896, 2,000 gold-hunters had descended on Turnagain Arm at the mouth of Sixmile Creek. The Governor recounted what happened: "About the 20th of June the snow disappeared. . . . Little or no gold being found, disappointment and misfortune was the lot of 95 percent of all those who had gone to this unfortunate field."[85]

That same year George Washington Carmack, a prospector-trader, found gold on Rabbit Creek, later renamed Bonanza. Water from this inconspicuous stream quickly joined the Yukon, but for about a mile it mingled with an intermediary—a river named Klondike. Carmack was California-born. He had inherited the argonaut's itch from his forty-niner father and the gold-rush stories that circulated up and down San Francisco's waterfront. In the eighties George Carmack had joined the Juneau rush and then drifted northward into Canada's Yukon Territory. Like the other Americans floating back and forth across the 141st meridian, he was rarely conscious of being on some nation's sovereign soil. It was the wilderness that captivated him. Color-conscious contemporaries described him as a man who preferred red to white civilization. Carmack had indeed "gone native," or "Siwash." On August 17, 1896, together with his Indian "brothers-in-law," Skookum Jim and Tagish Charlie, Carmack uncovered pay dirt on Rabbit

Creek. If he only could have kept his mouth shut, Carmack might have avoided James Marshall's fate and possibly have garnered the pot of gold at the end of every prospector's rainbow. But no, Carmack hurried off to Forty Mile to boast of his find. Even before he recorded his claim Carmack shouted out the golden news to his barroom buddies. By the end of the summer, down-river communities like Canada's Forty Mile and America's Circle City had the word, "Gold on the Klondike." Their residents fled and Dawson City was born.[86] A Dawson resident, Father William Judge, observed that the Yukon "miners seem to be men who have been running away from civilization as it advanced westward in the States, until now they have no farther to go, and so have to stop here." The hard-working Roman Catholic priest had heard of one man "who although born in the States, has never seen a railroad, because he kept moving ahead of the railroads until he got here."[87]

Had Editor Frank F. Myers of the *Juneau City Mining Record* dictated Alaska's future, the territory would have had a railroad by 1900, one that ran right across Bering Strait to Russia. But Myers voiced his Jules Verne concept in 1893; three years later Juneau's boosters looked in only one direction—north to the Klondike.[88] The stampede that commenced in 1897 and peaked the next year has been correctly designated as a watershed in Alaskan history. Notwithstanding the fact that Dawson City mushroomed on Canadian soil, Alaska's historic nineteenth-century summit is usually marked by a large sign reading "Klondike." This is as it should be. Tens of thousands of North Americans participated in the Klondike madness. Within a few years millions of dollars were fed into the region, and millions more were drawn from it. Alaska benefited from this boom. Actually by the mid-nineties Southeastern Alaska already was capable of handling the flood of gold-seekers. When this tide ebbed, neither Juneau nor Sitka found itself a stranded mining ghost town. In other words, with or without the Klondike, by 1897, Southeastern Alaska had become socially, economically, and politically durable.

NOTES

1. *The Sitka Post*, December 20, 1876.
2. "Blaine and Cleveland," JScrap, Vol. 11, p. 128.
3. Septima M. Collis, *A Woman's Trip to Alaska: Being an Account of a Voyage through the Island Seas of the Sitkan Archipelago in 1890* (New York, 1890), 77–78; *The Alaskan*, December 12, 1891.
4. Ellis P. Oberholtzer, *A History of the United States Since the Civil War* (5 vols.; New York, 1917–1937), V, 155–156.
5. Good summaries of the dispute are: Thomas A. Bailey, *A Diplomatic History of the American People* (New York, 1954), 412–414 and 536–537; Julius W. Pratt, *A History of United States Foreign Policy* (New York, 1955), 355–359.
6. Stuart Ramsay Tompkins: *Alaska, Promyshlennik and Sourdough* (Norman, Okla., 1945), 209–212; Oberholtzer, *A History*, V, 157.
7. Charles S. Campbell, "The Anglo-American Crisis in the Bering Sea, 1890–91," *Mississippi Valley Historical Review*, XLVIII (December, 1961), 393–414; Ted C. Hinckley, "Rustlers of the North Pacific," *Journal of the West*, II (January, 1963), 22–30; *New York Times*, July 30, 1895. The sum of $425,000 was finally paid by the United States to the Canadian ship owners. *New York Times*, June 12, 1896.
8. Letter in possession of author. Robert N. De Armond to Ted C. Hinckley, March 30, 1963.
9. Hubert Howe Bancroft, *History of Alaska, 1730–1885* (San Francisco, 1886), 658; U.S. Treasury, *Commercial Alaska in 1901* (Washington, D.C., 1902), 3942–3943; *The West Shore*, June 7, 1890.
10. Elliott's view is well told in: Jeanne Van Nostrand, "The Seals Are About Gone," *American Heritage*, XIV (June, 1963), 10 ff.; Henry W. Elliott, *Report of Henry W. Elliott on Condition of Fur Seal Fisheries of Alaska* (Washington, D.C., 1896).
11. Thomas A. Bailey, "The North Pacific Sealing Convention of 1911," *Pacific Historical Review*, IV (March, 1935), 1–14. Russia had seal islands of her own to protect. To compensate Canada and Japan, a stipulated percentage of the annual kill was paid them.
12. Robert H. Wiebe, *The Search for Order, 1877–1920* (New York, 1967), 44.
13. Letter from B. G. McIntyre to Gentlemen [San Francisco head office], July 1, 1878, Alaska Commercial Company Papers, Kodiak Letterpress Volume, p. 163, University of Alaska, College, Alaska.
14. L. D. Kitchener, *Flag over the North: The Story of the Northern Commercial Company* (Seattle, 1954), 104.
15. "The Treadwell Mines," *Alaska-Yukon Magazine* (September, 1907), 73–81; U.S. Treasury, *Commercial Alaska in 1901* (Washington, D.C., 1902), 3959.
16. Clarence Hulley, *Alaska: Past and Present* (Portland, Ore., 1958), 6–7.
17. Howard M. Kutchin, *Report on the Salmon Fisheries of Alaska* (Washington, D.C., 1897), 26.

18. Jefferson F. Moser, *The Salmon and Salmon Fisheries of Alaska* (Washington, D.C., 1899), 19; *The Alaskan,* October 31, 1891.

19. *The West Shore,* February 7, 1891.

20. *Alaska Journal,* March 25, 1893.

21. Moser, *The Salmon,* 20.

22. Letter from John T. Brisbane to William F. Vilas, Secretary of the Interior, January 9, 1889, TAP, Roll I.

23. James A. Crutchfield and Giulio Pontecorvo, *The Pacific Salmon Fisheries: A Study of Irrational Conservation* (Baltimore, 1969), 90; Kutchin, *Report on the Salmon,* 26; Letter from John S. Batchelly to Acting Secretary of the Treasury, July 12, 1889, CHR, Vol. 34.

24. C. L. Andrews, "The Salmon of Alaska," *Washington Historical Quarterly,* IX (October, 1918), 251; Alfred H. Brooks, *Blazing Alaska's Trails* (Caldwell, Ida., 1953), 446; Kutchin, *Report on the Salmon,* 24–25.

25. Joseph Murray, *Seal and Salmon Fisheries and General Resources of Alaska* (4 vols.; Washington, D.C., 1898), II, 411 ff.

26. *Ibid.,* 406.

27. Homer E. Gregory and Kathleen Barnes, *North Pacific Fisheries: With Special Reference to Alaska Salmon* (San Francisco, 1939), 91.

28. John Green Brady, *Governor's Annual Report, 1897* (Washington, D.C., 1897), 13.

29. *Alaska Journal,* June 7, 1893.

30. Tarleton H. Bean, *Report on the Salmon and Salmon Rivers of Alaska, with Notes on the Conditions, Methods and Needs of the Salmon Fisheries* (Washington, D.C., 1890), 206.

31. Ted C. Hinckley (Ed.), "The Canoe Rocks—We Do Not Know What Will Become of Us," *Western Historical Quarterly,* I (July, 1970), 270–271.

32. Interview by author with Walter Soboloff, Juneau, Alaska, August 19, 1962.

33. Henry M. Field, *Our Western Archipelago* (New York, 1895), 139.

34. Maturin M. Ballou, *The New Eldorado: A Summer Journey to Alaska* (Boston, 1890), 270–271, 315.

35. *Alaska Journal,* September 23, 1893; *The Alaskan,* January 3, 1893 and April 7, 1894.

36. *Ibid.* Earl Pomeroy, *The Pacific Slope: A History of California, Oregon, Washington, Idaho, Utah, and Nevada* (New York, 1965), 126.

37. Murray Morgan, *Skid Road: An Informal Portrait of Seattle* (New York, 1951), 159–167. After the Klondike Rush began, Bauer engaged in commercial efforts at Dyea and Skagway and for awhile established residence at Sitka.

38. *The Alaskan,* October 24, 1891; U.S., Senate, *Report Relative to the Condition of Natives of Alaska,* 51st Cong., 2d Sess., Senate Exec. Doc. 14, December 16, 1890, p. 3. Instructive in regard to this kind of change are the letters from the Seal Islands in: James Judge Papers, Oregon Historical Society, Portland, Oregon.

39. Reprinted in: *Alaska Herald,* January 19, 1872.

40. *New York Times,* March 29, 1880.

41. Norman A. Chance, *The Eskimo of North America* (New York, 1966),

14–15; *The West Shore*, March 8, 1890; C. L. Andrews, "Alaska Whaling," *Washington Historical Quarterly*, IX (January, 1918), 3 ff.

42. William Bixby, *Track of the Bear* (New York, 1965), 84 ff; *Washington Post*, December 1, 1891; John F. Murphy, "Two Standards of Judgment," *U.S. Coast Guard Academy Alumni Association Bulletin* (September–October, 1965), 366–375; *Report of the Revenue–Marine Service, 1881* (Washington, D.C., 1881), 55–56.

43. *Report Relative to the Condition of Natives*, 4.

44. Dorothy Jean Ray, "Sheldon Jackson and the Reindeer Industry of Alaska," *Journal of Presbyterian History*, XLIII (June, 1965), 71–99, provides a balanced evaluation of Jackson's reindeer-raising program. The most detailed record may be found in the General Agent's own *Annual Reports*.

45. Letter from Sheldon Jackson to W. H. Foutes, November 24, 1890, National Archives, Bureau of Education, 1890, Unfiled Letters.

46. Letter from Sheldon Jackson to A. F. Robinson, November 13, 1890, *ibid.*

47. Letter from John G. Brady to Sheldon Jackson, June 7, 1880, JCorr., Vol. 10, p. 177; "Edward de Groff," *Alaska–Yukon Magazine* (October, 1907), 139–140.

48. *The Alaskan*, December 12, 1886, May 12, 1888, and August 3, 1895; Letter from Edward de Groff to M. L. Washburn, April 18, 1894, Miscellaneous File, ACC.

49. *The Alaskan*, January 7, 1891, February 11, 1891, December 5, 1891, July 23, 1892, January 13, 1894, June 12, 1897.

50. *Alaska Mining Record*, April 8, 1895.

51. Mrs. Eugene S. Willard, *Life in Alaska* (Philadelphia, 1884); Julia McNair Wright, *Among the Alaskans* (Philadelphia, 1883).

52. *Ibid.*, 196.

53. Wendell H. Oswalt, *Mission of Change in Alaska: Eskimos and Moravians on the Kuskokwim* (San Marino, Calif., 1964), 94.

54. Maurice Montgomery, "The Murder of Missionary Thornton," *Pacific Northwest Quarterly*, LVI (October, 1963), 167–173, ably summarizes this episode and the literature printed on it.

55. Driggs never became an ordained clergyman but was made a deacon in order to marry and baptize his Eskimo flock. Among them it must have made a world of difference.

56. *San Francisco Chronicle*, July 4, 1887.

57. *The Alaskan*, November 7, 1891.

58. *Ibid.*, January 16, 1892.

59. *Alaska Journal*, April 1, 1893.

60. *The Alaskan*, November 1, 1891.

61. Letter from Carrie Willard to Sheldon Jackson, August 23, 1889, JCorr., Vol. 15, p. 224; U.S., Senate, *Alleged Outrages in Alaska*, 50th Cong., 2d Sess., Senate Exec. Doc. 141; *Condition of Indian Women and Girls in Portions of Alaska as Seen by Different Eyes and Gleaned from Different Sources* (n.p., n.d.); *Alaska Free Press*, November 22, 1890.

62. *Alaska Journal*, September 23, 1893.

63. *Alaska Herald,* January 15, 1894.

64. Robert E. Coontz, *From the Mississippi to the Sea* (Philadelphia, 1930), 118.

65. *Ibid.,* 163–164.

66. *The Alaskan,* May 23, 1891; Miner W. Bruce, *Alaska: Its History and Resources, Gold Fields, Routes and Scenery* (Seattle, 1895), 18.

67. Letter from Sheldon Jackson to Senator Dolph, January 19, 1892, PUTS, Sheldon Jackson Letters, Vol. 2, p. 206; Lester Henderson, "The Development of Education in Alaska, 1867 to 1931" (unpublished Ed.D. dissertation, Stanford University, 1934–1935), 170–181.

68. U.S. Treasury, *Commercial Alaska in 1901* (Washington, D.C., 1902), 3977.

69. *Juneau City Mining Record,* December 15, 1891; *The Alaskan,* July 16, 1891.

70. Clipping, *Juneau City Mining Record,* June 29, 1893, in the M. A. Healy Scrapbook, Huntington Library, San Marino, California.

71. *The Alaskan,* July 22, 1893; *Juneau City Mining Record,* July 13, 1893.

72. *Alaska Journal,* May 13, 1893 and January 27, 1894.

73. *Alaska Herald,* March 19, 1894.

74. James Sheakley, *Governor's Annual Report, 1894* (Washington, D.C., 1894), 11.

75. Bancroft, *History of Alaska,* 738; Morris Zaslow, "The Yukon: Northern Development in a Canadian American Context" in Mason Wade (Ed.), *Regionalism in the Canadian Community, 1867–1967* (Toronto, 1969), 182 ff. John G. Brady, *Governor's Annual Report, 1897* (Washington, D.C., 1897), 30.

76. Letter from William Weinland to Elizabeth Yost, January 4, 1886, William Weinland Collection, Huntington Library, San Marino, California.

77. *The Alaskan,* November 28, 1891; *The West Shore,* May, 1889.

78. *Ibid.,* October 14, 1893; James Wickersham, *A Bibliography of Alaskan Literature, 1724–1924* (Cordova, Alaska, 1927), 270–271; Brooks, *Blazing Alaska's Trails,* 509–511; Donald J. Orth, *Dictionary of Alaska Place Names* (Washington, D.C., 1967), 947; Dora E. McLean, "Early Newspapers on the Upper Yukon Watershed: 1894–1907" (unpublished master's thesis, University of Alaska, May 27, 1963), 20 ff.

79. Richard Mathews, *The Yukon* (New York, 1968), 123 ff; A. C. Harris, *Alaska and the Klondike Gold Fields* (Washington, D.C., 1897), 224–225; Edward M. Jones, "Jack McQuesten," *Alaska Sportsman,* XXXIII (May, 1967), 18 ff; Brooks, *Blazing Alaska's Trails,* 320.

80. Harris, *Alaska and the Klondike,* 457; Letter from Ivan Petroff to Robert P. Porter, Supt. of Census, October 21 1890, AGP, Knapp, Vol. II.

81. Harris, *Alaska and the Klondike,* 279–280.

82. H. O. S. Heistand, *The Territory of Alaska* (Kansas City, 1898), 13.

83. C. L. Andrews, "Biographical Sketch of Captain William Moore," *Washington Historical Quarterly,* XXII (January, 1931), 39–41.

84. Leroy N. McQuesten, *Recollections of Leroy N. McQuesten of Life in*

the Yukon, 1871–1885 (Dawson City, Yukon Territory, Canada, 1952), 9.

85. *The Alaskan,* June 10, 1893; James Sheakley, *Governor's Annual Report, 1895* (Washington, D.C., 1895), 322, and Sheakley, *Annual Report, 1896,* 200.

86. Pierre Berton's book, *The Klondike Fever: The Life and Death of the Last Great Gold Rush* (New York, 1958), is already a classic account of this memorable event.

87. Charles J. Judge, *An American Missionary: A Record of the Work of William H. Judge, S.J.* (Boston, 1907), 162.

88. *Juneau City Mining Record,* March 2, 1893.

CHAPTER SEVEN

☆ ☆ ☆ ☆ ☆ ☆ ☆ ☆ ☆ ☆ ☆ ☆ ☆ ☆ ☆ ☆ ☆ ☆

Acceptance Within 1887-1897

The courts here stand as high and are as able as in any part of the United States, and crime is as surely punished here as elsewhere. Our juries are not composed of saloon keepers, but of miners and businessmen. The miner can always be relied upon to mete out equal and exact justice to all; hard working, large hearted, and just, it is a libel of the basest kind to call him lawless or the community in which he lives a lawless one. — Governor James Sheakley, Annual Report, *1896.*

ALASKA'S PIONEERS were curiously ambivalent about acknowledging that their Panhandle communities had become viable zones of settlement. Their noncontiguous location and their unprecedented place in American history, plus the constant harping by their press and politicians that Congress did not appreciate the Far North territory, had given them an inferiority complex. Washington, D.C., snapped one editor, treated them "worse than Gaul . . . at hands of the Roman Empire."[1] America's inherently agrarian mental set no doubt caused many pioneers to misinterpret the uniqueness of their northern frontier. "This is not a farming country," asserted Sheakley, "and there is [*sic*] no farmers and no rural population, no settlers came to this country to get land and make homes for themselves. . . . The white people all live in towns and mining camps and take but small interest in school or anything but what directly interests them."[2] Like so many other Alaskans born east of the Missouri, Sheakley could not realize that the traditional frontier phase had ended. Furthermore, America's noble yeoman was being eclipsed by the city-dweller. For more than half a century the urban frontier had been challenging the historic prominence of the rural frontier. Sheakley's belief that non-farmers would take "small interest in . . . anything but what directly interests them" further betrayed his agrarian frame of reference. On balance, the yeoman's historic social consciousness probably has been no greater than that of the average city-dweller.

In 1897 President William McKinley presented Alaska with a Governor who understood the enigmatic Great Land probably as well as any man then could. An abandoned New York City waif, John G. Brady had been raised in Indiana and educated at Yale and New York City's Union Theological Seminary. Even before he arrived in Alaska in the late seventies, Brady was a westerner in spirit. In 1897, after almost twenty years of Far North residence, his Christian outlook had been thoroughly seasoned by a pioneer's pragmatism. Brady had early experimented with cereal crops around Sitka; thereafter he continually encouraged research into the District's agricultural possibilities. He grudgingly realized that his adopted land promised limited agricultural profit (unless one included lumbering), at least for the foreseeable future. Brady well merited the governorship. He had no illusions about who had pushed his appointment in Washington, and while Brady disagreed with Sheldon Jackson on a few Alaska policies, especially Jackson's impractical liquor control views, Brady's respect for the General Agent was almost that of son to father.[3]

Like his predecessor, Sheakley, Brady had long since accommodated himself to the bizarre character of the Panhandle frontier. But where Sheakley bemoaned "there are no organized cities or towns in this territory," Brady overlooked legal niceties, saw the towns in fact, and pushed ahead. On the homestead question he was totally western. Replying to a Californian and prospective pioneer, he wrote,

Governor John G. Brady, 1897–1906. Governor Brady came to Alaska as a Presbyterian missionary, became a businessman in Sitka, and as Governor marked the peak of the "Presbyterian Hierarchy."

"There is no way to acquire land in Alaska. . . . If you find land unoccupied you have a squatters right."[4] It was a two-sided answer, but it was truthful; above all, it might mean another Alaskan.

The Far North in 1897 could be compared with a man on his thirtieth birthday, who pauses, tries to "see himself as others do," weighs his achievements, and considers his future. Excluding only the most masochistic of Alaskans, Panhandle residents could take heart at the progress of the last three decades, particularly in light of the District's massive geographical handicaps. Professor Morgan Sherwood has ably detailed how by the mid-nineties Schwatka's explorer successors had effectively torn off Alaska's veil of mystery.[5] Nor was the Great Land merely known from the Arctic Slope to the Gulf of Alaska in a crude physiographic dimension. For some years such agencies as the Smithsonian Institution, the United States Weather Bureau, the Bureau of Plant Industry, the United States Geological Survey, and the Bureau of Fisheries had engaged in studies throughout Alaska. More than ten thousand prominent citizens had visited the land. In 1896, Vice-President Adlai E. Stevenson brought the prestige of his office northward.[6]

But to feel truly accepted, and in considerable measure this was really what Alaskans wanted, one must accept himself as well as sense acceptance by others. Were Alaska's settlers in fact willing to accept themselves? The degree of relative comfort and community confidence enjoyed by Sitka and Juneau in 1897 indicates that they did.

If Sitka commemorated Alaska's past, Juneau marked her future. "Juneau is the larger, the metropolis of the territory," wrote a *New York Sun* reporter. "Sitka is the center of gayety and fashion. Juneau is the richer in business enterprise and commerce; Sitka has the finer grace of distinguished, social culture." It was true, and the venerable lady took care to note her brassy younger rival's shortcomings. Admiral Coontz recalled that the capital's public officials, "the missionaries and the naval families, made about one hundred in real society."[7] This minute cell, with its polyglot mutation of native, Russian, and American (which in Alaska also meant Caucasian, Mongolian, and Negroid) bloods was a fascinating social organism. Because it was so microscopic, even discerning David Starr Jordan overlooked its nucleus. "The town-meeting idea on which our democracy is organ-

These Creole-Aleut musicians show how the physical characteristics of their antecedents had become fused. By the 1890's it was difficult to distinguish Slav from native. (University of Alaska Museum Photograph)

ized," he declared, "could have no application in Alaska, for Alaska is not a region of homes and householders . . . a civic feeling akin to the civic life in the United States can in no way be built up."[8] Jordan saw only the miner chaff and missed the germinated seeds of Sitka and Juneau.

In many ways Alaska's capital reflected a typical late nineteenth-century American hamlet, not unlike a slow-paced Border State river town. Municipal requirements such as

streets, waterworks, and fire engines were settled by petitions, public meetings, and duly authorized committees. A
walk through the capital would have revealed churches, a
hospital, schools, barber shops, and even barefoot lads
"carrying sling-shots, and using them," as the local press
protested, "at every available opportunity, to the destruction
of window glass and the annoyance and danger of everybody." Jail prisoners, who could hardly have run away, repaired her wooden sidewalks, while costs of repairs for in-
solvent and damaged humans were met by fairs, card-
playing, auctions, magic shows, and on Christmas a special
"Sitka Feast of Childhood." Welfare demands were not required as an excuse for leisure-time activities. Sitka's Literary and Dramatic Association gave would-be thespians a
chance to perform. The Alaskan Society of Natural History
and Ethnology performed a very real service by its publications, quasi-scholarly meetings, and especially its protection of the General Agent's irreplaceable collection of
native artifacts. The community's Free Reading Room suffered from lack of regular hours, but its library boasted
almost a thousand volumes.[9]

Sitka, like every other settlement in Alaska, was predominantly a man's town. Naturally there was a men's club, The
Sons of the Northwest, and, of course, plenty of fishing and
hunting. Sometimes the latter was combined with a trip to
the "hot Sulphur Springs" sixteen miles south of the capital.
Men and boys alike made the most of Independence Day
and Decoration Day. Apparently only those unable to walk
were not included in the annual Fourth of July parade.[10]

Ironically, the festooned holidays that honored liberty
and equality revealed an ugly stain on the territory's history. Independence Day athletic events separated Indians
and whites. It seemed so natural, just like the way the District
press made occasional jibes at the territory's few Negroes.
By this time Indians at both Sitka and Juneau had not only
their own schools but their own churches. Jackson had ques-
tioned this trend, but tradition and overwhelming white

sentiment had brought it to pass. Even the Russians had built and operated a segregated church for Sitka's Ranche Indians. The superiority of the white race was accepted as a social truism.[11] Nevertheless, Sitka had achieved considerable inter-cultural fusion. No less an authority than William Dall recognized that the "mission Indians" with their skills and missionary-promoted bungalows were better off than their parents had been in 1867. De Groff was proud to call the Chinaman Sing Lee his friend, and capital children keenly anticipated the noisy Chinese New Year celebration.[12] Despite these cheerful moments, the clash of cultures was at times very harsh. At the bottom of the social order was the aboriginal. White, yellow, and black — all sold the redman liquor. In 1897 the *Alaskan* reported, "The lightning kill me quick they got this time was the most poisonous and fatal they have had for years . . . one of the Indians managed to throw up the stuff by running an eagle feather down his throat and a dog standing by lapped up the vomit was immediately thrown into convulsions." Sitka's doctor worked all night once to save the victims of poisonous alcohol, but still two of the Ranche Indians died.[13]

Fortunately, the capital's revolting spectacles were now outshone by its decorous balls and gay receptions. On any pretext, be it the final meeting of Miss Baker's Dancing Academy or a governor's housewarming, Sitkans produced evening attire, the music of Rugg and Hanlan's orchestra, and hours of conviviality. Decorations featured the national colors, a picture of George Washington, and quantities of evergreen roping pleasing to both sight and scent. Smaller parties, for people leaving and arriving, followed the docking of almost every steamer. When the Navy vessels *Adams* and *Mohican* dropped their anchors, Sitka's ladies entertained with a ball that lasted until 2 A.M. The ships' officers promptly reciprocated with a "lunch and hop," first aboard the *Adams* and then the *Mohican*.[14] During much of the 1880's and 1890's, from October to spring, it was Alaska's pride, the trim little U.S.S. *Pinta*, with its youthful crew and shore-stationed Marine Guard, that supplied a dashing staple for capital society.[15] Seeing them, one steamer sight-seer reflected on an America that felt no need for a national defense based on preeminent military might.

Enforcing the law over such a vast region was an impossible charge, but the little U.S.S. Pinta *did her best to show the flag throughout the Alexander Archipelago. (Official Navy Photograph)*

It touched our patriotic pride as we drew up to the wharf to see the stars and stripes flying, and a little parade ground opposite the landing, with half a dozen field-pieces to fire a salute on the arrival and departure of "dignities," though the military establishment is not on a war footing, the whole force consisting of forty marines detailed from the Pinta, the small naval vessel that is considered sufficient to do duty in these waters. But there may be a very good government without an armament. If the old democratic saying be true, "That is the best government which governs least," the less display of power the better. There is not much need of soldiers, except to protect the peaceable inhabitants, and to maintain justice by the prompt arrest and punishment of crime."[16]

Marines were frequently on hand when sessions of the District Court were held at Juneau. In 1897, Sitka's *Alaskan* praised them "for their quiet conduct while on duty at Juneau, altho the city has many temptations."[17] An unkind cut, but true. Juneau continued to be essentially a miner's town well into the next century. Yet "miner" always had included every kind of human: Joe Juneau, Richard Harris, the William Moore men, John Boyd, John Treadwell, and soon Jack London.[18] Until the William Moore types outweighed the John Boyds, the violent, vulgar half of Americanization frequently ruled. This combustible element could still be seen sulking about Juneau throughout the 1890's. Periodically it showed its fangs. In 1892, "Dr. J. E. Connett, of the Friends' Mission at the Douglas [town on Douglas Island] Government School House Number 2 was waited upon," as Jackson described the assault, "by a band of outlaws styled the Vanguards of Civilization, called up out of bed, and deliberately taken out and tarred and feathered." Seattle's *Post Intelligencer* informed its readers of the cowardly crime:

This is a culmination of the trouble between the whisky smugglers of Alaska and the missionary element, which began with the killing of Charles H. Edwards, a school teacher; on January 10, . . . Connette [*sic*] had relieved Edwards at the Douglass [*sic*] island Quaker mission, and the latter had begun the establishment of a mission on Kake island among a wild and fierce tribe of Indians. Two whisky smugglers from Juneau appeared on the scene and disposed of a large quantity of liquor. Edwards remonstrated, and the drunken, infuriated savages killed him and his interpreter. [Actually Edwards was gunned down by a white, Malcolm Campbell of Douglas. Two Indians trying to assist Edwards were also killed by smuggler Campbell.] Connette took up the case and endeavored to bring the smugglers to justice. He published an account of the trouble in Eastern papers, which displeased the liquor element on Douglass island.

Late Sunday night, April 23, a messenger went to Dr. Connette's office at the mission and said a workman in one of the mines was dangerously wounded. As he emerged into the darkness a crowd seized, bound and gagged him. After a liberal application of tar and feathers assistance came and the crowd fled into the darkness and the woods.[19]

Jackson seethed, but he made no sweeping condemnation of Juneau's populace. "It has been said that this is a mining community and this is but what might be expected of miners. Such is not the case," he snapped. "The miners are producers; but there is a class here of non producers, who alone could be guilty of such a base and outrageous act. This class might be said as being more or less interested in the whiskey business, directly or indirectly; . . ." Jackson went on to praise the miners of Douglas Island. "As soon as the miners at Treadwell mines, Douglas City, heard how Dr. Connett had been got out of his home on the pretext of being called to aid a suffering miner, they had a meeting and resolved to raise $500.00 to assist in bringing to justice the perpetrators of this crime. . . ."[20] No one was ever punished for either the Edwards-Indians killings or the Connett outrage. Fortunately 1892 marked the crest of this kind of license.

By the mid-nineties Juneau had become a funnel for many of the Americans itching to follow the advice of the Yukon Valley prospectors, "Go north, young man, go north." Unlike Sitka, which rested in a quiet socio-economic eddy, Juneau vibrated with the eager anticipation and half-checked recklessness of men about to confront the dangerous unknown. The town radiated the same booster spirit that Sitka had voiced in 1868. With a population exceeding the capital's, a far larger and more diverse economy, and a location better suited to tap the interior traffic, Juneau could afford to be cocky. In fact, for some time now a group of what Sitkans referred to as "unscrupulous speculators" had been trying to have the District capital transferred to Juneau.

By the mid-1880's Juneau had become an embryo boom town. Across the Gastineau Channel the smoke of the Treadwell works signaled the beginnings of what would soon become one of the largest mining complexes in the world.

Ten years later Juneau was still growing. A Russian Orthodox church can be seen (right of center). Saloons were aplenty, but in this picture may also be seen the ubiquitous schoolhouse and church structures. The mansard-roofed building (center right) reflected a sense of civic confidence. (University of Alaska Museum Photograph)

How often had a state or territory's second wave of settlers politicked to move their commonwealth's capital? Abe Lincoln had in Illinois, and victory had crowned his exertions. Bernard M. Behrends was no Lincoln, but by the mid-nineties he was playing a part in the growing effort to move Alaska's capital. Certainly Behrends gave Juneau's missionary-home builder faction real cause for rejoicing. Born in Germany in 1862, Behrends emigrated to Nebraska with his parents in 1878. The next decade he joined the prospector crowd in California, and in 1887 came to Alaska. Two years later Behrends married one of Jackson's teachers; the General Agent himself officiated at their wedding. During the nineties, Behrends' merchandising successes at Juneau encouraged him to start a bank. His timing was excellent.[21] Most definitely Juneau had arrived when it could generate its own investment capital.

A robust town, Juneau also demanded virile entertainment. It attested to this by a wide selection of "houses of ill fame," saloons, sometimes identified as "drug stores," and other less taxing outlets for masculine entertainment, such as prize fights and baseball. Proof that the frontier had passed was easy to discern. There was electrified street lighting, and the Occidental Hotel prided itself on "all the modern conveniences." Author and Alaska enthusiast Charles Hallock congratulated "two negro men of nerve (praise to the race!) under stress of local pressure, have instituted a very creditable barbershop at Juneau."[22] For theatrical entertainment, native children in castoffs mumbled recitations from *Uncle Tom's Cabin*, while a "large and select audience gave full approval to the emotional drama 'East Lynne,' . . . presented . . . by a capable company with full and complete scenic equipment." Juneau vaunted not only the territory's only Grand Army of the Republic post but a Longfellow Literary Society.[23]

Notwithstanding her disheveled appearance and not infrequent bawdy behavior, Juneau had become a proud example of democratic self-management. Merchants maintained the board-walks adjoining their shops and helped support a municipal hospital; men such as Slim Jim, who owned the Opera House, unhesitatingly volunteered their facilities and purses to build their hometown. "Juneau presents the singular exception," recorded one visitor, "of a city well ordered, well improved, well kept, without municipal government, without taxation, without police."[24] Unquestionably, it was a tribute to the best of Americanization. When Tlingit chief Kah-du-shan journeyed to Juneau, he also talked about Americanization, but in a quite dissimilar vein:

The missionaries and teachers tell us that no one but God make the people. We know that the same God made us. And the God placed us here. White people are smart; our people are not as smart as white people. They have a very fine name; they call themselves white people. Just like the sun shining on this earth. They are powerful. They have the power. They have men of wars. It is not right for such powerful people as you are to take away from poor people like we are, our creeks and hunting grounds.[25]

There still remained an element that delighted in condemning the missionary faction. "If only these damn people would stop confusing the dirty Indians"—if only the Christians would stop injecting moral questions into everything! Most of those who disliked "killjoy missionaries" now preferred to copy ex-Governor Swineford, who, although continuing to attack Sheldon Jackson, admitted the good done by his followers. Missionaries had also begun to forgive past political spats. As Governor Brady wrote to the General Agent, "He [Swineford] and I are on good terms now."[26]

Jackson's fame was secure. In 1897 the Presbyterian Church gave him its pinnacle recognition: Moderator of the General Assembly. At the ceremony none other than Benjamin Harrison stepped forward to acclaim Jackson's achievements. Two other victories won in 1897 by the new Moderator marked that year as one of great professional and personal triumph. President William McKinley appointed Jackson protegé John G. Brady to the District governorship, and Edward Marsden, a full-blooded Northwest Coast Indian and product of the Sitka Industrial School, demonstrated how successfully the native could walk the white man's path. Like Brady, Marsden was also a Jackson protegé. After graduating from Marietta College, the indefatigable youth had finished his ministerial training at Lane Theological Seminary and been ordained by the Presbyterian Church. In 1898, Marsden commenced a mission to his own people in Southeastern Alaska.[27]

For all the District's stability, whether represented by its "Presbyterian hierarchy," or Behrend's deposits, the territory's population continued to possess a large percentage of transients. Juneau had more than it liked to admit, particularly of the light-fingered variety. Even "old-timers" occasionally found the combination of community freedom and local bullion too much to withstand. Frank Jurgens, a five-year employee of the Alaska Treadwell Gold Mining Company, skimmed $7,500 of gold from the clean-up tank at the chlorination works and fled southward. Understandably, Sitkans made much of "Juneau lawlessness." Such disparagement could not hide their very real envy. It took no Merlin to foresee that the future favored Juneau. As early as 1891, the capital's newspaper had predicted the consequences of a road to the Yukon interior. "Should that highway be opened as a result of mining enterprise, which is bound to gradually develop in Central Alaska, great benefits will be reaped therefrom by Juneau our sister city as it is lying on the direct route between Puget Sound and the Chilkat River." Two years later, in 1893, Juneau's *Alaska Journal* devoted three whole pages to the bright prospects shimmering from the interior and the ways in which Juneau must gain therefrom.[28]

The Klondike rush of 1897–1898 inevitably accelerated the human traffic to America's Far North. With considerable fluctuation, this movement had been in process since the 1867 purchase of Russian America. Notwithstanding that the Klondike diggings were located on foreign soil, the impact of the world-publicized rush on Alaskan history marked a totally new era. For the moment, at least, any question of Alaska's proper acceptance without or within was drowned out by steamer whistles and the cries of effusive goldseekers headed north. The overland trek to Dawson would be brutally arduous. What a sharp contrast it was to the relatively comfortable shipboard phase of the 1897–1898 miners' pilgrimages. Many who steamed north would travel directly from a West Coast city to the Bering Sea, ascend the Yukon River, and thus never visit Sitka and Juneau. A majority of those single-minded argonauts who passed through these two Alexander Archipelago towns were probably not impressed with what they saw. "Nothing other than tacky port villages" would have been a common judgment. Yet, these settlements had been tested by a quite different type of pioneering process. No farmers produced this Americanization. If the Southeastern region's maturation was indicative, Alaska's future would witness a socio-economic transformation that was fundamentally urban-oriented.

Neither Sitka nor Juneau had flourished, but they had taken root and grown. In 1897 the Panhandle's pioneer stage had ended. The Great Land's frontiers lay northward and westward.

NOTES

1. *The Alaskan,* September 10, 1892.

2. Letter from James Sheakley to William T. Harris, Commissioner of Education, October 24, 1890, JCorr., Vol. 15, p. 288.

3. *Alaska Appeal,* December 1, 1879; John G. Brady, *Governor's Annual Report, 1897* (Washington, D.C., 1897), 7; Letter from John G. Brady to Sheldon Jackson, December 14, 1896, JCorr., Vol. 17, p. 384; Letter from Sheldon Jackson to President of the United States [Benjamin Harrison], January 8, 1891, JCorr., Vol. 25, p. 255; interview by author with Governor Brady's sons, John and Hugh, summers 1962 and 1968.

4. Letter from Gov. James Sheakley to Senator George Perkins, March 28, 1896, AGP, Box 6; Letter from John G. Brady to William Murray, February 17, 1898, AGP, Box 11.

5. Morgan B. Sherwood, *Exploration of Alaska, 1865–1900* (New Haven, Conn., 1965).

6. See the indispensable work by James Wickersham, *A Bibliography of*

Alaskan Literature, 1724–1924 (Cordova, Alaska, 1927), for a listing of the significant government scientific reports prior to 1898; also Brady, *Governor's Annual Report, 1897,* 21.

7. Quoted in: *The Alaskan,* October 14, 1893; Robert E. Coontz, *From the Mississippi to the Sea* (Philadelphia, 1930), 120.

8. David Starr Jordan, *Imperial Democracy: A Study of the Relation of . . . Democracy to the Demands of a Vigorous Foreign Policy and Other Demands of Imperial Dominion* (New York, 1899), 184.

9. *The Alaskan,* October 10, 1891; *ibid.,* November 19, 1887, November 21, 1891, August 26, 1893. E. Katharine Bates, *Kaleidoscope: Shifting Scenes from East to West* (London, 1889), 255. Jeannette Stewart, "Library Service in Alaska: A Historical Study" (unpublished master's thesis, University of Washington, 1957), 15.

10. *The Alaskan,* November 12, 1887, December 5, 1891, June 4, 1892, February 10, 1894.

11. *Alaska Times,* June 4, 1869; *The Alaskan,* July 9, 1892. Miscellaneous letters from Sheldon Jackson during late 1888, National Archives, Washington, D.C., General Agent, Letterpress Vol. I, 405 ff. Henry Wood Elliott, *Our Arctic Province: Alaska and the Seal Islands* (New York, 1886), 40–41.

12. William H. Dall, "Alaska Revisited," *The Nation,* LXI (July 4, 1895), 6–7; *The Alaskan,* April 25, 1891.

13. *Ibid.,* August 28, 1897.

14. *Ibid.,* June 26, 1886, October 13, 1888, October 17, 1891, May 21, 1892; *Alaska Journal,* June 10, 1893.

15. R. N. De Armond, "They Were Named for Pinta," *Alaska Sportsman,* XXVIII (February, 1962), 29–30.

16. Henry M. Field, *Our Western Archipelago* (New York, 1895), 135.

17. *The Alaskan,* December 25, 1897.

18. Jack London arrived with the Klondikers. His story is well told in Franklin Walker's *Jack London and the Klondike: The Genesis of an American Writer* (San Marino, Calif., 1966). Letter from Sheldon Jackson to Attorney General, September 29, 1892, JCorr., Vol. 25, p. 524.

19. *The Post Intelligencer,* May 12, 1892. See also following day's issue.

20. Letter from Sheldon Jackson to Attorney General, JCorr., Vol. 25, p. 526.

21. *The Alaskan,* September 26, 1891. R. N. De Armond, *Some Names Around Juneau* (Sitka, Alaska, 1957), 7–8.

22. Charles Hallock, *Our New Alaska: Or Seward Purchase Vindicated* (New York, 1886), 63.

23. Henry T. Finck, *The Pacific Coast Scenic Tour: From Southern California to Alaska. . . .* (New York, 1890), 241; *The Alaskan,* September 17, 1892; *Alaska Journal,* March 3, 1893 and April 8, 1893; *Alaska Searchlight,* December 19, 1896; *The Alaskan,* October 17, 1891; and *Alaska Journal,* March 11, 1893.

24. Mrs. Frederick Schwatka, "Around About Alaska's Metropolis," *Midland Monthly,* VIII (October, 1897), 358; William C. Gray, *Musings by Campfire and Wayside* (Chicago, 1902), 255.

25. Ted C. Hinckley (Ed.), "The Canoe Rocks—We Do Not Know What Will Become of Us," *Western Historical Quarterly*, I (July, 1970), 271–272.

26. Letter from John G. Brady to Sheldon Jackson, May 2, 1895, JCorr., Vol. 17, p. 141.

27. William Gilbert Beattie, in his *Marsden of Alaska: A Modern Indian* (New York, 1955), recounts this intriguing biography.

28. *Juneau City Mining Record*, February 3, 1894; *The Alaskan*, November 21, 1891; and *Alaska Journal*, March 18, 1893.

CHAPTER EIGHT

Conclusion

Already Alaska beckons on the north, and pointing to her wealth of natural resources asks the nation on what new terms the new age will deal with her.—Frederick Jackson Turner, Commencement Address, University of Washington, 1914.

THE SAME YEAR that the Great Land was purchased, Nebraska won statehood. Between 1870 and 1890 the population of that Great Plains state increased nearly nine times. For the same two decades, the Dakotas' settlers skyrocketed in number from 14,000 to more than half a million. Pig's Eye, Minnesota, had long since become thriving St. Paul, while Montana's Last Chance Gulch was renamed Helena and honored as the Territory's capital. What about New Archangel, Russian America's old capital, long since called Sitka? It still counted its white citizens in the hundreds. In 1895, Alaska's Governor, "by the most careful estimate," computed the District's total white population to be 8,000.[1]

Far too much has been made over how a bad press injured the Great Land's development. The very year of its purchase, the *New York Times* predicted the coming importance of Alaska's "strategical advantages."[2] It is true that throughout the first thirty years under the American flag there were ludicrously negative reports about "a country so barren and poor that scarcely any grass will grow upon it, so utterly worthless . . . that the savages find it scarce worth hunting over."[3] Clearly, Alaskans were disturbed by the District's negative image. In 1868 a Panhandle pioneer went to the trouble to write Honolulu's *Pacific Commercial Advertiser* to correct the "vague and erroneous opinion . . . in regard to the climate of Sitka."[4] By the mid-seventies Alaska's advocates probably outnumbered her critics. As early as 1872, W. H. Dall posed the editorial question, "Is Alaska a Paying Investment?" After carefully weighing all of the District's annual costs, his reply was a scholarly *Yes.*[5]

But if Alaska had great value and people who cared to inform themselves were apprised of this fact, why was her development retarded? For one thing, it joined the national pageant too soon. When Gilded Age America acquired the Far North frontier, the United States was preoccupied, filling up the vast Great Plains–Great Basin West, patching up the wounds of its most savage war, and erecting an industrial-urban complex that would make it the world's preeminent manufacturer. The struggle toward any one of these achievements would have been a prodigious national burden. David Starr Jordan said Alaska's retardation stemmed from "neglect."[6] "Neglect" has a negative ring; he should have used "irrelevance."

Since the nation's birth, pioneers have damned Congress for its lethargy in the face of frontier wants. Their privations were usually quite real, and like humans everywhere, they felt most keenly their own sacrifices. Alaska was like a teenager who desires adulthood's socio-economic freedom without possessing the maturity to handle such responsibility. To constantly blame the national government for its growing pains may have been good catharsis, but it definitely was not a complete nor even a fair explanation of the reasons for Alaska's deficiencies.

Unfortunately, historians have echoed the nineteenth-century charge of grave national neglect and how it severely injured Alaska's growth. One is reminded of scholars of the American Revolution who for so long parroted the charges listed in the Declaration of Independence and laid the blame for the Revolution at the feet of George III. England's king is now seen to have been a rather minor cause of the Revolution, and the grievances listed against him by the Declaration of Independence were so exaggerated as to rank as propaganda. Sitka's tyro politicians resorted to a similar propaganda weapon during their Icarus flight from 1867 to 1873. Their safest and often most effective attention-getting device was to blame an outsider for District backwardness. Occasionally it was the Alaska Commercial Company. Increasingly it was a homeland that had "forgotten her northern stepchild." What began as a typical frontier chant for larger national consideration, Sheldon Jackson and Alaska's Governors turned into a symphony. The melody could be maudlin or strident, or both at the same time.

By the 1890's this cacophony ranged from high-pitched, almost hysterical notes to tones so deep and pure that they rang like heavenly peals. Swineford drummed, "What is the matter?" and answered with the leitmotiv, "Simply the detestable legislation enacted by Congress." "Defective transportation was the sole reason for the undeveloped . . . state of the land," piped E. J. Glave.[7] In 1897, Brady harped, "Perhaps nothing has so retarded the true and substantial growth of Alaska as this helplessness . . . to obtain titles to their homes."[8] "Alaska," he trumpeted in an article published that same year, "has not been properly appreciated."[9] The shrill wails of the Russian Orthodox *American Messenger* have resounded down through the years. "The thirty years which have elapsed since the Russian flag was taken down, have brought the aborigines to the last depth of destitution. All that was created here by Russian civilization has been ruthlessly destroyed."[10]

Such statements, for all the emotional conviction of those who mouthed them, were frequently gross exaggerations. Professor Earl Pomeroy has written that the American pioneer did not always wait "for what was legal and safe." He impetuously pushed out of the settled regions and made ceaseless demands on the federal government. Pomeroy's generalization surely applies to Alaska. Quite as applicable is the opinion of Western historian Thomas D. Clark. Frontiersmen, he believes,

developed a remarkably self-pitying attitude toward themselves because of their treatment by the remainder of the country. Isolation blinded them to general national conditions; they had only limited intercourse with people of other sections, and they were dependent upon their own slender intellectual and political resources in the solution of their everyday problems.[11]

The opening of the Alaskan frontier was also synonymous with a rising Victorian crescendo over the fate of the "Vanishing American." Jackson capitalized on this. No missionaries succeeded in emulating Duncan's Metlakatla triumph; that they cushioned the aboriginals' acculturation shock, however, is indisputable. Above all else, the Christian teachers courageously reproved their fellow whites for their racism and exploitation of the natives. As one Yukon prospector complained, "Why, it's got so . . . that a man can't give a squaw a drink of whiskey and take her out in the brush without getting into trouble."[12] Before long, Jackson's tireless campaign to protect the native population compelled him to adopt the cause of Alaska. His emphasis on the shameful neglect of the land was not only politically sound but also guaranteed him an even wider audience among the press, businessmen, and reform-minded Americans everywhere.[13] Understandably, one Governor after another took up Jackson's battle cry. Alaska's needs were, and remain, colossal. But if we are to discern the historical truth, the Great Land's geographic and historic handicaps must be placed in balance beside her very real economic, social, and political strides. Once this is done, and her growth and treatment are viewed in relation to the development of other western territories during the years 1867 to 1897, her progress seems reasonable enough.

The Americanization of Alaska, and of every western frontier, had seen an intermingling of the more stable eastern way of life with fluid western forces. Across the Missis-

sippi Valley, the Yankee had interacted with diverse indigenes and venerable Roman Catholic societies. In comparison, Alaska's aboriginal inhabitants proved to be considerably more heterogeneous. The impact on Alaska of her
relative handful of Russians was inconsequential as con-
trasted with the incalculable effects of the Franco–Spanish
stock on the Mississippi Valley. After the Great Land was
wedded to the Union, it had to compete for public attention
with America's booming Far West, and particularly the
Pacific Slope region. As a result, the District's population
expanded at a snail's pace at the same time that her southern
sister commonwealths doubled and then redoubled their
citizenry. In 1890, William M. Thayer strung together an
engrossing tome, *Marvels of the New West: A Vivid Portrayal
of the Stupendous Marvels in the Vast Wonderland West of the
Missouri River*. Thayer was satisfied that "the New West
will decide the destiny of our land." He worried over the
threat of "Mammonism, Mormonism, Socialism, Skep-
ticism and Atheisim," yet was comforted that "the holy
trinity of Liberty, Education and Christianity in which the
Anglo-Saxon race believe, will prove more than a match
for them all in the future conflict for supremacy."[14] Thayer
never mentioned the Far North frontier. In light of his
apprehensions, maybe it was just as well.

Nineteenth-century Alaska spokesmen were fond of com-
paring England's "favorable treatment" of her Asian-
Pacific colonies with the American policy toward the development of Alaska. It was invariably, if unfairly, an invidi-
ous comparison. Professor Archibald Grenfell Price has
now correctly categorized the nineteenth-century Alaskan
frontier as typical of the white man's sojourner civilization.[15]
Price referred in particular to the Russian occupation, but
until the 1880's this was true of the American period as
well. The *Alaska Appeal* described the sojourners as men who
"have got into the habit of conducting their affairs as a sort
of 'grab all and give nothing' principle. . . . they have failed
. . . owing mainly to their shortsighted policy."[16] Happily, a

tiny residual group did look ahead, sacrificed, and made the Great Land their home.

Like Australians in their pioneer age, Alaskans preferred not to admit that their immense homeland's isolated location then made them unimportant to the nation as a whole. Among themselves Alaskans could afford to speak truthfully. John Callbreath's pessimistic and lonely note, written in 1886, sounds as though it came straight from the Australian bush. "I see but little prospect of ever getting out of this country. Anybody who has money enough to buy me out has too much sense to anchor himself here."[17] Nevertheless, within a quarter of a century after their British and American occupancy, the Land Down Under and the Great Land boasted viable settlements. Australia had its sheep, Alaska its fish and gold. By 1896 the northern territory even possessed slight national political leverage. That year both the Democratic and Republican conventions recommended that a District delegate be seated in Congress.[18] Although no Alaskan was nominated for the Presidency, a citizen from the Trans-Missouri West was!

From 1867 to 1897, Alaska should be seen as a part of the United States, understood in relation to what historian Henry Steele Commager has called America's "watershed period." The energy which had dominated a continent had spread outward over the Pacific Basin. Some of this drive had been applied to the Far North frontier. Yet Alaska's rich opportunities had proved elusive. In order to exploit them, old habits and pioneer attitudes had to be modified. Fortunately for the Great Land, the traditional primacy of agrarian thought and economics across the United States was already largely subordinated to commerce and industry. Rural America was being supplanted by urban America. Regionalism was breaking down before interdependency. Trained civil servants were replacing spoils system appointees. Simple, small-scale planning had become dangerously archaic, and gigantic new problems demanded revolutionary new solutions. When scholars William H. Dall and David Starr Jordan urged that the needs of Alaska be made subject "to study and appropriate legislation," they also could have included such contemporary "watershed" problems as municipal planning, the rights of national and racial minorities, and industrial concentration.[19] It is obvious that Alaska's settlement would have been facilitated by intelligent planning and conscientious and consistent administration. But had any frontier up to that time been guided by such methodical deliberation? Had any frontier's geography approximated that of Alaska's? To each question the answer is clearly *No*. Frederick Jackson Turner wrote that the states were artificial in their relation to the national government and what genuinely counted were the sections, what he called "potential nations." Turner was probably not thinking of Alaska, yet his admonition needs be applied to the Far North frontier.[20]

Only in the political realm is there some justification for the charge of neglect. Even here the indictment must be softened in light of relative circumstances. Sheer space seemed to amplify every report, good or bad, that came from the North Country. Illustrative is the case of a Treasury Agent sent north to investigate the "violence and bloodshed . . . from the fierce competition of the three competing companies engaged in taking salmon at [Karluk]." The "lurid stories of death and destruction," he discovered, "were the vain imaginings of some aspirant to an elevated place among the romanticists."[21] Visitors often interpreted the territory's demands for more official consideration as evidence that the District was mismanaged. This charge enraged one Sitkan. "Lord deliver us from the eastern importations, who never describe things as they are, but mix the geography of the country up with some heart rending tales of official malfeascence in one long maze of sinuous entanglement and untruthful and diabolical misrepresentation."[22] Self-government, despite Alaska's howls about "an aloof Washington, D.C.," *was* the traditional pattern. *The Alaskan* admitted as much when it stated:

Luckily the Anglo-Saxon race, as the history of the past centuries plainly shows, is well able to govern itself. We who have lived here a quarter of a century under no law, misfit law, non-applicable law and non-enforced law, well know this. In spite of the jobbers and lobbyists, deals and combinations Alaska will grow.[23]

How prone pre-Vietnam Americans were to believe that all a society needed to advance was an application of United States governmental institutions. These techniques have indeed been tested by centuries and are among the world's best. They rest, however, on harsh socio-economic facts of life. In 1867, Congress should have promptly given the Far North territory a more sophisticated government and set of laws than it did. To presume that this would have significantly sped up Alaska's subsequent rate of growth overlooks both southside as well as District economics. Ivan Petroff wisely observed in 1892, "Upon the whole it would appear that until the country [Alaska] gives proof of further development, and until it shall have been decided whether any further revenue will flow from Alaska as an offset to expenditures, we have granted [her] enough. . . ."[24] In 1896, Editor Sylvester, always one for bluntness, frankly admitted "that Juneau's Board of Trade doesn't know whether it is alive or not. If it does no one else is aware of the fact."[25]

The next year the Klondike stampede awakened even the most somnolent of Juneau merchants. It is significant that some of the goldseekers who arrived in the Great Land were surprised to learn the Klondike was not on United States soil. A *sine qua non* to Alaska's wise development was an understanding of her diverse geography. Yet for most Americans, it had to be experienced to be appreciated. The effect of such a gigantic land on one's personality was unpredictable. The brilliant naturalist Robert Kennicott exulted in the freedom of the remote Yukon Valley because "it provides an excellent opportunity for the study of the relationship of North American and Asiatic flora and fauna."[26] A few months later he killed himself.

America's Gilded Age "go-gettum spirits," reinforced by modern technology and a concurrent diminution of the historic contiguous western frontier, had abetted Alaska's late nineteenth-century development. From the outset, America's historic disrespect for geographic limitations doomed any rational, comprehensive, space age occupation plan. Instead of having the Panhandle emerge as a distinct state to be followed eventually by yet other Far North states to the north and west, with the remaining territory treated as Canada has sensibly done with her Northwest Territories, it once again was all or nothing. Neither Alaska's exuberant frontier promoters nor a disinterested federal government took the Great Land's Americanization seriously enough. Two years before the Spanish-American War bestowed a Pacific empire on the United States, the prominent Sitkan, John G. Brady, sensed his countrymen's limitations. "Some of us in Alaska," he declared in 1896, "who have been willing to see Cuba and Canada and the Sandwich Islands brought under the American flag are beginning to doubt the ability or genius of our government to manage or control detached portions of territory."[27]

Because of the unprecedented swiftness with which the Trans-Missouri West was occupied, too many Alaskans mistakenly surmised that their territory would shortly enjoy as rapid a settlement. In 1867, an excessively sanguine group of Pacific Slope town boosters believed that Sitka might mushroom into a Portland or San Francisco. The discerning James Bryce understood that the occupation of America's Far West had in fact been too fast. The result, as historian John D. Hicks has observed, was that the West "was immediately confronted with problems that it could not comprehend."[28] How especially germane to the Far North is his generalization. It would be decades before the Far West was really settled, and even longer before the Far North became critically important as a Pacific Basin resource zone for both Japan and the United States.

Alaska's enormous size made men talk big and think big.

CONCLUSION

Such hyperbole would be needed to subdue America's "last frontier." In 1867, Alaska was an economic sleeper. By the 1970's the dizzying rise of the world's population was helping spark the forty-ninth state's take-off. Could the "last frontier" be maintained as "a place for high thoughts and generous inspirations to all," as one American dreamed it would? One hundred years ago, a correspondent to the *New York Times* wistfully hoped Alaska might. "Let us at least try," he wrote, "to choose the noblest part of the physical creation for our most solicitous care."[29] Now, a century later, the frightening consumption of the earth's resources and shrinking living space make it absolutely imperative that Alaska receive her countrymen's "most solicitous care."

NOTES

1. James Sheakley, *Governor's Annual Report, 1895* (Washington, D.C., 1895), 18. The 1890 Census listed a total of 6,121 ("white" plus "mixed") Alaskans. Robert P. Porter (Supt.), *Compendium of the Eleventh Census: 1890* (Washington, D.C., 1892), Pt. I, 918–919.

2. *New York Times*, May 4, 1877.

3. "Scenes in Alaska," *Harper's Weekly*, XXIII (October 4, 1879), 791. This 1879 article frankly admits that its earlier harsh criticism (from which this quotation was drawn) was excessive.

4. *Pacific Commercial Advertiser*, October 24, 1868.

5. William H. Dall, "Is Alaska a Paying Investment," *Harper's New Monthly Magazine*, XLIV (January, 1872), 252–257.

6. David Starr Jordan, *Imperial Democracy: A Study of the Relation of . . . Democracy to the Demands of a Vigorous Foreign Policy and Other Demands of Imperial Dominion* (New York, 1899), 212.

7. E. J. Glave, "Pioneer Packhorses in Alaska," *The Century Magazine*, XXII (September, 1892), 671.

8. John G. Brady, *Governor's Annual Report, 1897* (Washington, D.C., 1897), 3.

9. John G. Brady, "Alaska," *The Chautauquan*, XXIII (September, 1896), 729.

10. Quoted in *The Alaskan*, October 9, 1897.

11. Earl S. Pomeroy, *The Territories and the United States, 1861–1890: Studies in Colonial Administration* (Philadelphia, 1947), 95; Thomas D. Clark, *Frontier America: The Story of the Westward Movement* (New York, 1959), 168. See also the insightful discussion by Gene M. Gressley, "Colonialism: A Western Complaint," *Pacific Northwest Quarterly*, LIV (January, 1963), 1–8.

12. Hudson Stuck, *A Winter Circuit of Our Arctic Coast: A Narrative of a Journey with Dog-sleds around the Entire Arctic Coast of Alaska* (New York, 1920), 71.

13. It should never be overlooked that Jackson was only the most vivacious and successful of numerous late nineteenth-century Americans promoting Alaska. Lacking television and the movies, residents of Washington, D.C., found a lecture on Alaska exciting entertainment. Sometimes the audience included the President. *The National Republican*, April 16, 1880.

14. William M. Thayer, *Marvels of the New West* (Norwich, Conn., 1890), 715.

15. A. Grenfell Price, *The Western Invasions of the Pacific and Its Continents: A Study of Moving Frontiers and Changing Landscapes, 1513–1958* (Oxford, 1963).

16. *Alaska Appeal*, July 30, 1879.

17. Letter from John C. Callbreath (at Telegraph Creek) to John Cook, September 2, 1886, John C. Callbreath Collection, Letterpress Vol. 4, University of Washington, Seattle.

18. K. H. Porter and D. B. Johnson (Comps.), *National Party Platforms, 1840–1960* (Urbana, Ill., 1960), 99 and 109.

19. Henry Steele Commager, *The American Mind: An Interpretation of American Thought and Character Since the 1880's* (New Haven, Conn., 1954), 41; William H. Dall, "Alaska As It Was and Is, 1865–1895," *Philosophical Society of Washington Bulletin*, XIII (1895–1900), 123–161; David Starr Jordan, *Imperial Democracy*, 212; however, to be fair, read also, pp. 193–194.

20. Frederick Jackson Turner, *The Frontier in American History* (New York, 1962), 158.

21. Howard M. Kutchin, *Report on the Salmon Fisheries of Alaska* (Washington, D.C., 1898), 6.

22. *The Alaskan*, November 21, 1891.

23. *Ibid.*, March 26, 1898.

24. Ivan Petroff, "Twenty-five Years of Alaska," *North American Review*, CLIV (May, 1892), 630.

25. *Alaska Searchlight*, December 12, 1896.

26. Richard Mathews, *The Yukon* (New York, 1968), 83.

27. John G. Brady, "Alaska," *The Chautauquan*, XXIII (September, 1896), 737.

28. James Bryce, *The Study of American History* (New York, 1922), 35, as quoted in John D. Hicks, *The Populist Revolt* (Lincoln, Nebr., 1961), 2.

29. Henry M. Field, *Our Western Archipelago* (New York, 1895), 102; *New York Times*, December 11, 1869. A synthesis of the continuing and inevitable conservation confrontation is: Richard A. Cooley, *Alaska: A Challenge in Conservation* (Madison, Wis., 1966). Already dated but very useful for understanding the difficulties that await those brave enough to prognosticate on Alaska affairs is: George W. Rogers, *The Future of Alaska: Economic Consequences of Statehood* (Baltimore, 1962).

☆ ☆ ☆ ☆ ☆ ☆ ☆ ☆ ☆ ☆ ☆ ☆ ☆ ☆ ☆ ☆ ☆ ☆

Bibliography

PRIMARY SOURCES

Manuscript Collections

Alaska Commercial Company Papers. University of Alaska, College, Alaska.

Alaska Governors Papers. Federal Records Center, Seattle, Washington.

Andrews, C. L., Collection. Sheldon Jackson College Library, Sitka, Alaska.

Bancroft, Hubert Howe, Scrapbooks. Bancroft Library, University of California, Berkeley, California.

Brady, John Green, Collection. Beinecke Library, Yale University, New Haven, Connecticut.

Callbreath, John C., Papers. University of Washington, Seattle, Washington.

Cole, Cornelius, Collection. University of California, Los Angeles, California.

Healy, M. A., Collection. Huntington Library, San Marino, California.

Indian Affairs, Office, Alaska Division of the U.S. Office of Education, 1877–1900. U.S. National Archives, Washington, D.C.

Jackson, Sheldon, Correspondence and Scrapbook Collections. Presbyterian Historical Society, Philadelphia, Pennsylvania.

Jackson, Sheldon, Miscellany. Sheldon Jackson Museum and Library, Sheldon Jackson College, Sitka, Alaska.

Jackson, Sheldon, Papers. Speer Library, Princeton Theological Seminary, Princeton, New Jersey.

Judge, James, Papers. Oregon Historical Society. Portland, Oregon.

Kinkead, John H., "In Nevada and Alaska," etc. Bancroft Library, University of California, Berkeley, California.

Lopp, William Thomas, Papers. University of Oregon, Eugene, Oregon.

Marsden, Edward, Papers. San Francisco Theological Seminary, San Anselmo, California.

Meade, Richard Worsam, Papers. New York Historical Society, New York, N.Y.

Miller, John Franklin, Papers. Stanford University, Stanford, California.

Petroff, Ivan, "Questions," etc. Bancroft Library, University of California, Berkeley, California.

Pilz, George E., "Reminiscences: Pioneer Days in Alaska." University of Alaska, College, Alaska.

Ricks, Melvin, Collection. Alaska Methodist University, Anchorage, Alaska.

Seward, William Henry, Papers. University of Rochester, Rochester, New York.

Shattuck, Agnes, Collection. Juneau, Alaska.

Sitka Town Records. Alaska State Historical Library, Juneau, Alaska.

Thwing, Clarence, Papers. San Francisco Theological Seminary, San Anselmo, California.

United States Army, Department of Alaska. National Archives, Microfilm selections from Record Groups No. 94 and No. 98, Washington, D.C.

United States Customs Service Records. Alaska State Historical Library, Juneau, Alaska.

United States Interior Department, Territorial Papers, Alaska, 1869–1911. National Archives, Microcopy No. 430, Washington, D.C.

Weinland, William Henry, Collection. Huntington Library, San Marino, California.

United States Government Documents

Alaska Boundary Tribunal. *Proceedings of the Alaska Boundary Tribunal, Convened at London.* Vol. I. Washington, D.C.: Government Printing Office, 1904.

Alaska, Governors. *Annual Reports, 1884–1900.* Washington, D.C.: Government Printing Office, 1884–1900.

Bailey, George W. *Report upon Alaska and Its People 1879.* Washington, D.C.: Government Printing Office, 1880.

Bean, Tarleton H. *Report on the Salmon and Salmon Rivers of Alaska, with Notes on the Conditions, Methods and Needs of the Salmon Fish-*

eries. Washington, D.C.: Government Printing Office, 1890.

Congressional Globe and after 1873 *Congressional Record, 1867–1897.* Washington, D.C.: Government Printing Office, 1867–1897.

Education, United States Commissioners. *Annual Reports, 1879–1900.* Washington, D.C.: Government Printing Office, 1880–1901.

Education for Alaska, General Agent. *Annual Reports, 1878–1900.* Washington, D.C.: Government Printing Office, 1879–1901.

Elliott, Henry Wood. *Report of Henry W. Elliott on Condition of Fur Seal Fisheries of Alaska.* Washington, D.C.: Government Printing Office, 1896.

Indian Affairs, Commissioners. *Annual Reports, 1881–1888.* Washington, D.C.: Government Printing Office, 1881–1889.

Kutchin, Howard M. *Report on the Salmon Fisheries of Alaska.* Washington, D.C.: Government Printing Office, 1897.

Moser, Jefferson F. *The Salmon and Salmon Fisheries of Alaska.* Washington, D.C.: Government Printing Office, 1899.

Murray, Joseph. *Seal and Salmon Fisheries and General Resources of Alaska.* Vol. II. Washington, D.C.: Government Printing Office, 1898.

Porter, Robert P. (Supt.) *Compendium of the Eleventh Census: 1890.* Washington, D.C.: Government Printing Office, 1892.

Report of the Operations of the Revenue-Marine Service, 1881. Washington, D.C.: Government Printing Office, 1881.

Schwatka, Frederick. *Report of a Military Reconnaissance in Alaska, Made in 1883.* Washington, D.C.: Government Printing Office, 1885.

U.S., Congress, House, *Message in Relation to the Transfer of Territory from Russia to the United States.* 40th Cong., 2d Sess., Ex. Doc. No. 125, January 28, 1868.

U.S., Congress, House, *Russian America,* 40th Cong., 2d Sess., Ex. Doc. No. 177, February 19, 1868.

U.S., Congress, House, *Jurisdiction of the War Department over the Territory of Alaska* by William W. Belknap, 44th Cong., 1st Sess., Ex. Doc. No. 153, February 29, 1876.

U.S., Congress, House, *Population and Resources of Alaska, etc.* by Ivan Petroff, 46th Cong., 3d Sess., Ex. Doc. No. 40, January 15, 1881.

U.S., Congress, House, *Report of United States Naval Officers Cruising in Alaska Waters,* 47th Cong., 1st Sess., Ex. Doc. No. 81, February 24, 1882.

U.S., Congress, Senate, *Report of a Special Agent on the Territory of Alaska and the Collection of the Customs-Revenue Therein,* 44th Cong., 1st Sess., Ex. Doc. No. 37, March 20, 1876.

U.S., Congress, Senate, *Report upon the Customs District Public Service, and Resources of Alaska Territory* by William Gouverneur Morris, 45th Cong., 3d Sess., Ex. Doc. No. 59, February 14, 1879.

U.S., Congress, Senate, *Reports of Commander L. A. Beardslee . . . June 15, 1879 to January 22, 1880* by L. A. Beardslee, 46th Cong., 2d Sess., Ex. Doc. No. 105, March 5, 1880.

U.S., Congress, Senate, *Report of Capt. L. A. Beardslee, U.S. Navy, Relative to Affairs in Alaska, and . . . U.S.S. Jamestown . . .* , 47th Cong., 1st Sess., Ex. Doc. No. 71, January 24, 1882.

U.S., Congress, Senate, *Alleged Outrages in Alaska,* 50th Cong., 2d Sess., Ex. Doc. No. 141, March 1, 1889.

U.S., Congress, Senate, *Report Relative to the Condition of the Natives of Alaska* by Sheldon Jackson, 51st Cong., 2d Sess., Ex. Doc. No. 14, December 16, 1890.

U.S. Treasury. *Commercial Alaska in 1901.* Washington, D.C.: Government Printing Office, 1902.

Books

Aldrich, Herbert L. *Arctic Alaska and Siberia, or Eight Months with the Arctic Whalemen.* Chicago: Rand, McNally, 1889.

Arctander, John W. *The Apostle of Alaska: The Story of William Duncan of Metlakahtla.* New York: Fleming H. Revell, 1909.

Ballou, Maturin M. *Footprints of Travel, or, Journeying in Many Lands.* Boston: Ginn & Co., 1896.

———. *The New Eldorado: A Summer Journey to Alaska.* 2nd ed. Boston: Houghton Mifflin, 1890.

Bancroft, Hubert Howe. *History of Alaska, 1730–1885.* Vol. XXXIII of *The Works of Hubert Howe Bancroft.* San Francisco: A. L. Bancroft & Co., 1886.

Barnum, Francis. *Life on the Alaska Mission with an Account of the Foundation of the Mission.* Woodstock, Md.: Woodstock College Press, 1893.

Bates, E. Katharine. *Kaleidoscope: Shifting Scenes from East to West.* London: Ward & Downey, 1889.

Bowles, Samuel. *Our New West.* Hartford, Conn.: Hartford Publishing Co., 1869.

Brevig, Tollef Larson. *Apaurak in Alaska.* Translated by J. W. Johnshoy. Philadelphia: Dorrance & Co., 1944.

Broke, Horatio G. *With Sack and Stock in Alaska*. London: Longmans, Green, 1891.

Bruce, Miner W. *Alaska: Its History and Resources, Gold Fields, Routes and Scenery*. Seattle: Lowman & Hanford, 1895.

Cody, H. A. *An Apostle of the North: Memoirs of the Right Reverend William Carpenter Bompas. . . .* New York: E. P. Dutton, 1908.

Collis, Mrs. Septima M. *A Woman's Trip to Alaska: Being an Account of a Voyage Through the Inland Seas of the Sitkan Archipelago in 1890*. New York: Cassell Publishing Co., 1890.

Coontz, Robert E. *From the Mississippi to the Sea*. Philadelphia: Dorrance & Co., 1930.

Crosby, Rev. Thomas. *Up and Down the North Pacific Coast by Canoe and Mission Ship*. Toronto, Canada: The Missionary Society of the Methodist Church, 1914.

Dall, William H. *Alaska and Its Resources*. London: Sampson, Low, Son and Marston, 1870.

Elliott, Henry Wood. *Our Arctic Province: Alaska and the Seal Islands*. New York: Charles Scribner's Sons, 1886.

Field, Henry M. *Our Western Archipelago*. New York: Charles Scribner's Sons, 1895.

Finck, Henry T. *The Pacific Coast Scenic Tour: From Southern California to Alaska. . . .* New York: Charles Scribner's Sons, 1890.

Gray, William Cunningham. *Musings by Campfire and Wayside*. Chicago: Fleming H. Revell, 1902.

Hallock, Charles. *Our New Alaska: or Seward Purchase Vindicated*. New York: Forest and Stream Publishing Co., 1886.

———. *Peerless Alaska: Our Cache Near the Pole*. New York: Broadway Publishing Co., 1908.

Harris, A. C. *Alaska and the Klondike Gold Fields. . . .* Washington, D.C.: J. R. Jones, 1897.

Harrison, Carter H. *Summer's Outing and the Old Man's Story*. Chicago: Donohue, Henneberry & Co., 1891.

Heistand, H. O. S. *The Territory of Alaska*. Kansas City, Mo.: Hudson Kimberly Publishing Co., 1898.

Jackson, Sheldon. *Alaska and Missions on the North Pacific Coast*. New York: Dodd, Mead, 1880.

James, Bushrod Washington. *Alaska: Its Neglected Past, Its Brilliant Future*. Philadelphia: Sunshine Publishing Co., 1897.

Jordan, David Starr. *Imperial Democracy: A Study of the Relation of . . . Democracy to the Demands of a Vigorous Foreign Policy and Other Demands of Imperial Dominion*. New York: D. Appleton & Co., 1899.

Judge, Charles J. *An American Missionary: A Record of the Work of*

Rev. William H. Judge, S.J. 2nd ed. Boston: Catholic Foreign Mission Bureau, 1907.

Krause, Aurel. *The Tlingit Indians: Results of a Trip to the Northwest Coast of America and the Bering Straits.* Translated by Erna Gunther. Seattle: University of Washington Press, 1956.

Laufe, Abe (Ed.). *An Army Doctor's Wife on the Frontier: Letters from Alaska and the Far West 1874–1878.* Pittsburgh: University of Pittsburgh Press, 1962.

McQuesten, Leroy N. *Recollections of Leroy N. McQuesten of Life in the Yukon, 1871–1885.* Dawson City, Yukon Territory, Canada: Yukon Order of the Pioneers, 1952.

Muir, John. *Travels in Alaska.* Boston: Houghton Mifflin, 1915.

Niblack, Albert P. *The Coast Indians of Southern Alaska and Northern British Columbia. Annual Report . . . Smithsonian Institution . . . June 30, 1888.* Washington, D.C.: Government Printing Office, 1890.

Rollins, Alice W. *From Palm to Glacier.* New York: G. P. Putnam's Sons, 1892.

Scidmore, Eliza Ruhamah. *Alaska: Its Southern Coast and the Sitkan Archipelago.* Boston: D. Lothrop & Co., 1885.

————. *The Guide-Book to Alaska and the Northwest Coast.* London: William Heinemann, 1893.

Sessions, Francis C. *From Yellowstone Park to Alaska.* New York: Welch, Fracker Co., 1890.

Seward, Frederick W. *Seward at Washington, as Senator and Secretary of State.* New York: Derby and Miller, 1891.

Shepard, Isabel S. *The Cruise of the U.S. Steamer "Rush" in the Behring Sea: Summer of 1889.* San Francisco: Bancroft Co., 1889.

Stewart, Robert Laird. *Sheldon Jackson: Pathfinder and Prospector of the Missionary Vanguard in the Rocky Mountains and Alaska.* New York: Fleming H. Revell, 1908.

Stuck, Hudson. *The Alaska Missions of the Episcopal Church.* New York: Domestic and Foreign Mission Society, 1920.

————. *A Winter Circuit of Our Arctic Coast: A Narrative of a Journey with Dog-sleds around the Entire Arctic Coast of Alaska.* New York: Charles Scribner's Sons, 1920.

Swineford, Alfred P. *Alaska: Its History, Climate and Natural Resources.* Chicago: Rand McNally, 1898.

Teichmann, Emil. *A Journey to Alaska in the Year 1868.* Edited by Oskar Teichmann. New York: Argosy-Antiquarian, 1963.

Thayer, William M. *Marvels of the New West.* Norwich, Conn.: Henry Bill Publishing Co., 1890.

Thornton, Harrison Robertson. *Among the Eskimos of Wales, Alaska,*

1890–93. Edited by Neda S. Thornton and William M. Thornton, Jr. Baltimore: Johns Hopkins Press, 1931.

Villard, Henry. *A Journey to Alaska.* New York: Reprinted from *The New York Evening Post,* 1899.

Wardman, George. *A Trip to Alaska: A Narrative of What Was Seen and Heard during a Summer Cruise in Alaskan Waters.* Boston: Lee and Shepard Publishers, 1885.

Wellcome, Henry S. *The Story of Metlakahtla.* London: Saxon & Co., 1887.

Whymper, Frederick. *Travel and Adventure in the Territory of Alaska.* New York: Harper & Bros., 1868.

Wiley, Sara King, and William H. *The Yosemite, Alaska, and the Yellowstone.* New York: John Wiley & Sons, 1893.

Willard, Mrs. Eugene S. *Life in Alaska.* Edited by Mrs. Eva McClintock. Philadelphia: Presbyterian Board of Publications, 1884.

Woodman, Abby Johnson. *Picturesque Alaska: A Journal of a Tour Among the Mountains, Seas and Islands of the Northwest from San Francisco to Sitka.* Boston: Houghton Mifflin, 1889.

Wright, Julia McNair. *Among the Alaskans.* Philadelphia: Presbyterian Board of Publications, 1883.

Wright, Lewis (Ed.) *Lewis and Dryden's Marine History of the Pacific Northwest.* Portland, Ore.: Lewis and Dryden Printing Co., 1895.

Young, S. Hall. *Alaska Days with John Muir.* New York: Fleming H. Revell, 1915.

_____. *Hall Young of Alaska: An Autobiography.* New York: Fleming H. Revell, 1927.

Pamphlets

Ball, M. D. *To the House of Representatives: Strike But Hear Me.* n.p., n.d.

Briggs, Horace. *Letters from Alaska and the Pacific Coast.* Buffalo: *Commercial Advertiser,* 1888.

Great Northern Railroad. *Alaska: Land of Gold and Glaciers.* Chicago: Poole Bros., 1898.

Hamilton, J. Taylor. *The Beginning of the Moravian Mission in Alaska.* Bethlehem, Pa.: Comenius Press, 1890.

Jackson, Sheldon. *Alaska and Its Inhabitants.* n.p., n.d.

_____. *Condition of Indian Women and Girls in Portions of Alaska, as Seen by Different Eyes and Gleaned from Different Sources.* n.p., n.d.

_____. *Facts about Alaska: Its People, Villages, Missions, Schools.* New York: Woman's Board of Home Missions of the Presbyterian Church, 1903.

_____. *The Presbyterian Church in Alaska: An Official Sketch of Its Rise and Progress, 1877–1884, with the Minutes of the First Meeting of the Presbytery of Alaska.* Washington, D.C.: Thomas McGill & Co., 1886.

_____. *A Statement of Facts Concerning the Difficulties at Sitka, Alaska, in 1885.* Washington, D.C.: Thomas McGill & Co., 1886.

Lopp, W. T. *A Year Alone in Alaska, 1892.* New York: American Missionary Association, n.d.

Lukens, Matilda Barns. *The Inland Passage: A Journal of a Trip to Alaska.* Privately printed, 1889.

McWhinnie, Mrs. James. *History of Kadiak Orphanage, Wood Island, Alaska: 1892–1906.* Published by Woman's American Baptist Home Mission Society, n.d.

Pacific Coast Steamship Company. *All about Alaska.* San Francisco: Goodall, Perkins, 1888.

United States Military Academy, West Point Association of Graduates. *Twenty-fourth Annual Reunion.* New York: West Point, 1893.

Newspapers

The Alaska Appeal
The Alaska Bulletin
Alaska Free Press
Alaska Herald
The Alaska Journal
Alaska Searchlight
The Alaska Times
The Alaskan
Alta California
Chicago Tribune
Juneau, Alaska Mining Record
The Metlakahtlan
The National Republican
The New York Daily Tribune
New York Herald
New York Times
The North Star
The Pacific Commercial Advertiser
Portland Standard
Rocky Mountain Presbyterian
The Sitka Post
The Sitka Times
Sacramento Daily Union
San Francisco Chronicle

BIBLIOGRAPHY.

Territorial Dispatch and Alaska Times
Weekly Astorian
The West Shore

Articles and Periodicals

Blake, Theodore A. "Notes on Alaska," *Proceedings of the California Academy of Sciences,* IV (January, 1868), 13–15.

Bloodgood, C. Delavan. "Eight Months at Sitka," *The Overland Monthly,* II (February, 1869), 175–186.

Brady, John G. "Alaska," *The Chautauquan,* XXIII (September, 1896), 729–737.

Dall, William H. "Alaska as It Was and Is, 1865–1895," *Philosophical Society of Washington Bulletin,* XIII (1895–1900), 123–161.

_____. "Alaska Revisited," *The Nation,* LXI (July 4, 1895), 6–7.

_____. "Is Alaska a Paying Investment?" *Harper's New Monthly Magazine,* XLIV (January, 1872), 252–257.

Eaton, John. "Sheldon Jackson," *The Alaska and Northwest Quarterly,* I (April, 1899), 137–142.

"Edward de Groff," *Alaska–Yukon Magazine* (October, 1907), 139–140.

Elliott, Henry Wood. "Ten Years' Acquaintance with Alaska," *Harper's,* LV (November, 1877), 801–816.

Forrest, George F. "Juneau the Capital of Alaska," *Alaska–Yukon Magazine,* Special Gastineau Number (September, 1907), 13–15.

Glass, Henry. "Naval Administration in Alaska," *U.S. Naval Institute Proceedings,* XVI (January, 1890), 1–19.

Glave, E. J. "Pioneer Packhorses in Alaska," *The Century Magazine,* XXII (September 1892), 671–682.

Jackson, Sheldon. "Alaska," *The Chautauquan,* I (November, 1880), 70–75.

_____. "Alaska," *Goldthwaite's Geographical Magazine,* III (February, 1892), 139–141.

_____. "Alaska," *The Truth,* January 31, 1880.

_____. "Missionary Work in Alaska," *The Treasury,* XIII (May, 1895), 15–24.

_____. "What Missionaries Have Done for Alaska," *The Missionary Review of the World* (July, 1903).

Muir, John. "The Alaska Trip," *The Century Magazine,* LIV (August, 1887), 513–526.

Petroff, Ivan. "Alaska as It Is," *The International Review,* XII (February, 1882), 111–124.

————. "Twenty-five Years of Alaska," *North American Review,* CLIV (May, 1892), 628–630.

Sessions, F. C. "Alaska," *Magazine of Western History,* V (December, 1886), 270–282; (January, 1887), 384–391.

"Scenes in Alaska," *Harper's Weekly,* XXIII (October 4, 1879), 791.

Seton-Karr, H. W. "A Fresh Field for the Sportsman," *Fortune,* XLVII (March, 1887), 394–406.

Schwatka, Mrs. Frederick. "Around About Alaska's Metropolis," *Midland Monthly,* VIII (October, 1897), 353–360.

"The Treadwell Mines," *Alaska–Yukon Magazine* (September, 1907), 73–81.

SECONDARY SOURCES

Bibliographic Aids

Bancroft, Hubert Howe. *History of Alaska, 1730–1885.* San Francisco: A. L. Bancroft, 1886.

Brann, Harrison A. "A Bibliography of the Sheldon Jackson Collection in the Presbyterian Historical Society," *Journal of the Presbyterian Historical Society,* XXX (September, 1952), 139–164.

Caswell, John Edwards. "Materials for the History of Arctic America," *Pacific Historical Review,* XX (August, 1951), 219–226.

Frederick, Robert A. "Caches of Alaskana: Library and Archival Sources of Alaskan History," *Alaska Review,* II (Fall and Winter, 1966–67), 39–79.

Fuller, Grace Hadley, and Hellman, Florence S. (Comps.). *Alaska: A Selected List of References.* Washington, D.C.: Library of Congress, 1943.

Judson, Katherine Berry. *Subject Index to the History of the Pacific Northwest and of Alaska as Found in the United States Government Documents, Congressional Series, in the American State Papers, and in Other Documents, 1798–1881.* Prepared for Seattle Public Library. Olympia, Wash., 1913.

Lada-Mocarski, Valerian. *Bibliography of Books on Alaska Published Before 1868.* New Haven: Yale University Press, 1969.

Lindgard, Elmer (Comp.). *Preliminary Inventory of the Records of the Office of the Governor of Alaska, 1884–1958.* Seattle: General Services Administration, 1968.

National Archives. *Interior Department Territorial Papers Alaska, 1869–1911* (pamphlet). Washington, D.C.: Government Printing Office, 1964.

Rowe, Howard Marshall. "A Preliminary Draft of a Subject Index to Historical Material of the Pacific Northwest and Alaska to be Found in the United States Congressional Series and Other Public Documents from 1881–1931." Unpublished master's thesis, Department of History, Idaho University, 1938.

Tremaine, Marie. *Arctic Bibliography.* 14 vols. U.S., Department of Defense. Washington, D.C.: Government Printing Office, 1953–1969. Currently continued by Montreal, Canada: McGill-Queen's University Press.

Wickersham, James. *A Bibliography of Alaskan Literature, 1724–1924.* Cordova, Alaska: Cordova Daily Times, 1927.

Winther, Oscar O. *A Classified Bibliography of the Periodical Literature of the Trans-Mississippi West (1811–1957).* Bloomington: Indiana University, 1961.

Collected Documents and Atlases

Baker, Marcus. *Geographic Dictionary of Alaska.* 2nd edition. Washington, D.C.: Government Printing Office, 1906.

Barker, Fred W. (Comp.). *Compilation of the Acts of Congress and Treaties Relating to Alaska.* . . . Washington, D.C.: Government Printing Office, 1906.

Carter, Thomas H. *The Laws of Alaska.* . . . Chicago: Callaghan and Co., 1900.

Dall, William H., and Patterson, Carlisle P. *Pacific Coast Pilot: Coasts and Islands of Alaska, U.S. Coast and Geodetic Survey.* Washington, D.C.: Government Printing Office, 1879.

Documents Relative to the History of Alaska. 15 vols. University of Alaska History Research Project, 1936–1938. MS in the University of Alaska Library and the Library of Congress.

Gruening, Ernest (Ed.). *An Alaskan Reader: 1867–1967.* New York: Meredith Press, 1966.

Henning, Bob. *The Milepost, Alaska Highway Guidebook.* 17th revised edition. Juneau, Alaska: Northwest Publishing Co., 1965.

Orth, Donald J. *Dictionary of Alaska Place Names.* Washington, D.C.: Government Printing Office, 1967.

Richardson, James D. (Ed.). *A Compilation of the Messages and Papers of the Presidents.* 22 vols. New York: Bureau of National Literature, 1911.

Books

Alexander, Mary Charlotte. *Dr. Baldwin of Lahaina.* Berkeley: Privately printed, 1953.

Andrews, Clarence L. *Wrangell and the Gold of the Cassiar: A Tale of Fur and Gold in Alaska.* Seattle: Luke Tinker, 1937.

————. *The Story of Alaska.* Caldwell, Ida.: Caxton Printers, 1953.

Andrews, Ralph W., and Larssen, A. K. *Fish and Ships.* New York: Bonanza Books, 1959.

Athearn, Robert G. *High Country Empire: The High Plains and the Rockies.* New York: McGraw-Hill, 1960.

Bailey, Thomas A. *A Diplomatic History of the American People.* New York: Appleton-Century-Crofts, 1954.

Barth, Gunther. *Bitter Strength: A History of the Chinese in the United States, 1850–1870.* Cambridge, Mass.: Harvard University Press, 1964.

Beattie, William Gilbert. *Marsden of Alaska: A Modern Indian.* New York: Vantage Press, 1955.

Beaver, R. Pierce. *Church, State and the American Indians.* St. Louis, Mo.: Concordia Publishing House, 1966.

Berton, Pierre. *The Klondike Fever: The Life and Death of the Last Great Gold Rush.* New York: Alfred A. Knopf, 1958.

Billington, Ray Allen. *Westward Expansion: A History of the American Frontier.* New York: Macmillan, 1960.

Bixby, William. *Track of the Bear.* New York: David McKay, 1965.

Brooks, Alfred H. *Blazing Alaska's Trails.* Caldwell, Ida.: Caxton Printers, 1953.

————. *The Geography and Geology of Alaska.* Washington, D.C.: Government Printing Office, 1906.

Calasanctius, Sister Mary Joseph. *The Voice of Alaska: A Missioner's Memories.* Lachine, Quebec: Sisters of St. Ann Press, 1935.

Chance, Norman A. *The Eskimo of North Alaska.* New York: Holt, Rinehart and Winston, 1966.

Chase, Will H. *Reminiscences of Captain Billie Moore.* Kansas City, Mo.: Burton Publishing Co., 1947.

Chevigny, Hector. *Lord of Alaska: Baranov and the Russian Adventure.* New York: Viking Press, 1944.

————. *Russian America: The Great Alaskan Venture, 1741–1867.* New York: Viking Press, 1965.

Chiu, Ping. *Chinese Labor in California, 1850–1880: An Economic Study.* Madison: State Historical Society of Wisconsin, 1963.

Clark, Henry W. *History of Alaska.* New York: The Macmillan Co., 1930.

Clark, Thomas D. *Frontier America: The Story of the Westward Movement.* New York: Charles Scribner's Sons, 1959.

Collison, William H. *In the Wake of the War Canoe.* London: Seeley, Service & Co., Ltd., 1915.

BIBLIOGRAPHY

Commager, Henry Steele. *The American Mind: An Interpretation of American Thought and Character Since the 1880's.* New Haven, Conn.: Yale University Press, 1954.

Cooley, Richard A. *Alaska: A Challenge in Conservation.* Madison: University of Wisconsin Press, 1966.

————. *Politics and Conservation: The Decline of the Alaska Salmon.* New York: Harper & Row, 1963.

Coolidge, Mary B. *Chinese Immigration.* New York: Henry Holt & Co., 1909.

Coulter, John Wesley. *The Pacific Dependencies of the United States.* New York: Macmillan Co., 1957.

Crutchfield, James A., and Pontecorvo, Giulio. *The Pacific Salmon Fisheries: A Study of Irrational Conservation.* Baltimore: Johns Hopkins Press, 1969.

De Armond, R. N. *Some Names Around Juneau.* Sitka: Sitka Printing Co., 1957.

————. *The Founding of Juneau.* Juneau: Gastineau Channel Centennial Assn., 1967.

Dillon, Richard H. *The Hatchet Men: The Story of the Tong Wars in San Francisco's Chinatown.* New York: Coward-McCann, 1962.

Dodds, Gordon B. *The Salmon King of Oregon: R. D. Hume and the Pacific Fisheries.* Chapel Hill: The University of North Carolina Press, 1959.

Drucker, Philip. *Cultures of the North Pacific Coast.* San Francisco: Chandler Publishing Co., 1965.

Drury, Clifford M. *Presbyterian Panorama: One Hundred and Fifty Years of National Missions History.* Philadelphia: Presbyterian Board of Christian Education, 1952.

Eblen, Jack E. *The First and Second United States Empires: Governors and Territorial Government, 1784–1912.* Pittsburgh: University of Pittsburgh Press, 1968.

Evans, Stephen H. *The United States Coast Guard, 1790–1915: A Definitive History.* Annapolis, Md.: U.S. Naval Institute, 1949.

Farrar, Victor J. *The Annexation of Russian America to the United States.* Washington, D.C.: W. F. Roberts Co., 1937.

Friis, Herman R. (Ed.) *The Pacific Basin: A History of Its Geographical Exploration.* New York: American Geographical Society, 1967.

Fritz, Henry E. *The Movement for Indian Assimilation, 1860–1890.* Philadelphia: University of Pennsylvania Press, 1963.

Glanz, Rudolf. *The Jews in American Alaska, 1867–1880.* New York: The author, 1953.

Goodykoontz, Colin Brummitt. *Home Missions on the American Frontier: With Particular Reference to the American Home Missionary Society.* Caldwell, Ida.: Caxton Printers, 1939.

Gregory, Homer E., and Barnes, Kathleen. *North Pacific Fisheries: With Special Reference to Alaska Salmon.* San Francisco: American Council, Institute of Pacific Relations, 1939.

Gruening, Ernest. *The State of Alaska.* New York: Random House, 1954.

———. *An Alaska Reader, 1867–1967.* New York: Meredith Press, 1967.

Gunther, Erna. *Northwest Coast Indian Art: An Exhibit at the Seattle World's Fair Fine Arts Pavilion.* Seattle: n.p., 1962.

Hafen, LeRoy R., and Rister, Carl Coke. *Western America: The Exploration, Settlement and Development of the Region Beyond the Mississippi.* 2nd Edition. Englewood Cliffs, N.J.: Prentice-Hall, 1950.

Hagan, William T. *American Indians.* Chicago: University of Chicago Press, 1961.

———. *Indian Police and Judges: Experiments in Acculturation and Control.* New Haven: Yale University Press, 1966.

Hardy, Osgood, and Dumke, Glenn S. *A History of the Pacific Area in Modern Times.* Boston: Houghton Mifflin Co., 1949.

Hawgood, John A. *America's Western Frontiers: The Exploration and Settlement of the Trans-Mississippi West.* New York: Alfred A. Knopf, 1967.

Heller, Herbert L. (Ed.). *Sourdough Sagas: The Journals, Memoirs, Tales and Recollections of the Earliest Alaskan Gold Miners, 1883–1923.* Cleveland: World Publishing Co., 1967.

Hicks, John D. *The Populist Revolt.* Lincoln: University of Nebraska Press, 1961.

Hodge, Frederick Webb. (Ed.) *Handbook of American Indians North of Mexico.* (Smithsonian Institution, Bureau of American Ethnology, Bulletin 30.) Washington, D.C.: Government Printing Office, 1907.

Hulley, Clarence C. *Alaska: Past and Present.* Portland, Ore.: Binfords & Cort, 1958.

Johnston, Samuel P. *Alaska Commercial Company 1868–1940.* San Francisco: n.p., 1940.

Keithahn, Edward L. *Monuments in Cedar: The Authentic Story of the Totem Pole.* Ketchikan, Alaska: Roy Anderson, 1945.

Kitchener, L. D. *Flag over the North: The Story of the Northern Commercial Company.* Seattle: Superior Publishing Co., 1954.

Kuykendall, Ralph S. *The Hawaiian Kingdom 1778–1854: Foundation and Transformation.* Honolulu: University of Hawaii Press, 1957.

Lafeber, Walter. *The New Empire: An Interpretation of American Expansion 1860–1898.* Ithaca: Cornell University Press, 1964.

Lamar, Howard Roberts. *Dakota Territory 1861–1889: A Study of*

Frontier Politics. New Haven, Conn.: Yale University Press, 1956.

Latourette, Kenneth Scott. *The Great Century in Europe and the United States of America A.D. 1800–A.D. 1914*. Vol. IV, *A History of the Expansion of Christianity*. New York: Harper & Bros., 1941.

Lavender, David. *Bent's Fort*. New York: Doubleday, 1954.

Lazell, J. Arthur. *Alaskan Apostle: The Life Story of Sheldon Jackson*. New York: Harper and Bros., 1960.

Lemert, Edwin M. *Alcohol and the Northwest Coast Indians*. Berkeley: University of California Press, 1954.

Lewis, Oscar. *George Davidson, Pioneer West Coast Scientist*. Berkeley: University of California Press, 1954.

Luciw, Wasyl, and Luciw, Theodore. *Agapius Honcharenko and the Alaska Herald*. Stamford, Conn.: Slavia Library, 1963.

Mack, Gerstle. *Lewis and Hannah Gerstle*. New York: Profile Press, 1953.

Marx, Leo. *The Machine in the Garden: Technology and the Pastoral Ideal in America*. New York: Oxford University Press, 1964.

Mathews, Richard. *The Yukon*. New York: Holt, Rinehart and Winston, 1968.

Morgan, Murray. *Skid Road: An Informal Portrait of Seattle*. New York: The Viking Press, 1951.

Morison, Samuel Eliot. *The Maritime History of Massachusetts, 1783–1860*. Boston: Houghton Mifflin Co., 1961.

Nash, Roderick. *Wilderness and the American Mind*. New Haven, Conn.: Yale University Press, 1967.

Neill, Stephen. *Christian Missions*. Baltimore: Penguin Books, Ltd., 1964.

Newell, Gordon. *Pacific Steamboats*. New York: Bonanza Books, 1958.

Nichols, Jeannette Paddock. *Alaska: A History of Its Administration, Exploitation, and Industrial Development During Its First Half Century under the Rule of the United States*. Cleveland: Arthur H. Clark Co., 1924.

Oberholtzer, Ellis Paxson. *A History of the United States Since the Civil War*. 5 vols. New York: Macmillan, 1937.

Ogden, Adele. *The California Sea Otter Trade, 1784–1848*. Berkeley: University of California Press, 1941.

Okun, S. B. *The Russian–American Company*. Translated by Carl Ginsburg. Cambridge, Mass.: Harvard University Press, 1951.

Oswalt, Wendell H. *Mission of Change in Alaska: Eskimos and Moravians on the Kuskokwim*. San Marino, Calif.: Huntington Library, 1964.

Paul, Rodman Wilson. *Mining Frontiers of the Far West 1848–1880*. New York: Holt, Rinehart & Winston, 1963.

Plesur, Milton. "Rumblings Beneath the Surface: America's Outward Thrust, 1865–1890," in H. Wayne Morgan (Ed.), *The Gilded Age: A Reappraisal.* Syracuse, N.Y.: Syracuse University Press, 1963.

Pomeroy, Earl. *In Search of the Golden West: The Tourist in Western America.* New York: Alfred A. Knopf, 1957.

_____. *The Pacific Slope: A History of California, Oregon, Washington, Idaho, Utah and Nevada.* New York: Alfred A. Knopf, 1965.

_____. *The Territories and the United States, 1861–1890: Studies in Colonial Administration.* Philadelphia: University of Pennsylvania Press, 1947.

Porter, Kirk H., and Johnson, Donald Bruce (Comps.) *National Party Platforms 1840–1960.* Urbana: University of Illinois Press, 1960.

Pratt, Julius W. *A History of United States Foreign Policy.* New York: Prentice-Hall, 1955.

Price, A. Grenfell. *The Western Invasions of the Pacific and Its Continents: A Study of Moving Frontiers and Changing Landscapes, 1513–1958.* Oxford: Oxford University Press, 1963.

Priest, Loring Benson. *Uncle Sam's Step-Children: The Reformation of the United States Indian Policy, 1865–1887.* New Brunswick, N.J.: Rutgers University Press, 1942.

Prucha, Francis Paul. *The Sword of the Republic: The United States Army on the Frontier, 1783–1846.* London: The Macmillan Co., 1969.

Reid, Virginia Hancock. *The Purchase of Alaska: Contemporary Opinion.* Long Beach: Press-Telegram Printers, 1940.

Rickard, T. A. *Through the Yukon and Alaska.* San Francisco: Mining and Scientific Press, 1909.

Ricks, Melvin B. *Directory of Alaska Post Offices and Postmasters.* Ketchikan: Tongass Publishing Co., 1965.

Rogers, George W. *The Future of Alaska: Economic Consequences of Statehood.* Baltimore, Md.: Johns Hopkins Press, 1962.

Schoenberg, Wilfred P. *A Chronicle of the Catholic History of the Pacific Northwest: 1743–1960.* Spokane: Gonzaga Preparatory School, 1962.

Sherwood, Morgan B. (Ed.). *Alaska and Its History.* Seattle: University of Washington Press, 1967.

_____. *Exploration of Alaska, 1865–1900.* New Haven, Conn.: Yale University Press, 1965.

Smith, Page. *As a City upon a Hill: The Town in American History.* New York: Alfred A. Knopf, 1966.

Spicer, George Washington. *The Constitutional Status and Govern-

ment of Alaska. Vol. XLV in *Johns Hopkins University Studies in History and Political Science.* Baltimore: Johns Hopkins Press, 1927.

Stewart, George R. *Names on the Land: An Historical Account of Place Naming in the United States.* Boston: Houghton Mifflin, 1967.

Thomas, Benjamin Platt. *Russo-American Relations 1815–1867. Johns Hopkins University Studies in Historical and Political Science.* Baltimore, Md.: Johns Hopkins Press, 1930.

Thomas, Tay (Mrs. Lowell Thomas, Jr.) *Cry in the Wilderness: "Hear Ye the Voice of the Lord."* Anchorage: Color Art Printing Co., 1967.

Tompkins, Stuart Ramsay. *Alaska: Promyshlennik and Sourdough.* Norman: University of Oklahoma Press, 1945.

Turner, Frederick Jackson. *The Frontier in American History.* New York: Holt, Rinehart and Winston, 1962.

U.S. Army. *Building Alaska with the United States Army: 1867–1962.* Alaska: Information Office, Hdqtrs., [Anchorage], 1962.

Van Deusen, Glyndon G. *William Henry Seward.* New York: Oxford University Press, 1967.

VanStone, James W. *Eskimos of the Nushagak River: An Ethnographic History.* Seattle: University of Washington Press, 1967.

———. *Point Hope, An Eskimo Village in Transition.* Seattle: University of Washington Press, 1962.

Wade, Mason (Ed.) *Regionalism in the Canadian Community, 1867–1967.* Toronto: University of Toronto Press, 1969.

Walker, Franklin. *Jack London and the Klondike: The Genesis of an American Writer.* San Marino, Calif.: Huntington Library, 1966.

White, Leonard D. *The Republican Era, 1869–1901: A Study in Administrative History.* New York: Macmillan, 1958.

Wiebe, Robert H. *The Search for Order, 1877–1920.* New York: Hill and Wang, 1967.

Winther, Oscar Osburn. *The Great Northwest: A History.* New York: Alfred A. Knopf, 1956.

Wolfe, L. M. *Son of the Wilderness: The Life of John Muir.* New York: Alfred A. Knopf, 1951.

Wright, Louis B. *Culture on the Moving Frontier.* Bloomington: Indiana University Press, 1955.

Pamphlets

Farrar, Victor T. *The Purchase of Alaska.* Washington, D.C., n.p., 1934.

Mayberry, Genevieve. *Sheldon Jackson Junior College: An Intimate History.* New York: Board of National Missions, 1953.

Piet, Joseph M. *The Land of the Midnight Sun—Alaska: The Missions of Alaska.* Spokane: n.p., 1925.

Articles

Anderson, Charles A. (Ed.) "Letters of Amanda R. McFarland," *Journal of the Presbyterian Historical Society,* XXXIV (June and December, 1956), 83–102 and 226–244.

Andrews, C. L. "Alaska Whaling," *Washington Historical Quarterly,* IX (January, 1918), 3–10.

———. "Biographical Sketch of Captain William Moore," *Washington Historical Quarterly,* XXI (July and October, 1930), 195–203 and 271–280; XXII (January, 1931), 32–41; XXII (April, 1931), 99–111.

———. "Marine Disasters in Alaska," *Washington Historical Quarterly,* VII (January, 1916), 21–37.

———. "The Salmon of Alaska," *Washington Historical Quarterly,* IX (October, 1918), 243–256.

Athearn, Robert G. "An Army Officer's Trip to Alaska in 1869," *Pacific Northwest Quarterly,* XL (January, 1949), 44–64.

Bailey, Alvin K. "Sheldon Jackson, Planter of Churches," *Journal of the Presbyterian Historical Society,* XXVI (September and December, 1948), 129–148, 193–214, XXVII (March, 1949), 21–40.

Bailey, Thomas A. "The North Pacific Sealing Convention of 1911," *Pacific Historical Review,* IV (March, 1935), 1–14.

———. "Why the United States Purchased Alaska," *Pacific Historical Review,* III (March, 1934), 39–49.

Buzanski, Peter. "Alaska and Nineteenth Century American Diplomacy," *Journal of the West,* VI (July, 1967), 451–467.

Campbell, Charles S. "The Anglo-American Crisis in the Bering Sea, 1890–91," *Mississippi Valley Historical Review,* XLVIII (December, 1961), 393–414.

Crain, Mel. "When the Navy Ruled Alaska," *United States Naval Institute Proceedings,* LXXXI (February, 1955), 198–203.

De Armond, R. N. "They Were Named for Pinta," *Alaska Sportsman,* XXVIII (February, 1962), 29–30.

Dozer, Donald Marquand. "Anti-Expansionism During the Johnson Administration," *Pacific Historical Review,* XII (September, 1943), 253–275.

Dunning, William A. "Paying for Alaska: Some Unfamiliar Incidents in the Process," *Political Science Quarterly,* XXVII (September, 1912), 385–398.

BIBLIOGRAPHY

Farrand, Max. "Territory and District," *American Historical Review*, V (July, 1900), 676–681.

Gilbert, Benjamin F. "The Confederate Raider Shenandoah: The Elusive Destroyer in the Arctic and the Pacific," *Journal of the West*, IV (April, 1965), 169–182.

Golder, Frank A. "Mining in Alaska Before 1867," *Washington Historical Quarterly*, VII (January, 1916), 233–238.

_____. "The Purchase of Alaska," *American Historical Review*, XXV (April, 1920), 411–425.

Gressley, Gene M. "Colonialism: A Western Complaint," *Pacific Northwest Quarterly*, LIV (January, 1963), 1–8.

Harjunpa, Toivo. "The Lutherans in Russian America," *Pacific Historical Review*, XXXVII (May, 1968), 123–146.

Hinckley, Ted C. (Ed.) "The Canoe Rocks–We Do Not Know What Will Become of Us," *Western Historical Quarterly*, I (July, 1970), 265–290.

_____. "The Early Alaskan Ministry of S. Hall Young, 1878–1888," *Journal of Presbyterian History*, XLVI (September, 1968), 175–196.

_____. "Ice from Seward's Icebox," *Pacific Historian*, XI (Summer, 1967), 28–38.

_____. "The Inside Passage: A Popular Gilded Age Tour," *Pacific Northwest Quarterly*, LVI (April, 1965), 67–74.

_____. "The Presbyterian Leadership in Pioneer Alaska," *Journal of American History*, LII (March, 1966), 742–756.

_____. "Prospectors, Profits and Prejudice," *American West*, II (Spring, 1965), 58–65.

_____. "Publicist of the Forgotten Frontier," *Journal of the West*, IV (January, 1965), 27–40.

_____. "Punitive Action at Angoon," *Alaska Sportsman*, XXIX (January, 1963), 8 ff; concluded (February, 1963), 14 ff.

_____. "Reflections and Refractions: Alaska and Gilded Age America," *Frontier Alaska: A Study in Historical Interpretation and Opportunity*. Ed. by Robert A. Frederick. Anchorage, Alaska: Alaska Methodist University Press, 1968.

_____. "Rustlers of the North Pacific," *Journal of the West*, II (January, 1963), 22–30.

_____. "Sheldon Jackson and Benjamin Harrison," *Pacific Northwest Quarterly*, LIV (April, 1963), 66–74.

_____. "Sheldon Jackson, Presbyterian Lobbyist for the Great Land of Alaska," *Journal of Presbyterian History*, XL (March, 1962), 3–23.

_____. "Sheldon Jackson as Preserver of Alaska's Native Culture,"

Pacific Historical Review, XXXIII (November, 1964), 411–424.
_____. "The United States Frontier at Sitka, 1867–1873," *Pacific Northwest Quarterly*, LX (April, 1969), 57–65.
Hinckley, Theodore C. and Caryl (Eds.) "Ivan Petroff's Journal of a Trip to Alaska in 1878," *Journal of the West*, V (January 1966), 25–70.
Howay, F. W. "A List of Trading Vessels in the Maritime Fur Trade, 1785–1825," *Transactions of the Royal Society of Canada*, XXIV (Section II, 1930), 111–134; XXV (Section II, 1931), 117–149; XXVI (Section II, 1932), 43–86; XXVII (Section II, 1933), 119–147; XXVIII (Section II, 1934), 11–49.
_____. "The Introduction of Intoxicating Liquors Amongst the Indians of the Northwest Coast," *British Columbia Historical Quarterly*, VI (July, 1942), 159–169.
Jackson, C. Ian. "The Stikine Territory Lease and Its Relevance to the Alaska Purchase," *Pacific Historical Review*, (August, 1967), 289–306.
Jensen, Billie Barnes. "Alaska's Pre-Klondike Mining: The Men, the Methods and the Minerals," *Journal of the West*, VI (July, 1967), 417–431.
Jones, Edward M. "Jack McQuesten," *Alaska Sportsman*, XXXIII (May, 1967), 17–19.
Jones, Gordon P. "Cod Bangers to Alaska," *Alaska Sportsman*, XXXII (March, 1966), 8 ff.
Keithahn, E. L. "Alaska Ice, Inc.," *Pacific Northwest Quarterly*, XXXVI (April, 1945), 121–131.
Mazour, Anatole G. "The Prelude to Russia's Departure from America," *Pacific Historical Review*, X (September, 1941), 311–319.
_____. "Review of *The Russian American Company* by S. B. Okun," *Pacific Historical Review*, XXI (May, 1952), 190.
Montgomery, Maurice. "The Murder of Missionary Thornton," *Pacific Northwest Quarterly*, LIV (October, 1963), 167–173.
Monroe, Robert D. "An Excursion to Wrangell, 1896," *Pacific Northwest Quarterly*, L (April, 1959), 48–52.
Murphy, John F. "Two Standards of Judgment," *U.S. Coast Guard Academy Alumni Association Bulletin*, XXVII (September–October, 1965), 366–375.
Murray, Andrew E. "Presbyterian History in Colorado," *Journal of the Presbyterian Historical Society*, XXVIII (March, 1950), 1–20.
_____. "Presbyterian Expansion in Colorado," *Journal of the Presbyterian Historical Society*, XXVIII (June, 1950), 79–103.
_____. "Colorado's Changing Frontier and Presbyterianism,"

Journal of the Presbyterian Historical Society, XXVIII (September, 1950), 147–165.

Pierce, Richard A. "Prince D. P. Maksutov: Last Governor of Russian America," *Journal of the West,* VI (July, 1967), 403–411.

Ray, Dorothy Jean. "Sheldon Jackson and the Reindeer Industry of Alaska," *Journal of Presbyterian History,* XLIII (June, 1965), 71–99.

Shenitz, Helen A. "Vestiges of Old Russia in Alaska," *Russian Review,* XIV (January, 1955), 55–59.

Sherwood, Morgan B. "Ardent Spirits: Hooch and the Osprey Affair at Sitka," *Journal of the West,* IV (July, 1965), 301–344.

_____. "George Davidson and the Acquisition of Alaska," *Pacific Historical Review,* XXVIII (May, 1959), 141–154.

_____. "A Pioneer Scientist in the Far North: George Davidson and the Development of Alaska," *Pacific Northwest Quarterly,* LIII (April, 1962), 77–80.

Steckler, Gerald G. "The Case of Frank Fuller: The Killer of Alaska Missionary Charles Seghers," *Pacific Northwest Quarterly,* LIX (October, 1968), 190–202.

Stewart, George R. "The Name Alaska," *Names, Journal of the American Name Society,* IV (December, 1956), 193–201.

Stone, K. H. "Populating Alaska—The United States Phase," *Geographical Review,* XLII (July, 1952), 384–404.

Van Nostrand, Jeanne. "The Seals Are About Gone," *American Heritage,* XIV (June, 1963), 10–17 and 78–80.

Welch, Richard E., Jr. "American Public Opinion and the Purchase of Russian America," *The American Slavic and East European Review,* XVII (December, 1958), 481–494.

Wilson, Clifford. "The Surrender of Fort Yukon One Hundred Years Ago," *The Beaver,* Outfit 300 (Autumn, 1969), 47–51.

Wilson, William H. "Alaska's Past, Alaska's Future: The Uses of Historical Interpretation," *Alaska Review,* IV (Spring and Summer, 1970), 1–11.

Wolfenden, Madge, and Hamilton, J. H. "The Sitka Affair," *The Beaver,* Outfit 286 (Winter, 1955–1956), 3–7.

Unpublished Manuscripts

De Armond, Robert. "Summary of Sitka Record Book—Deeds." Unpublished manuscript, Alaska State Historical Library, Juneau, Alaska.

Donnelly, Joseph Peter, S. J. "The Liquor Traffic among the Aborigines of the New Northwest, 1800–1860." Unpublished doctoral dissertation, St. Louis University, 1940.

Henderson, Lester D. "The Development of Education in Alaska 1867–1931." Unpublished doctoral dissertation, Stanford University, 1934–1935.

McLean, Dora Elizabeth. "Early Newspapers on the Upper Yukon Watershed: 1894–1907." Unpublished master's thesis, University of Alaska, 1963.

Murton, Tom. "The Administration of Criminal Justice in Alaska 1867–1902." Unpublished master's thesis, University of California, Berkeley, 1965.

Stewart, Jeannette. "Library Service in Alaska: A Historical Study." Unpublished master's thesis, University of Washington, 1957.

Stubbs, Valerie K. "The United States Army in Alaska 1867–1877: An Experiment in Military Government." Unpublished master's thesis, The American University, May, 1956.

Interviews

Personal interview with Mrs. Agnes Shattuck [daughter of Governor Alfred P. Swineford], August 4, 1962, Juneau, Alaska.

Personal interview with Walter A. Soboloff, August 19, 1962, Juneau, Alaska.

Personal interviews with the sons and daughters of John Green Brady, 1963–1970.

Index